Longman

21st Century Science

Science GCSE Higher

Series Editor:
Penny Johnson

Peter Ellis
Michele Francis
Sue Kearsey
Penny Marshall
Michael O'Neill
Gary Philpott
Steve Woolley

This book also includes
Active **Book**

PEARSON
Longman

Edinburgh Gate
Harlow, Essex

Contents

How to use this book   6

B1 **You and your genes**

B1.1	You and your genes	8
B1.2	Genes and DNA	10
B1.3	One parent or two?	12
B1.4	Sex chromosomes	14
B1.5	Specialised cells	16
B1.6	Alleles	18
B1.7	Inherited diseases	20
B1.8	Healthy children?	22
B1.9	Genetic testing	24
B1.10	Modifying genes	26
B1.11	Cloning	28
B1.12	Using embryos	30
B1.13	Gene clinic	32

C1 **Air quality**

C1.1	Air quality	34
C1.2	Looking at data on air quality	36
C1.3	Air – a mixture	38
C1.4	Checking the pollutants	40
C1.5	Making new compounds	42
C1.6	Burning fuels	44
C1.7	Making pollutants	46
C1.8	Air pollutants and the environment	48
C1.9	Air pollution and health	50
C1.10	Pollution and power stations	52
C1.11	Pollution and transport	54
C1.12	Making choices about air quality	56
C1.13	Looking at air quality	58

P1   The Earth in the Universe

P1.1	The Earth in the Universe	60
P1.2	The face of the Earth	62
P1.3	Continental drift	64
P1.4	Plate tectonics	66
P1.5	Weighing the evidence	68
P1.6	Geohazards 1 – Volcanoes	70
P1.7	Geohazards 2 – Earthquakes	72
P1.8	The Solar System	74
P1.9	Asteroid impact!	76
P1.10	Studying the stars	78
P1.11	The Sun and other stars	80
P1.12	The Universe	82
P1.13	Planet for sale!	84

B2   Keeping healthy

B2.1	Keeping healthy	86
B2.2	Microorganisms and disease	88
B2.3	Body defences	90
B2.4	Fighting off infection	92
B2.5	Vaccines	94
B2.6	The good and bad side of vaccination	96
B2.7	Choosing to vaccinate	98
B2.8	Antibiotics	100
B2.9	Testing treatments	102
B2.10	The testing debate	104
B2.11	Heart disease	106
B2.12	Finding the cause	108
B2.13	A doctor's day	110

C2   Material choices

C2.1	Material choices	112
C2.2	Fit for the job	114
C2.3	Comparing properties	116
C2.4	More properties	118

C2.5	Plastics, rubbers and fibres	120
C2.6	Synthetic materials	122
C2.7	Refining oil	124
C2.8	Making polymers	126
C2.9	Inside polymers	128
C2.10	Changing polymers	130
C2.11	Life cycle of a polymer	132
C2.12	Polymer decisions	134
C2.13	A shopping trip	136

P2 Radiation and life

P2.1	Radiation and life	138
P2.2	The electromagnetic spectrum	140
P2.3	Heating with radiation	142
P2.4	Mobile phones and microwaves	144
P2.5	Ionising radiation	146
P2.6	The ozone layer	148
P2.7	Photosynthesis	150
P2.8	The carbon cycle	152
P2.9	The greenhouse effect	154
P2.10	A warmer Earth	156
P2.11	The global warming debate	158
P2.12	The way forward	160
P2.13	Staying safe	162

B3 Life on Earth

B3.1	Life on Earth	164
B3.2	Starting out	166
B3.3	Evolution of life on Earth	168
B3.4	Evolution by natural selection	170
B3.5	Darwin's theory of evolution	172
B3.6	Sensor and effector cells	174
B3.7	Communication systems	176
B3.8	Human evolution	178
B3.9	Food webs	180
B3.10	Extinction	182

B3.11 Humans and extinctions 184

B3.12 Biodiversity 186

B3.13 Earth, life and humans 188

C3	Food matters

C3.1 Food matters 190

C3.2 Producing food 192

C3.3 Intensive farming 194

C3.4 Organic farming 196

C3.5 Food additives 198

C3.6 Additives and safety 200

C3.7 Chemical contaminants 1 202

C3.8 Chemical contaminants 2 204

C3.9 Digestion 206

C3.10 Using food 208

C3.11 Diabetes 210

C3.12 Diet and health 212

C3.13 Food and its uses 214

P3	Radioactive materials

P3.1 Radioactive materials 216

P3.2 Radioactivity 218

P3.3 Three types of radiation 220

P3.4 Activity and half-life 222

P3.5 Ionising effects of radiation 224

P3.6 Exposure to radiation 226

P3.7 Are we safe? 228

P3.8 Fossil fuels and electricity 230

P3.9 Renewable energy resources 232

P3.10 Nuclear power 234

P3.11 Renewable or non-renewable? 236

P3.12 Sustainable development 238

P3.13 Power for the people 240

Glossary 242

Index 251

Acknowledgements 255

How to use this book

Each module starts with a double page that introduces some of the ideas that you will learn more about in the module.

It also has questions that will help you to start thinking about the ideas in the module.

Each module is divided into 12 topics. Each topic is a double page.

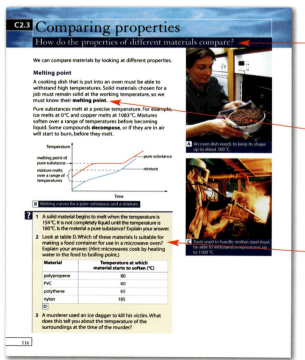

You should be able to answer this question when you have finished this topic.

The words in **bold** are important scientific words. You can check their meanings by looking at the glossary at the end of the book.

The questions will help you to understand what is on the page.

These boxes give you ideas for practical work or other activities.

Some questions ask you to give more than one answer, to help you think harder about what you are learning.

The last question is more difficult than the others, to see how well you understand the topic.

The summary will help you remember all the ideas you need from this topic. Keep the answers to the summaries for when you are revising for tests or examinations.

The last two pages have revision questions that will help you check how much you have remembered from this module.

Health news, 1 April 2056

Non-IVF to be banned?

Law proposed to ban 'natural' conception

The 'Right to Health' group is campaigning for a new law to ban the old 'natural' method of conception, where a sperm cell fertilises an egg cell inside the woman's body.

The modern era started back in 1978 with the birth of Louise Brown, the world's first 'test tube baby'. The official name for the treatment is 'In-Vitro Fertlisation', which means 'fertilisation in glass'! Egg cells were taken from Louise's mother and fertilised in a glass laboratory dish. The fertilised egg cell was placed back in her uterus for the embryo to grow in the normal way.

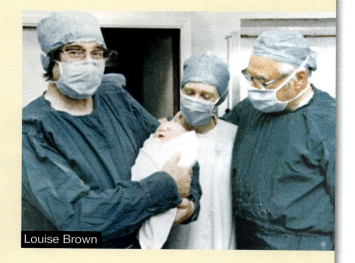

Louise Brown

In those days, IVF was only used to help couples who could not conceive 'normally'. The early techniques weren't always successful. Even in the year 2010, only one fifth of the treatments resulted in a live birth. Today, though, the treatments always work, and offer so many benefits that now over 95% of all babies are conceived by IVF.

Women only have their egg cells harvested once – these can be stored, and fertilised when they are wanted. The DNA of the embryos is tested, and parents can choose the ones with the healthiest genes, or the ones of the sex or appearance that the parents want. Parents can even have themselves cloned, if they wish. If necessary, the genes of the embryos can be modified before they are implanted into the mother's uterus. Any embryos not wanted for babies can be used for spare body tissues in case the other children suffer from a disease later in life.

Some opponents say that this way of reproducing is un-natural, and should not be allowed. Right to Health campaigners point out that there are far fewer cases of inherited diseases today than there were 50 years ago, and future children should not be denied the right to health, good looks and happiness. IVF treatments do cost a lot of money, but the Health Services have saved even more money by not having to care for people with genetic diseases.

We don't know what will happen in the future, but scientists are discovering more about us and our genes all the time. The way of reproducing described in the news report could happen at some time in the future.

However, just because something *can* be done, does not mean that it *should* be done. People will have to decide whether genetic testing and cloning are morally right. Decisions like this are called **ethical decisions**. They will need to know something about genes and how they work to help them to decide.

?

1 Describe how humans normally reproduce, in as much detail as you can.

2 a What does IVF mean?
  b How is IVF done?

3 a What are the advantages of IVF described in the article?
  b Write down some arguments against using IVF in this way.

4 What is your opinion about the article?

5 Write down a list of things you would need to find out about to help you to decide whether you would be for or against the new law.

Genes and DNA

What do genes do?

A

We all started off from a pair of **gametes** (a sperm cell and an egg cell), but we all look different to one another. We may have different coloured eyes or hair, different shaped faces, or different skin colours. These things are our **characteristics**. Many of our characteristics are caused by **genes**, which control how our bodies grow. We all have slightly different genes.

Most of our characteristics depend on combinations of several genes working together, and some characteristics are affected by **environmental factors** as well. For example, your height depends on the effect of several genes, and may also depend on whether or not you got enough food when you were growing.

Most of the **cells** in your body have a **nucleus**, and the nucleus contains **chromosomes**. Chromosomes are made of long molecules of a chemical called **DNA**. Genes are sections of chromosomes.

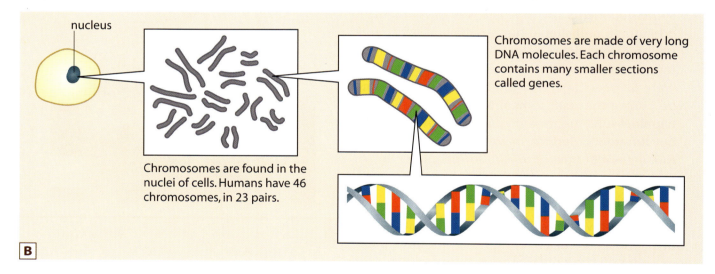

nucleus

Chromosomes are made of very long DNA molecules. Each chromosome contains many smaller sections called genes.

Chromosomes are found in the nuclei of cells. Humans have 46 chromosomes, in 23 pairs.

B

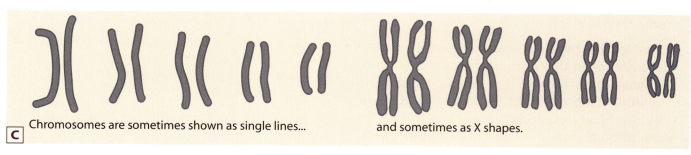

Chromosomes are sometimes shown as single lines...

and sometimes as X shapes.

C

You can think of genes as chapters in a book. Each chapter (gene) contains an instruction that controls one of our characteristics. The chapters (genes) are collected together into books (chromosomes), so each chromosome carries the instructions for lots of characteristics.

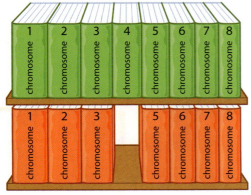

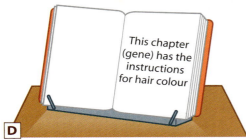

This chapter (gene) has the instructions for hair colour

D

E Sometimes criminals leave hairs, blood or bits of skin at the scene of a crime. Forensic scientists can analyse the DNA and see if it matches DNA samples taken from criminals.

Genes and proteins

Genes carry the instructions for making **proteins**. Proteins are important chemicals because they make up parts of your body such as muscles, skin and hair. These are called **structural proteins**.

There are other important proteins called **enzymes**. Enzymes control the chemical reactions that happen in your body. Nearly everything that happens in your body depends on enzymes. For example, enzymes:

- help to break down food in your digestive system
- help to build new cells
- keep your nerves and brain working.

Summary

Write definitions for all the words in bold on these two pages.

?

1 a Where are chromosomes found?
  b How many chromosomes are there in a normal body cell?

2 a What do genes do?
  b What are they made from?

3 Drawing D shows an analogy that helps you to think about genes and what they do. Describe a different analogy where a gene is represented by a piece of music.

4 a What are enzymes?
  b Why are enzymes important?

5 Write these things in order of size, and explain your answer: DNA molecule, nucleus, chromosome, gene

6 Forensic scientists can match a criminal's DNA from a sample of blood, but not from red blood cells. Find out the explanation for this statement.

One parent or two?

What are sexual and asexual reproduction?

Most animals produce offspring by **sexual reproduction**, when male and female gametes **fuse** to form a fertilised egg. Offspring produced by sexual reproduction **inherit** half of their genes from their mother, and half from their father. This is why the offspring look similar to their parents, but are not identical to them.

Some animals can also reproduce **asexually**. This means that one animal can produce offspring without needing a mate of the opposite sex.

The offspring produced by asexual reproduction only have one parent, so they get all their genes from this parent. All the offspring have the same genes as each other and their parent. The offspring are said to be **clones**.

B Female aphids can give birth to live young which have developed without fertilisation by a male aphid.

A These puppies have inherited characteristics from both their parents.

Bacteria and plants

Bacteria mostly reproduce asexually. If you have food poisoning, all the bacteria in you that are making you ill are likely to be clones, because they have been produced by asexual reproduction.

Sexual reproduction in plants happens when an egg cell is fertilised by pollen from another plant, and grows into a seed. The plant that grows from the seed will have genes from both the parent plants.

Many plants can reproduce asexually as well. We can grow new plants from **cuttings** (parts cut off a plant), which will grow roots and develop into new plants. This is possible because many cells in plants are not specialised – they can develop into different kinds of cell.

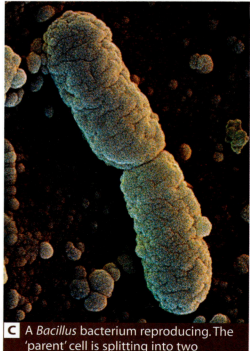

C A *Bacillus* bacterium reproducing. The 'parent' cell is splitting into two genetically identical cells (magnification ×20 000).

E *Bryophyllum* plants grow tiny plantlets on the edges of their leaves, which can grow into new plants.

runners

D Strawberry plants put out runners, which produce roots and eventually grow into a new plant.

A Are leaves the only parts of plants that can be used for cloning?
• How would you find out?
• What apparatus would you need?

Clones of an organism all have the same genes, but they may not always look the same because environmental factors can affect how an organism grows.

Summary

Draw a concept map to summarise what happens in sexual and asexual reproduction. You can start your map like this:

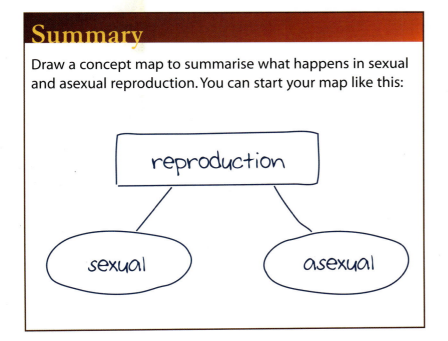

? 1 Why are the offspring of sexual reproduction:
   a) similar to their parents
   b) not identical to their parents?

2 What is asexual reproduction?

3 Write down two ways that clones of plants can be produced.

4 Suggest a reason why a gardener might wish to reproduce plants asexually.

5 Identical twins have the same genes as each other. Write down at least four environmental factors that could make them look different from each other.

6 One pea plant is bigger than another. Write down as many explanations for this statement as you can.

7 Find out about other animals that can reproduce asexually. You could start with the hydra.

Sex chromosomes

How do genes produce boys and girls?

A A peahen (female) and a peacock (male).

When animals reproduce, the offspring develop into either males or females. The male and female of a species can look very different.

The **gender** of a human depends on **sex chromosomes**. There are two types of sex chromosomes, called X and Y. Women have two X chromosomes, and men have one X and one Y. We say that women are XX and men are XY.

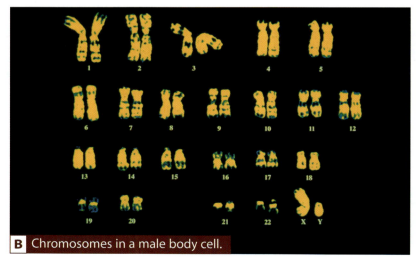

B Chromosomes in a male body cell.

Normal body cells have 23 *pairs* of chromosomes. Gametes only have one chromosome from each pair, so that when they combine the fertilised egg cell has the correct number of chromosomes. This is why offspring inherit characteristics from both parents.

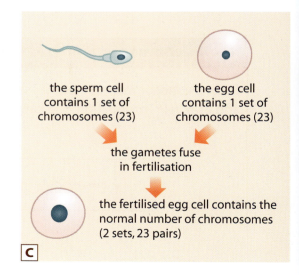

the sperm cell contains 1 set of chromosomes (23)

the egg cell contains 1 set of chromosomes (23)

the gametes fuse in fertilisation

the fertilised egg cell contains the normal number of chromosomes (2 sets, 23 pairs)

C

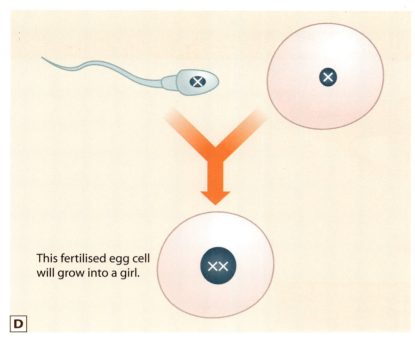

This fertilised egg cell will grow into a girl.

D

Sperm cells form in pairs, and each sperm cell gets one of each pair of chromosomes. This means that one sperm cell from each pair gets an X sex chromosome, and one gets a Y. When egg cells are formed, they all have one X sex chromosome. The gender of a baby depends on which kind of sperm cell fertilises the egg cell.

A When a couple have a baby by IVF, the doctors could test the embryos to find out if they are male or female. Parents could choose whether to have a boy or girl.
- Should parents be allowed to choose the gender of their children?
- Why might parents want to choose?
- What advantages could there be to choosing the gender?
- What disadvantages could there be?
- What might happen in cultures where boys are valued more than girls?

Summary

Draw a poster for a doctor's surgery to explain why parents are just as likely to have a girl as a boy.

?

1. In humans, how many chromosomes are there in:
   a a normal body cell
   b a sperm cell
   c an egg cell
   d a fertilised egg cell?

2. Look at diagram D. Draw a similar diagram to show how the gametes could produce a boy.

3. Why do egg cells never contain a Y chromosome?

4. 'Half of all babies born are girls.'
   a Explain why you would expect this statement to be true.
   b How could you find out if *exactly* half the babies born are girls?

5. Which is the odd one out: egg cell, sperm cell, body cell? Explain your answers.

6. A couple have had four boys. Explain why their chances of having a girl next time are still only 50:50.

7. a How many different combinations of chromosomes could you get in offspring from parents who only had one pair of chromosomes? (*Hint*: the mother could contribute either one of her pair of chromosomes.)
   b How many combinations would there be if each parent had two pairs of chromosomes?

Specialised cells

Why are there so many different kinds of cell?

A These skaters need to use their sight and hearing to dance to the music. They need to use their bones, muscles and nerves to move their bodies, and their brains to remember the moves.

Our bodies have over 200 different kinds of cell. The different kinds of cell are **specialised**, which means they have features that they need for their particular function. For example:

• some cells detect light and sound
• some help our bodies to move
• some carry oxygen around our bodies
• some help us to reproduce.

? 1 List five different kinds of cell, and explain how each one is specialised for its function.

B Rod cells in the retina of the eye.   Muscle cells.   Nerve cells.

After an egg cell is fertilised, it divides to make copies of itself. About four days after fertilisation there is a ball of cells called an **embryo**. At this stage the cells are not specialised – they can develop into any kind of cell. These cells are called **embryonic stem cells**. These cells can be extracted from embryos left over after IVF treatments and grown in the laboratory. Scientists are researching ways of using embryonic stem cells to treat illnesses such as diabetes, heart disease and spinal injuries.

The cells in the embryo continue to divide, but they soon begin to specialise. All the cells still have the same genetic instructions, but different cells follow different parts of the instructions. The genes that provide instructions that are not needed are permanently 'switched off'. Some cells develop into muscle cells, some develop into nerve cells and others specialise in different ways.

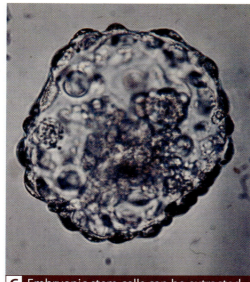

C Embryonic stem cells can be extracted from embryos at this stage of development.

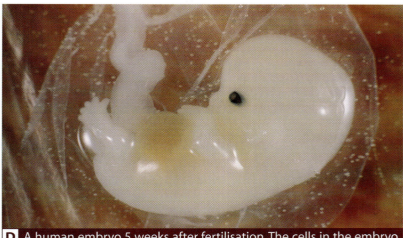

D A human embryo 5 weeks after fertilisation. The cells in the embryo are becoming specialised.

Some of the cells in your body are still dividing, so that you can grow and replace damaged cells. When a body cell divides, it produces a cell just like itself. Once human cells have become specialised, they cannot change into different types of cell.

Sex organs

Some cells in the early embryo become specialised into sex organs. The embryo develops the beginnings of both male **testes** and female **ovaries**. A Y chromosome contains a gene called SRY. This causes the production of certain **hormones** (chemicals which affect cells). One hormone (testosterone) causes the testes to develop, and another hormone (MIS) causes the tiny female ovaries to wither away. If these hormones are not present, female reproductive organs form.

?

2 a What are embryonic stem cells?
  b How are they obtained for medical research?

3 Why will your cells need to divide even after you have stopped growing?

4 a Which gene controls sex determination?
  b Where is this gene found?
  c Why don't females develop testes?

5 Which is the odd one out: nerve cell, egg cell, muscle cell? Explain your answers.

6 Some people think that embryonic stem cells should not be used for research or treatment. Suggest some reasons why they may think this.

Summary

Write encyclopaedia entries for all the words in bold on these pages.

Alleles

What are dominant and recessive alleles?

The characteristics of an organism depend on its genes. For instance, in pea plants there is a gene that controls the colour of the flowers. Some pea plants have red flowers and some have white ones, so there must be two different versions of this gene. The different versions of a gene are called **alleles**.

The chromosomes in body cells are in pairs. Each chromosome of the pair contains the same genes (such as flower colour) in the same order, but some of the genes may be different alleles (such as red and white). If an organism has two alleles of the same kind, it is said to be **homozygous**. If it has one of each kind of allele, it is **heterozygous**.

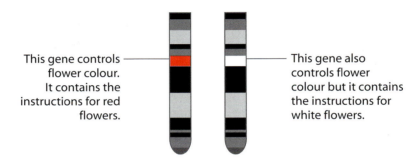

This gene controls flower colour. It contains the instructions for red flowers.

This gene also controls flower colour but it contains the instructions for white flowers.

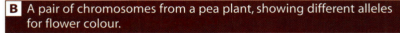

B A pair of chromosomes from a pea plant, showing different alleles for flower colour.

A Pea flowers.

The chromosomes in diagram B have one allele for red flowers and one for white flowers. The different instructions do not mix to produce pink flowers. The allele for red flowers is **dominant** (it does not allow the other allele to work), and so the pea plant has red flowers. The allele for white flowers is called a **recessive** allele. We use letters to represent the different alleles. The dominant allele always has a capital letter.

The characteristics of a recessive allele can only be seen if the organism has a copy on both chromosomes in the pair (it is homozygous). Pea plants will only have white flowers if both alleles of the gene are for white flowers.

If you breed two pea plants together, the colour of the flowers of the offspring depends on which alleles the parent plants have. Diagram C shows what happens when you cross a plant that is homozygous for red flowers with a plant that is homozygous for white flowers.

? 1 What is an allele?

2 What colour flowers would each of these pea plants have?
   a RR
   b Rr
   c rr

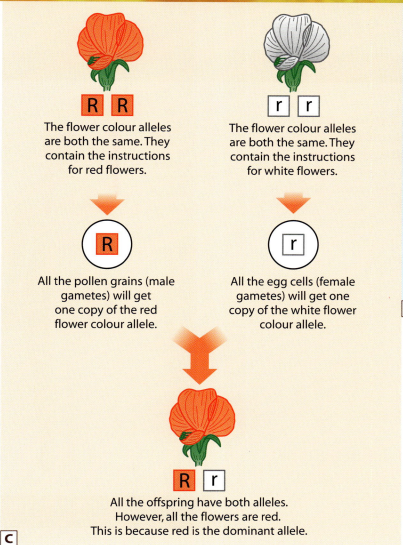

The flower colour alleles are both the same. They contain the instructions for red flowers.

The flower colour alleles are both the same. They contain the instructions for white flowers.

All the pollen grains (male gametes) will get one copy of the red flower colour allele.

All the egg cells (female gametes) will get one copy of the white flower colour allele.

All the offspring have both alleles. However, all the flowers are red. This is because red is the dominant allele.

C

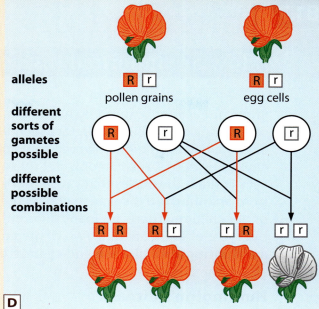

alleles

pollen grains

egg cells

different sorts of gametes possible

different possible combinations

D

Some plants with red flowers are heterozygous and have one allele for white flowers and one for red flowers. You cannot see the effects of the allele for white flowers because it is recessive. When the gametes from these plants fuse to make a new organism, some of the offspring will end up with two alleles for white flowers, and so their flowers will be white.

The offspring from the pea plants shown in diagram D are not all the same, because they inherited different combinations of alleles from the parent plants.

? 3 Why do pea plant gametes only have one allele for flower colour?

4 A pea plant has red flowers. Write down all the possible combinations of genes for flower colour in its *parent* plants.

5 Short pea plants always have short offspring. Tall pea plants can have tall or short offspring. Explain why this happens in terms of dominant and recessive alleles.

Summary

Write a short article for a gardening magazine explaining why planting pea seeds from plants with red flowers will sometimes produce white flowers.

Inherited diseases

How are inherited diseases passed on?

Some diseases are caused by bacteria or viruses, and some can be caused by lifestyle factors such as smoking or not eating a balanced diet. However, some diseases can be caused by genes. You can only get these diseases if your cells contain the alleles that cause them. Someone suffering from an **inherited disease** may pass the disease on to his or her children. There are many different inherited diseases, but most of them are rare. Two of the more common ones are **Huntington's disease** and **cystic fibrosis**.

Huntington's disease

Huntington's disease slowly destroys nerves. People with the allele for Huntington's disease are not affected until they are about 40 years old. They first start to shake and jerk uncontrollably, and their brains are also affected. They usually die within 10 years of showing the symptoms. There is no cure for Huntington's disease, and nothing that doctors can yet do to slow it down.

Huntington's disease is caused by a dominant allele. If a child inherits one copy of the allele he or she will get the disease.

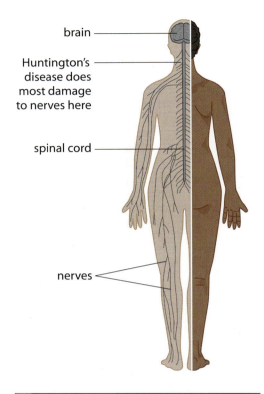

brain

Huntington's disease does most damage to nerves here

spinal cord

nerves

A Huntington's disease damages the nervous system.

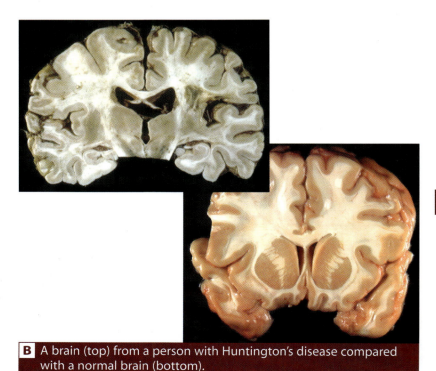

B A brain (top) from a person with Huntington's disease compared with a normal brain (bottom).

?
1 **a** What is an inherited disease?
  b What other ways are there of getting a disease?

2 What are the symptoms of Huntington's disease?

3 Nadia has the allele for Huntington's disease. What percentage of her children would you expect to get the disease?

Cystic fibrosis

Cystic fibrosis is an inherited disease that makes mucus produced by certain cells in the body thick and sticky instead of runny. Mucus sticks in the lungs, and can also block some tubes in the digestive system. People with cystic fibrosis often suffer from lung infections, and may only live to about 30 years of age. There is no cure for cystic fibrosis yet.

B Cystic fibrosis sufferers have their back or chest hit to loosen the mucus so they can cough it up.

Cystic fibrosis is caused by a recessive allele. This means that a person will only get the disease if they are homozygous (have two copies of the allele). A person who is heterozygous for the allele is a **carrier** of the disease, but they do not get the symptoms. If both parents are carriers, some of their children may get two copies of the gene and so suffer from the disease.

parents' alleles

James   Helen

children's alleles

Mark   Chloe   Lee

C A family with cystic fibrosis alleles. The normal allele is shown with an **F**, and the recessive allele that causes the disease is shown with an **f**.

?

4 Why do cystic fibrosis sufferers have difficulty:
   a digesting their food
   b breathing?

5 Look at Diagram C.
   a Why don't James and Helen have cystic fibrosis?
   b Which child has cystic fibrosis?
   c Which child is a carrier of the disease?

6 Sanjay and Nita are both carriers of the cystic fibrosis allele. What proportion of their children would you expect to get the disease?

7 Haemophilia is an inherited disease. Find out why women do not normally suffer from haemophilia.

Summary

Draw a table to summarise the information about the diseases described on these two pages. Include the symptoms and whether the allele is dominant or recessive.

Healthy children?

How can we stop inherited diseases being passed on?

Cystic fibrosis is an inherited disease caused by a recessive allele. Diagram A shows the four ways that Tony and Cleo's alleles can combine. There is a 25% chance that each baby will have the disease.

Huntington's disease is caused by a dominant allele. Janet has just one allele for this disease.

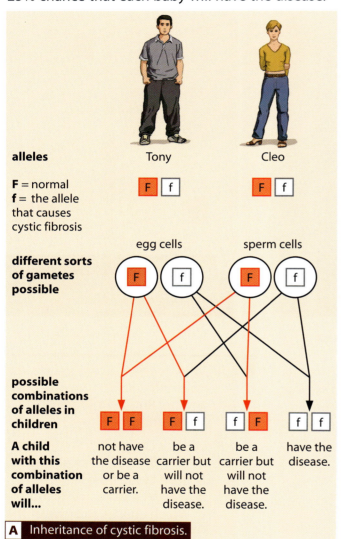

A Inheritance of cystic fibrosis.

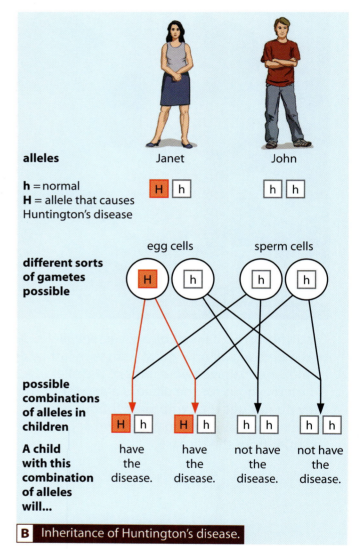

B Inheritance of Huntington's disease.

?

1. Look at diagram A. Which combinations of alleles will produce:
   a a carrier
   b a child with the disease?

2. What is the probability that a child of Janet and John will have Huntington's disease?

3. Why is it that people with the Huntington's allele can pass the disease on to their children before they realise there is a risk of doing so?

A Not everyone who might be carrying the Huntington's allele wants to be tested.
- Why might having the test be a good idea?
- Why might someone not want to know if they have the allele?

Scientists can test a person's genes to find out if they are carrying certain alleles. Janet would know that she might have the allele for Huntington's disease when she was still young, because one of her parents or grandparents may have the symptoms. Janet could ask for a genetic test before she has any babies. If her result is **positive** (meaning that she does have the allele) she might choose not to have any children.

A genetic test may show that there is a risk of passing on a disease. A woman might decide to get pregnant and then have the fetus tested to see if it has the allele for the disease. A doctor carefully takes a cell from the developing fetus while it is still in the uterus, and examines its alleles. If the test is positive the parents could choose to **terminate** the pregnancy (have an **abortion**).

Alternatively, the couple could use IVF to have a baby. In IVF a number of egg cells are taken from the woman and fertilised. One cell can be taken from each embryo and tested. Only healthy embryos are implanted in the woman to start a pregnancy. This is known as **pre-implantation genetic testing**.

A

C

• What would parents have to think about before asking for a fetus to be tested?

?

4 Write down one reason why a person may choose:
 a to have a test for a genetic disease
 b not to have a test
 c to have a fetus tested
 d not to have a fetus tested.

5 a Why might an employer want to see the results of genetic tests on someone being considered for a job?
 b Why might the potential employee not want the employer to see a report?

6 Why do some people consider that pre-implantation genetic testing is more ethical than testing a fetus in the uterus?

Summary

Write a leaflet for a doctor's surgery to explain the differences between testing an adult, a fetus and an IVF embryo for a disease, and what a person needs to think about before asking for a test.

Genetic testing

What are the arguments for and against genetic testing?

Scientists can now carry out tests for many genetic diseases, but people do not always agree that these tests should be done! In many areas of science we need to consider **ethical issues** to decide whether or not something should be done.

For example, some people think that abortions should not be allowed at all, or should only be allowed if having the baby would put the mother's life in danger. Abortion is an ethical issue, and it is something we need to think about when we are discussing genetic testing.

There are lots of different views about genetic testing.

Abortion is wrong, no matter what the reason! There is no point in testing fetuses. If a married couple want to be sure of healthy babies they should have themselves tested to see if they have faulty genes.

We want a family, but we want to be certain our babies will be healthy! We would rather try to adopt a baby than have a child of our own who will suffer from a nasty disease like cystic fibrosis.

Sally and Jim.

Father O'Hara.

No genetic test is absolutely certain. There is still a chance that the test results may be incorrect. A 'false positive' is where the test says there is a problem when there is not. A 'false negative' is where the test says there is no problem when there is one.

Testing my fetus may harm it – I could have a miscarriage because of the test. And I'm not sure if I could have an abortion even if the test was positive. It would be like killing the baby!

Dr Chandak.

Mrs Kapoor.

There is a test to see if I am likely to get a genetic disease. What happens if I am? I won't be able to stop myself getting it – I would just be so depressed if I knew I was going to become ill.

Mr Brandon.

We want to have a baby using IVF treatment. The doctor says they can test the embryos before they implant them, so we can be sure that we will not pass on Marcia's cystic fibrosis gene. Choosing which embryos to implant is not like having an abortion!

Carlton and Marcia.

I have cystic fibrosis. I wouldn't wish it on anybody, but I don't like the idea that my parents might not have wanted me if they had found out about my illness before I was born!

Andy.

I don't think abortion is always wrong – it all depends! A fetus isn't a person until it is nearly ready to be born. Anyway, the law says that I could have an abortion any time until I am 24 weeks pregnant, and even later if there is something wrong with the fetus. They must have considered things carefully before they made that law. They know a lot more of the facts than I do.

Zoe.

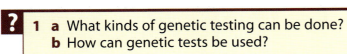

?

1 a What kinds of genetic testing can be done?
  b How can genetic tests be used?

2 What are some of the ethical issues we need to think about?

3 Choose one ethical issue connected with genetic testing.
  a Write down two opposite views on this issue.
  b Suggest an argument for and against each view that you wrote down in part **a**.

4 Find out more about how abortions are carried out. Does knowing what happens in an abortion change your view about when (or whether) abortions should be allowed?

Summary

Write two letters to your MP: one from a person who agrees with genetic testing, and one from someone who is against it.

Modifying genes

How can genetic modification be used to treat diseases?

Scientists have developed ways to modify genes in animals. They are trying to find ways to modify genes in humans to cure some genetic diseases.

Modifying body cells

If scientists know which gene causes an inherited disease, they can try to cure the disease by putting new genes into the cells that need them. Before **gene therapy** can be used, scientists have to work out:

• which gene is causing the problem and how to modify it
• how to get the modified gene into cells without harming the patient.

A These GloFish went on sale in 2003 as pets. They have been genetically modified to glow red.

B Ashanti DeSilva had gene therapy in 1990, when she was four yeas old. She was treated for a genetic disease that stopped her immune system working properly.

C Jesse Gelsinger died when he received gene therapy for a liver problem.

?

1 What is gene therapy?

2 Write down two problems that scientists have to solve before gene therapy can work.

3 A person who has had gene therapy to modify body cells to cure an inherited disease could still pass the disease on to their offspring. Explain why.

Modifying embryos

If an allele in an embryo is modified, all the new cells formed as the embryo grows will have the modified allele. The individual that grows from the egg could pass on the modified version of the gene to their offspring. This technique has only been used on animals so far, but in the future it could be used on human embryos.

D Eduardo Kac asked scientists to create Alba as a work of 'transgenic art'. She glows green when blue light shines on her.

Designer babies

If it could be done safely, most people would agree that modifying an embryo to replace the allele that causes inherited diseases would be a good idea. However, it may also be possible to modify genes in embryos to make sure the children grow up to be tall, to have blond hair, or to be good at sport. This use of gene modification is sometimes called making 'designer babies'.

Summary

Draw a table to summarise points for and against gene therapy, and for and against modifying embryos.

A Should scientists be allowed to change the genes in embryos?
- What are the arguments for allowing this?
- What reasons might people have for opposing it?

?

4 How could a modified embryo pass on the new gene to its offspring?

5 a What is a 'designer baby'?
   b Why are there no designer babies at present? Give as many reasons as you can.

6 Look at photograph A and D. Do you think these animals should have been created? Explain the reasons for your answer.

7 Think of a plus, a minus and an interesting point about this statement: A baby's genes have been modified to make it good at maths.

8 Find out how scientists are trying to deliver modified genes to the organs in the body that need them.

Cloning

How are clones made?

Some animals can reproduce asexually, by producing clones of themselves. The offspring are clones because they contain exactly the same genetic information as the parent animal. The offspring may not be exactly the same as each other, as environmental factors will also affect the way they develop.

In animals that reproduce sexually, the cells of an embryo can sometimes separate naturally to form two separate organisms, called **identical twins**. Identical twins have exactly the same set of genes as each other, because they both started out as part of the same embryo.

Clones can also be made using an egg cell and a cell from an adult animal. The first mammal to be cloned was Dolly the sheep. Diagram B shows how Dolly was created.

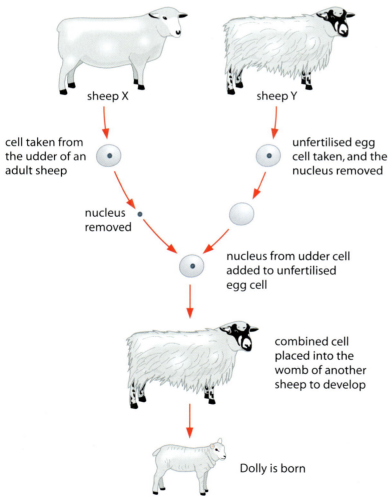

sheep X

sheep Y

cell taken from the udder of an adult sheep

unfertilised egg cell taken, and the nucleus removed

nucleus removed

nucleus from udder cell added to unfertilised egg cell

combined cell placed into the womb of another sheep to develop

Dolly is born

B

A These identical twins have the same set of genes.

C Dolly the sheep (5.7.96–14.2.03).

? 1 a How are identical twins formed?

b Explain why identical twins are clones of each other.

c Explain why identical twins are not clones of their parents.

2 Look at Diagram B. Which sheep has identical genes to Dolly?

Single cells can be cloned in the laboratory. Embryonic stem cells needed for medical research are grown this way.

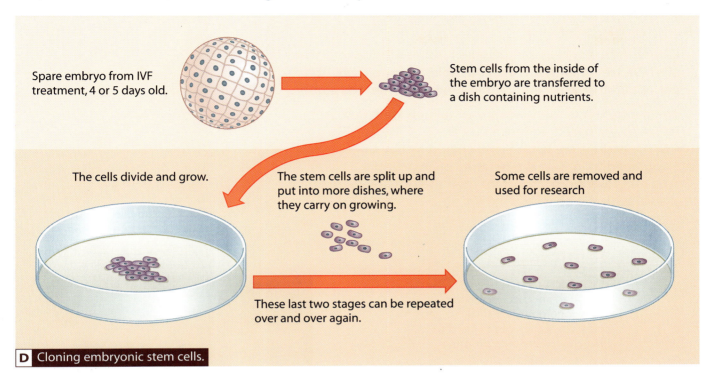

Spare embryo from IVF treatment, 4 or 5 days old.

Stem cells from the inside of the embryo are transferred to a dish containing nutrients.

The cells divide and grow.

The stem cells are split up and put into more dishes, where they carry on growing.

Some cells are removed and used for research

These last two stages can be repeated over and over again.

D Cloning embryonic stem cells.

? **3** Explain how an embryo which contains only a few cells can be used to produce hundreds of stem cells.

It may be possible one day to use embryonic stem cells to treat various diseases. Such treatments could eventually replace the need for organ transplants, and could also cure diseases that have no cure at the moment.

One problem with organ transplants is that the patient's immune system recognises the donated organ as an 'invader' and attacks it. Patients have to stay on drugs that suppress their immune systems for the rest of their lives, and this may make them more likely to catch other diseases.

A similar problem could exist with embryonic stem cells. One way to avoid this problem is to make a clone from one of the patient's cells, and then use embryonic stem cells from this clone for treatment. This is known as **therapeutic cloning**.

? **4** What advantage would using stem cells for treatment have over organ transplants? (*Hint*: think about the supply of organs).

5 a Stem cell 'lines' already exist that have been cloned from spare IVF embryos. Why may these not be suitable for treating patients?

b How can this problem be avoided? Explain your answer.

6 Blood from umbilical cords contains some stem cells, which could be used to treat some diseases.

a Why would some people think that using these stem cells is better from an ethical point of view than using embryonic stem cells?

b Why do some people want to freeze blood from their baby's umbilical cord when it is born?

Summary

Write an encyclopaedia entry on therapeutic cloning.

Using embryos

Should human embryos be used for treating illnesses?

Embryonic stem cells can be taken from embryos left over after IVF treatments. It is also possible to clone a cell from a patient and 'harvest' embryonic stem cells from the clone.

Some arguments for or against obtaining stem cells from embryos are based on these ideas:

- Some actions are wrong, and should not be taken.
- You need to look at the benefits of an action – if the benefits are more important than the possible harm, then go ahead and do it.

> We have five embryos that the clinic are keeping frozen for us. Even if we don't need them, it doesn't seem right to use them for experiments. They could have been human beings!

> I feel too old to go through another pregnancy. I'm never going to use those frozen embryos. If they can be used to develop treatments for other people, that's great!

Felicity's son was born using IVF.

Gina and Atsu used IVF to have their babies.

> Human life is a sacred gift from our Creator. We will not encourage destruction of human embryos that have at least the potential for life.

George Bush, President of the USA (2001–2009). He announced that government money could only be used for research using stem cells that already existed. No new embryos were to be killed to obtain stem cells.

The concept of farming human life for medical purposes is revolting – it's almost like cannibalism!

Patrick took part in an email debate about cloning.

Using stem cells from embryos neither creates nor destroys life – a ball of cells is not a human being. What it does do is to give hope to millions of living human beings suffering from conditions like juvenile diabetes and Alzheimer's.

Michelle's mother has Alzheimer's disease.

Bella

Embryos created for IVF will be destroyed anyway if they are not used. Many fertilised human eggs never implant anyway. However, I don't think it is right to create new embryos on purpose for research – that's not the same thing at all!

? When you are answering these questions, you can use your own ideas as well as some of the ideas on this page.

1 Write down some of the ethical issues involved when we are discussing using embryonic stem cells. You might need to look back at page 24 to remind yourself about ethical issues.

2 Write down some opinions about using embryonic stem cells that are based on these ideas:
   a Using embryonic stem cells is wrong.
   b The benefits of using embryonic stem cells are greater than the harm it may do.

3 What is *your* opinion about using embryonic stem cells? Give reasons for your answer.

4 Embryonic stem cells may one day be used to treat diseases such as Parkinson's or Alzheimer's. Find out more about one of these diseases.

Summary

Write a short paragraph to explain why people need to consider whether embryonic stem cell treatments *should* be used, even if the technical problems are solved.

GENE CLINIC

Are you planning a family? Don't want a 'surprise package'?

Come and talk to us first – we can make sure your baby is healthy and happy, and just the way you want it!

We offer:

- genetic screening of you and your embryos
- selection of suitable embryos
- genetic modification to correct defects in health or appearance.

The services advertised by the Gene Clinic are not available yet, but they may be in the future.

The advert refers to a 'surprise package' because parents can never know exactly what their baby will be like.

Genes control a person's characteristics. They are lengths of DNA found on chromosomes.

1 Genes carry the instructions for making proteins.
  a Name two different things that are made from structural proteins.
  b Enzymes are proteins. What do enzymes do?

2 Genes are passed on in gametes.
  a Explain why a child inherits characteristics from both parents.
  b How many chromosomes does a gamete contain? Explain your answer.
  c Which chromosomes determine the gender of a fetus?
  d How is the development of sex organs controlled by genes?

3 a How are identical twins formed?
  b Why would you expect identical twins to look the same as each other?
  c Why don't identical twins look exactly alike?

The advert offers genetic screening, which means that genes can be tested to make sure there are no alleles that cause inherited diseases.

4 Huntington's disease is caused by a dominant allele.
  a What is an allele?
  b What does dominant mean?
  c What are the symptoms of Huntington's disease?
  d Jeff has the Huntington's allele but his wife does not. Copy and complete the diagram below to show the different combinations of alleles possible if the couple have a child. Use **H** to represent the allele that causes Huntington's disease, and **h** to represent the normal allele.

Jeff

	H	h

Jeff's wife

5 Adults could have their genes tested before starting a family.
  a Give one reason why they might want to do this.
  b Give one reason why they may not want to do this.

6 Cystic fibrosis is caused by a recessive allele.
  a What are the symptoms of cystic fibrosis?
  b What is a 'carrier' of cystic fibrosis?
  c Explain why there is only a risk of a baby getting the disease if both parents have the allele. Draw a diagram to illustrate your answer.
  d What are the chances of a couple who are both carriers having a baby with the disease?

7 If a couple are having a baby, the fetus could be tested to find out if it has two copies of the allele that causes cystic fibrosis.
  a Give one reason why parents may choose to have a fetus tested.
  b Give one reason why they may not wish to have the test.
  c If the couple are having a baby using IVF, the embryos could be tested before any of them are implanted. Why would some people be more likely to have this test than a test on a fetus?

There are often embryos left over after IVF treatments. Embryonic stem cells could be used in the future to treat illnesses. A patient's cell could also be cloned, and embryonic stem cells extracted from the clone.

8 a How are embryonic stem cells different to normal body cells?
  b Why could this be useful in treating diseases?

9 Describe how a clone of an adult animal can be made.

10 a Why are stem cells from a clone of a patient likely to be a more successful treatment than stem cells from an embryo that already exists?
   b Suggest why some people think that therapeutic cloning is not acceptable, whereas using stem cells from spare IVF embryos is acceptable.

Air quality

Why should we be concerned about the air?

Some of the ways that we affect air quality.

With each breath, we take in at least 500 cm³ of air and breathe out about the same volume. Without oxygen we would not be able to live. Nearly every other living thing on the Earth also needs oxygen – it is one of the essential resources. We know that air is necessary for life so you would think that we would take special care of it, but look what we do to it.

A **pollutant** is a substance that is produced by human activity and is harmful to the environment or health or both. Pollutants are found in places where they do not occur naturally or in amounts larger than normal. Pollutants in the air may be gases such as sulfur dioxide, liquids such as sulfuric acid or solids such as soot. They come from many sources but combustion is the main one.

A
- How much air goes in and out of your lungs every day?
- How can you measure lung capacity?

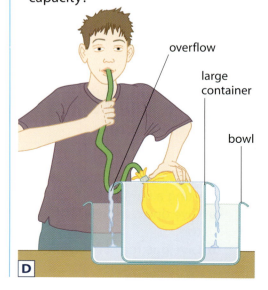

?

1. What do we do to affect the air?
2. How could changes to the air affect us?
3. What else do we need to know in order to answer questions **1** and **2** more fully?

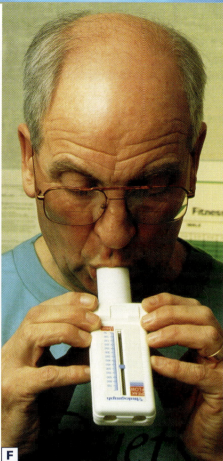

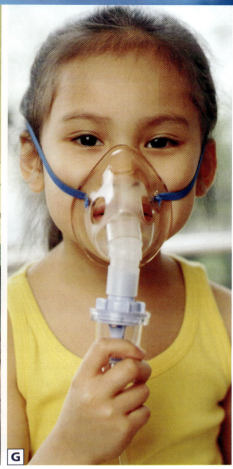

E

F

G

Not everyone takes breathing for granted. In some cities people wear masks to avoid breathing poisonous gases. Asthma sufferers have to check their breathing and some people have to be given extra oxygen to help them breathe.

Asthma is one of the diseases that can affect breathing. In an asthma attack the breathing tubes close up and the sufferer struggles to take in enough air. The number of asthma sufferers has increased in the last 50 years. Sometimes breathing in polluted air, such as from cars, can set off an asthma attack.

Someone buying a new car may think about how fast it will go, how reliable it is and how expensive it is to run. They may not stop to think about how much pollution it produces or whether it will make someone's asthma worse.

We have to make choices and later in this module we will look at what information we need in order to make the best choices for the future.

?

4 The gases given off by car exhausts are a major source of air pollution. There may be ways to reduce the amount of exhaust gases but they will probably make cars and fuel more expensive. People could use public transport instead of their own cars.
   a What can we do to reduce the air pollution caused by cars?
   b What other information do you need to give a better answer to part **a**?

5 Think of a plus, a minus and an interesting point about this statement: The air should be pure oxygen.

6 Sulfur dioxide is found in the air around volcanoes and around power stations that burn coal. In which environment is sulfur dioxide a pollutant? Explain your answer.

How can I find out about air pollution?

A

Cities such as Mexico City have days when the air quality is poor because of pollutants in the air. Information about air quality appears in newspapers, on television weather forecasts, on teletext or on the internet.

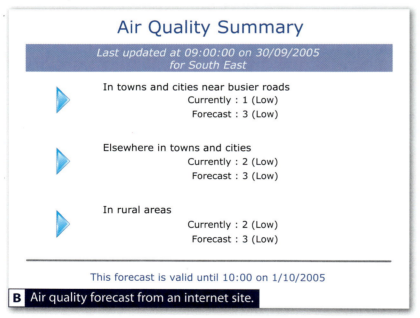

Air Quality Summary

Last updated at 09:00:00 on 30/09/2005
for South East

▷ In towns and cities near busier roads
Currently : 1 (Low)
Forecast : 3 (Low)

▷ Elsewhere in towns and cities
Currently : 2 (Low)
Forecast : 3 (Low)

▷ In rural areas
Currently : 2 (Low)
Forecast : 3 (Low)

This forecast is valid until 10:00 on 1/10/2005

B Air quality forecast from an internet site.

Measuring air quality

Air quality is measured by **sensors** across the UK. The instruments continuously record the amount of various substances in the atmosphere. The data is sent to a computer which averages it for each substance every hour. These readings are used to give the air pollution a number on a scale from 1 to 10, called the air **pollution index**. This data is combined with weather information to give a pollution forecast for the next few hours or days. Often, just a single word is used to describe the air pollution.

?
1 Why is air quality 'good' when the air pollution forecast is 'low'?

2 a Why is it a good idea to have a large number of air pollution measuring stations?

b Why are some sensors placed close to roads?

Index number	Band	Meaning
1–3	low	Pollutants are not noticeable, even to people who are sensitive to them.
4–6	medium	Sensitive people may notice the pollutants but no action is necessary.
7–9	high	Pollutants could cause some people breathing problems and they should stay indoors.
10	very high	Those people who are affected would experience worse problems.

C Pollution index.

A You can use a carbon monoxide sensor to measure how much carbon monoxide there is in the air.
• What sites would you choose to test?
• How many measurements should you take at each site?

There are always **errors** in measurements of air quality and other quantities. The last digit of a reading is usually unreliable, so readings are repeated to overcome some sources of error. Any measurement that seems to be much larger or smaller than the others is called an **outlier**. The outliers are not used when a mean is worked out. The largest and smallest of the remaining data form the **range** within which the true value should lie. The mean is the **best estimate** of the true value.

"Air Quality - Good"

"Air Pollution Forecast - Low"

"Air Pollution Forecast - Band 3"

Sulphur dioxide – 70 ppb, carbon monoxide – 8.0 ppm, particulates – 42 μg/m³

D Air quality can be described in different ways.

?

3 What effect might an air pollution index of 8 have?

4 a The readings of a sensor that can take measurements to an accuracy of 1 decimal place are 8.22 and 8.18. Would you count these readings as being different or the same? Explain your answer.
b The sensor produced three more readings of 8.24, 8.40 and 8.19. What is the best estimate of the true value and the range of the five readings? Explain how you get your answer.

5 An air quality sensor is giving a 'high' reading while others in the region are giving 'low' data. Consider all the possible reasons for this.

6 The detailed figures from sensors are not given in the air quality forecasts in newspapers or on TV. Discuss the reasons for this.

Summary

A List the ways in which information about air quality can be given and give an advantage and disadvantage for each.

B Write a short paragraph to describe why readings are repeated, and what is done with the readings.

Air – a mixture

What chemicals make up the air?

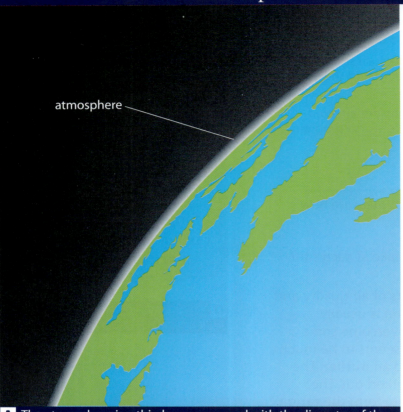

A The atmosphere is a thin layer compared with the diameter of the Earth.

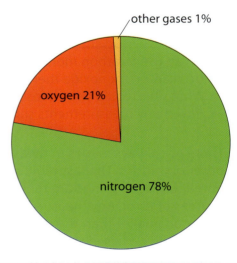

B The percentages of gases in dry air (air without water vapour).

The Earth is surrounded by a layer of gas called the **atmosphere** which is about 100 km deep.

The atmosphere is a mixture called air. The percentages of gases in the air remain at fairly constant levels but the amount of water vapour in the air can vary between 0 and 1%.

A How can you find the percentage of oxygen in the air?
• You can use this apparatus to remove oxygen from a volume of air.

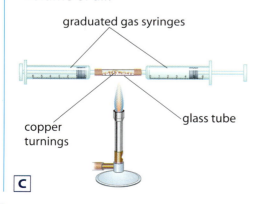

C

 1 The air is a mixture of gases. Explain what is meant by the words: mixture, gas.

2 Why are the percentages of gases in chart B given for dry air?

Life support

Oxygen would not remain in the atmosphere for long if it wasn't constantly replaced by plants by photosynthesis. Unlike oxygen, nitrogen is quite unreactive. Winds mix the gases in the air thoroughly so the amount of each gas only varies a little from place to place.

Trace gases

Argon wasn't discovered until 1894 because it is unreactive. It is used to fill filament light bulbs. The amount of carbon dioxide in the atmosphere is about 0.04% or 400 parts per million (ppm) and there are even tinier percentages (or **trace** amounts) of the other unreactive gases helium, neon, krypton and xenon.

E Oxygen and other gases are separated by distilling liquefied air. The gases are supplied to hospitals and industries.

There are also trace amounts of harmful gases in the air such as methane, carbon monoxide, sulfur dioxide and nitrogen oxides. These gases are formed by natural processes such as volcanic activity and decomposition of organic matter, and by human activities such as burning fuels.

Chemical reactions 15 km up in the atmosphere produce small quantities of the gas ozone. The ozone layer protects organisms on the surface from harmful ultraviolet rays from the Sun. Ozone is only formed at ground level by human activities and here it harms the environment and health.

Natural processes and human activities also produce particles of dust and soot which are small enough to float in the air. They are called **particulates**. Dust is made up of tiny particles of rock and bits of skin and hair.

D With just a little more oxygen in the atmosphere, forest fires would be more common.

?

3 Which gas in the air is used in respiration?

4 a Would you expect the amount of oxygen in the air over a city to be greater or less than that over a forest?
  b Explain your answer.

5 Which trace gases are pollutants? Explain your answer.

6 Why do houses get dusty?

7 Which is the odd one out: oxygen, carbon dioxide, argon? Explain your answers.

8 How would you expect the percentage of carbon dioxide to vary:
  a daily
  b during the year
  c over cities and rainforests?
  Explain your answers.

Summary

Draw a mind map to remind you of which gases are in the air. Add a statement about each of them.

Checking the pollutants

How do we decide which substances are pollutants?

A Scientists collecting samples on a volcano need to wear face masks.

If you ever get the chance to visit an active volcano you will notice that it smells odd. Volcanoes release sulfur dioxide, along with other gases, into the air. If you breathe in air containing sulfur dioxide it irritates the back of your throat and makes you cough. Just a whiff of the gas can set off an attack in asthma sufferers. Too much sulfur dioxide is harmful and affects the environment.

The amount of sulfur dioxide produced by volcanoes is not normally a problem unless you happen to be close to one when it erupts. However, sulfur dioxide produced by human activities is a concern. In this case it is called a pollutant.

Hazards and risks

Chemists do experiments to find out how substances react and how they affect health and the environment. They find out how much of a substance is required to produce serious harm. These are the **hazards** of a substance. Lists of hazards are published, for instance on **Hazcards**. Harmful substances produced by the chemical industry are labelled with a hazard symbol.

? 1 a When is sulfur dioxide a pollutant?
   b Many human activities produce water. Is water a pollutant? Explain your answer.
   c What information do we need to decide if substances in the air are pollutants?

97. SULFUR DIOXIDE

TOXIC

CORROSIVE

Toxic by inhalation. May cause burns. Irritating to the eyes and respiratory system. It is a choking gas with serious effects on the lungs and eyes, resulting in possible bronchitis and conjunctivitis. **Pupils with known breathing difficulties must not inhale the gas; it may trigger an asthmatic attack.**

B Part of a Hazcard for sulfur dioxide.

A **risk** is the actual danger to health caused by a chemical with a known hazard present in the air. A large amount of a substance with a low hazard could be more of a risk to health than a tiny amount of a very hazardous substance.

Pollutant	Hazard	Effect on health
sulfur dioxide	toxic	Irritates the eyes and respiratory system. Prolonged exposure is fatal.
nitrogen oxides	very toxic	Irritates the eyes and respiratory system. Prolonged exposure is fatal.
carbon monoxide	toxic and extremely flammable	Has no smell but replaces oxygen in blood. Prolonged exposure is fatal.
hydrogen sulfide	very toxic	Harms the nervous system. A small quantity can be fatal.

HARMFUL

FLAMMABLE

OXIDISING

TOXIC

CORROSIVE

C Hazard symbols.

Disasters every day

Major disasters where a very hazardous pollutant is released into the air are rare, but smaller pollution events are very common. Every day people produce pollutants as they go about their daily lives working in factories, farms and offices and travelling from place to place. Sometimes the amount of some pollutants can increase to a level that is a high risk to health and to the environment.

Summary

Write an answer to a question in a teenage magazine asking what a pollutant is and the meaning of the words hazard and risk.

?

2 Which hazard symbols should be used with carbon monoxide?

3 If equal amounts of carbon monoxide and hydrogen sulfide were present in the air, which would constitute the greatest risk to health? Explain your answer.

4 Explain the difference between a hazard and a risk.

5 How would you know if the health risk of breathing air in a particular place was high?

6 Chemists have discovered the substance dihydrogen monoxide in the air. How can we decide if it is a pollutant?

Making new compounds

How are pollutant molecules formed from other substances?

Millions of different chemicals make up the Earth, the oceans and the atmosphere. They are all made up from about 90 substances that cannot be broken into any simpler substances, called **elements**. Each element is made up of **atoms**. Atoms of different elements are different. Most substances are **compounds** in which two or more elements are joined together.

Molecules are groups of atoms joined together by a chemical bond. For instance, two atoms of oxygen are joined together in a molecule of oxygen gas. Carbon dioxide is made up of one atom of carbon and two atoms of oxygen. There are millions of ways of combining even small numbers of atoms of various elements.

The properties of compounds such as water and carbon dioxide are very different from those of the elements that make them up.

A In 1803 John Dalton said that atoms of elements were indestructible particles that could join together to form compounds.

oxygen

carbon dioxide

carbon monoxide

water

B Molecules of some common gases.

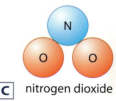
nitrogen oxide

nitrogen dioxide

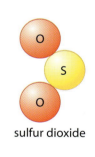
sulfur dioxide

C

It doesn't matter how the carbon dioxide is formed, the number and arrangement of the atoms in the molecules are always the same. The same is true for all other molecular substances including the pollutants carbon monoxide, sulfur dioxide, nitrogen monoxide and nitrogen dioxide.

Each molecule can be represented by a **formula** which shows the number of atoms of each element that are joined together in the molecule. For example, the formula for carbon dioxide is CO_2. This shows it has one atom of carbon and two atoms of oxygen.

In a **chemical reaction** the atoms are rearranged to make new substances. Some atoms that were joined together in molecules may become separated and may join together to form new molecules. Whatever happens, the same number of atoms of each element is present at the end of the reaction as was there at the beginning.

? 1 Carbon and oxygen are elements. Write down two statements about the atoms of carbon and oxygen.

2 Write down the formula for each of these molecules:
 a water
 b carbon monoxide
 c sulfur dioxide
 d nitrogen monoxide

For example, the element carbon burns in oxygen to form carbon dioxide gas. The atoms in the oxygen molecules separate. Two oxygen atoms join up with each carbon atom to make a molecule of carbon dioxide. Carbon and oxygen are the **reactants** and carbon dioxide is the **product** of the reaction.

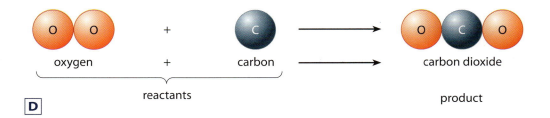

oxygen + carbon → carbon dioxide

reactants   product

D

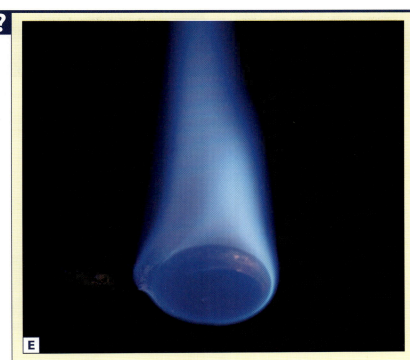

E

3 Sulfur burns in oxygen to form sulfur dioxide.
   a Which molecules have broken up?
   b Which atoms have joined together?
   c Draw a diagram to represent the atoms in the reaction, similar to diagram D.

4 At very high temperatures, nitrogen combines with oxygen to form nitrogen monoxide. Draw a diagram to represent the reaction.

5 Which is the odd one out: element, atom, molecule? Explain your answers.

6 How does carbon burning in the atmosphere change the composition of the air?

Summary

A Make a list of the differences between:
   i an element and a compound
   ii an atom and a molecule.

B Write some rules for how atoms behave in chemical reactions.

Burning fuels

What human activities release carbon dioxide and water into the air?

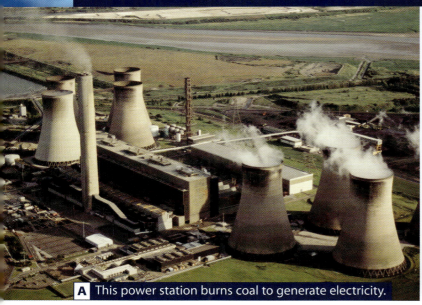

A This power station burns coal to generate electricity.

B Ships burn the hydrocarbons in fuel oil.

A **fuel** is a substance that burns in the air, releasing useful heat energy. **Fossil fuels** such as coal, oil and natural gas were formed many millions of years ago from the remains of plants and animals trapped in rocks.

Fossil fuels are made up of molecules called **hydrocarbons** which are compounds of hydrogen and carbon. Coal is mainly carbon with some hydrocarbons. Natural gas is largely a hydrocarbon called methane with the formula CH_4. The liquid fuels are more complex mixtures of hydrocarbons.

In industrialised countries the burning of fossil fuels provides most of the energy that humans need.

C Natural gas is burnt in our homes to cook food and to heat water in central heating systems.

methane

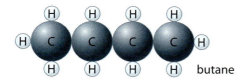

butane

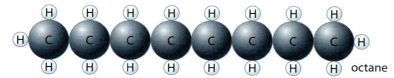

octane

D Some hydrocarbon molecules.

? **1** Why are liquid fuels such as petrol and diesel used in transport instead of solid fuels like coal?

2 Why is natural gas the most popular fuel for heating homes?

3 How many atoms of oxygen combine with every atom of carbon in coal when it is burned? (*Hint:* look back at page 43.)

A How could you show that carbon dioxide and water are formed when a hydrocarbon fuel is burned?

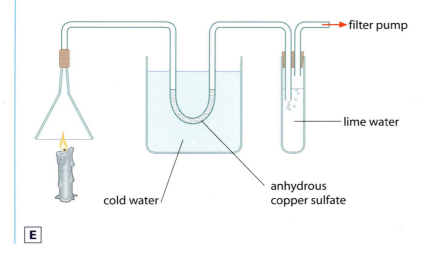

filter pump

lime water

anhydrous copper sulfate

cold water

E

Hydrocarbons burn in the air to form carbon dioxide and water:

hydrocarbon + oxygen → carbon dioxide + water

Burning 1 kg of petrol uses up about 3.5 kg of oxygen – the amount of oxygen in about 10 000 litres of air.

Graph F shows that we burn many millions of tonnes of coal, liquid fuels and natural gas. This takes out a huge amount of oxygen from the air and replaces it with carbon dioxide and water vapour. The combustion of fossil fuels is increasing the amount of carbon dioxide in the atmosphere. You can find out about the effects of carbon dioxide on the environment in Module P2. As damage to the environment indirectly affects humans, carbon dioxide is also classed as a pollutant.

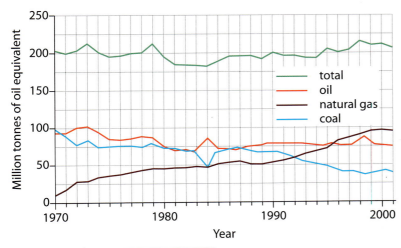

F UK fuel consumption 1970–2000.

?

4 A car travels about 10 km on 1 kg of petrol. What volume of air does it use up for every kilometre it travels?

5 What was the total fuel consumption in:
   a 1970
   b 2002?

6 Between 1970 and 2000, for which fuels has consumption:
   a increased
   b decreased?

7 When the same amounts of coal and natural gas are burned, coal gives off more carbon dioxide. How would this affect the choice of fuel for power stations?

8 Explain the changes you noted in questions **5** and **6**.

9 Think of a plus, a minus and an interesting point about this statement: The use of fossil fuels in developing countries has been increasing.

10 Draw a diagram to represent the reaction of a molecule of methane with molecules of oxygen.

Summary

Draw a mind map with 'fossil fuels' at the centre. Add the key words and ideas that you have met in this topic.

Making pollutants

What is the source of pollutants in the air?

A

The burning of hydrocarbons produces carbon dioxide and water but may produce other pollutants as well.

Carbon monoxide, CO

Students killed by faulty gas fire

B Carbon monoxide is a poisonous gas.

Fuels burnt in homes must have a good supply of air. If the amount of oxygen is limited, the atoms in the fuel and oxygen rearrange themselves to form carbon monoxide as well as carbon dioxide and water. When fuel is burnt in the small spaces inside vehicle engines the air supply is never enough to burn the fuel completely, so carbon monoxide is always formed.

Dust and soot

When coal is burnt it always leaves some ash and dust. Some of the carbon in fuels does not get burned and is given out as soot or **particulate carbon**. Particulates like dust and soot are made up of tiny particles of solid which float in the air.

A Sticky-backed plastic will trap particles of soot and dust.
- How could you use sticky-backed plastic to measure particulate pollution?

? 1 a How many atoms of carbon react with oxygen to form a molecule of carbon monoxide?
b Why is carbon monoxide formed instead of carbon dioxide when there is a poor supply of oxygen?

2 A yellow Bunsen burner flame produces soot.
a Is the air hole open or closed to produce a yellow Bunsen flame?
b How does this affect how much soot is formed?

Sulfur dioxide, SO$_2$

Sulfur is present in plants and animals so it is also found in fossil fuels. Coal in particular often contains a considerable amount of sulfur. When the fuel is burned, the sulfur burns too.

sulfur + oxygen → sulfur dioxide

Most of the sulfur can be removed from natural gas and liquid fuels.

high octane unleaded

super unleade

super unleaded
octane 97 Ron BS 7800

low emission
ultra low sulphur

city diesel

diesel
BS EN590

C Service stations now supply fuel with reduced amounts of sulfur.

Nitrogen oxides, NO and NO$_2$

Nitrogen doesn't burn in air unless the temperature is hot enough (about 1000 °C). Then nitrogen combines with oxygen to form nitrogen monoxide.

nitrogen + oxygen → nitrogen monoxide

This temperature is reached inside engines in cars and lorries and sometimes in power station furnaces. When the nitrogen monoxide mixes with cool air, some of it reacts with more oxygen to form nitrogen dioxide.

nitrogen monoxide + oxygen → nitrogen dioxide

The two oxides of nitrogen are together referred to as **NO$_x$**.

?

3 Why was a lot more sulfur dioxide released into the air up to about 20 years ago?

4 Draw a diagram to show how two nitrogen monoxide molecules react with an oxygen molecule to form two nitrogen dioxide molecules.

5 How is the formation of NO$_x$ different to the way in which other pollutants are formed by burning fuels?

6 a Which is the most serious source of air pollution – burning coal in power stations or burning liquid fuels in vehicle engines? Explain your answer.
   b What information do you need to give a better answer to this question?

D All these different gases are released into the air when fuels are burned.

Summary

Write two or three bullet points about each of the air pollutants described on these two pages.

Air pollutants and the environment
What happens to pollutants once they are in the air?

Once a substance is in the air:
- it may remain in the air
- it may react with other substances in the air
- it may dissolve in rainwater, or the oceans, or settle on the ground.

Particulates

Dust and soot do not remain in the air for very long. The particles settle on the ground, on plants or buildings, or in people's lungs. When coal was burnt in many homes and industries, buildings became blackened by soot. The tiny particles of soot given out by diesel engines are still a concern.

? 1 Why don't buildings get covered by soot as much today?

2 What happens to the soot in the air that you breathe?

A The Houses of Parliament used to be covered with soot…

B … but after cleaning the colour of the stone can be seen again.

Acid rain

Rain is normally weakly acidic because of carbon dioxide dissolved in it. Sulfur dioxide and nitrogen oxides react with oxygen and water vapour in the air to form sulfuric and nitric acids. These dissolve in raindrops to make a solution with a **pH** of about 4, which is a fairly strong acid.

C Many trees have died as a result of acid rain.

Acid rain can make rivers and lakes too acidic for fish. It can also dissolve harmful substances from soil and wash these into rivers and lakes, and it damages trees.

A How would you investigate the effects of acid rain on:
- buildings made from calcium carbonate
- machines made of steel
- the growth of a plant?

Carbon dioxide

Photosynthesis in land and water plants converts carbon dioxide and water into sugars and oxygen. Farmers give plants in greenhouses extra carbon dioxide to encourage growth, but plants may not be able to take up the extra carbon dioxide in the air across the whole of the Earth.

D Carbon dioxide from the Earth's ancient atmosphere is stored in these cliffs.

Carbon dioxide can dissolve in rainwater, and about half of the carbon dioxide that is released dissolves in the oceans. Shellfish use the carbon dioxide and calcium and magnesium compounds in the water to build their shells. If more carbon dioxide dissolves in the ocean then the water may become too acidic and the shells will dissolve. Without the processes of photosynthesis and dissolving, carbon dioxide might just remain in the atmosphere.

Summary

Copy and fill in the table below, showing what happens to pollutants when they are in the air.

Pollutant	Outcome

? 3 Pollutants produced in the UK are blown across the North Sea to Norway. What effect do you think this has on the forests of Norway?

4 Write a word equation for the reaction of photosynthesis.

5 What effect will destruction of the rainforests have on carbon dioxide levels?

6 There is a greater mass of microscopic plants in the oceans than the mass of all the trees on land. Why is this fact important?

7 Not all the carbon dioxide released by burning fossil fuels is in the air. Consider all the possible explanations for this.

8 **Residence time** is the time a substance stays in the air without changing. Which of the air pollutants has the longest residence time? Explain your answer.

Air pollution and health

What effects do air pollutants have on health?

Pollution kills

Smog is the name given to a thick brown fog. It was common at one time in cities, caused by burning smoky coal during damp, cold winters. In London, in 1952, a thick smog lasted for nearly a week. Table A shows the number of deaths in the area covered by the smog in 1952.

Disease	Number of deaths	
	Week before smog	Week of smog
bronchitis	74	704
influenza	47	192
tuberculosis	14	77
breathing problems	9	52
heart disease	206	525
others	595	934

A Smog deaths in 1952.

?

1 a Calculate the ratio in percentages for deaths from each disease before and during the smog

$$\% \text{ ratio} = \frac{\text{deaths in week of smog}}{\text{deaths before smog}} \times 100\%$$

b Which disease showed the biggest percentage change?

B A London smog in the 1950s.

The diseases shown in table A are caused by microbes or lifestyle but during the smog more people died of diseases they already had. The **correlation** was confirmed in other smogs. Scientists found that smog damages the breathing tubes so smog was the **cause** of death of people already weakened by disease. In 1956 the British Government banned the burning of smoky coal in cities. The smogs soon ceased.

?

2 Why is it wrong to say that the smog caused bronchitis?

Correlation, cause and outcome

Two factors are correlated if they follow a related pattern. A correlation shows a link but it does not always mean that one **factor** causes another. In 1952 the rise in the number of deaths from bronchitis was the **outcome** of incidents of smog. It was an **acceptable theory** that smog was a cause of the deaths.

In a laboratory, scientists do experiments to test **theories**. They control factors, change one factor at a time and look at the outcome. They decide which theory is acceptable. This process is not possible when looking at factors in diseases, because scientists cannot make a group of people do something that could harm their health.

Air pollution and asthma

One in eight children and one in 13 adults received medical attention in 2003 for the breathing disease, asthma. This is a big increase on 30 years ago. Many factors, including air pollution, trigger asthma attacks, but scientists are still seeking an acceptable theory for the cause of the disease.

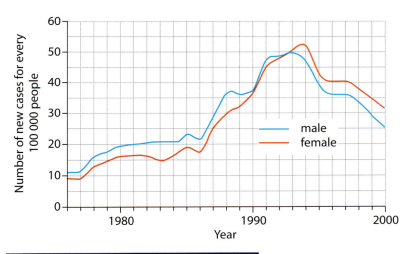

C New asthma cases in the UK, 1976–1999.

Summary

Explain, with examples, the meaning of the terms correlation, cause, factor, acceptable theory and outcome.

?

3   Has the number of asthma cases risen more in men or women? Explain your answer.

4   In which 5-year period on the graph did the number of new cases of asthma increase the fastest? Explain your answer.

5   Did more people have asthma in 1999 than in 1995? Explain your answer.

6   Look at graph F on page 45. Is there a correlation between the number of new asthma cases and:
   a the use of coal
   b the use of natural gas?
   Explain your answers.

7   What further information would be needed to show that a factor was the cause of increases in asthma cases?

8   Do you think the data given in the table on smog-related deaths was the only reason why the British Government passed the Clean Air Acts in 1956? Explain your answer.

Pollution and power stations

How can we cut pollution caused by power stations?

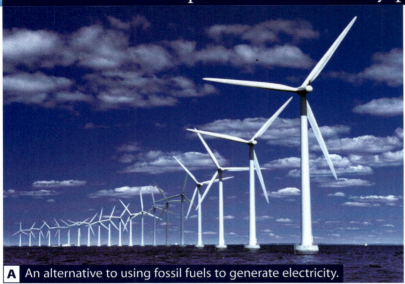

A An alternative to using fossil fuels to generate electricity.

The burning of fossil fuels is the major cause of poor air quality. A large proportion of the fossil fuels that are used are burnt in power stations to generate electricity. Electricity is used by industry, in offices, in hospitals, schools and in our own homes. We must look at ways of reducing the amount of pollutants given off by power stations.

The energy market

In the UK, power stations are owned by generating companies that sell electricity to consumers. The company makes a profit if the money it earns from selling electricity is greater than the costs of generating it. Companies want to make a profit and will only make changes to the way they produce electricity if:
- their profit would be bigger if they changed
- the government makes laws that the companies have to obey or else pay large fines.

There are a number of options the generating companies could use to improve air quality:

A produce less electricity

B remove sulfur from oil and natural gas

C remove sulfur dioxide and particulates from the gases given off by the burning fuel

D burn fuels that produce less pollutants

E produce electricity by methods other than by burning fuels, such as wind turbines, hydroelectric schemes or solar power.

?
1 Option A on the left means that we would have to use less electricity. How could we do this?

2 Look at charts **C** and **D** on page 53.
   a Describe how fossil fuel use changed from 1970 to 2000.
   b Which of the options A to E explains the change in fuel consumption? Explain your answer.

3 Which of the options listed would:
   a increase the costs of the generating companies
   b reduce the profits gained by the companies?

4 Which options would reduce the amount of carbon dioxide released into the air?

5 What alternatives to burning fossil fuels are there for generating electricity?

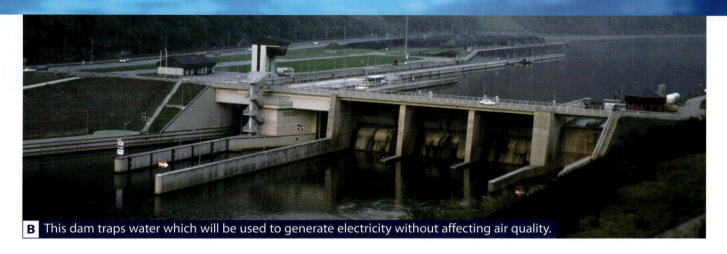

B This dam traps water which will be used to generate electricity without affecting air quality.

Controlling pollution

The air quality in the UK has improved in the last 30 years, as the government has passed laws controlling the amount of sulfur in fuels, and limiting the amounts of sulfur dioxide and nitrogen oxides that power stations are allowed to produce. There are targets to continue to reduce the amounts of these pollutants produced in the future.

The government also provides various financial incentives to companies generating electricity from renewable resources.

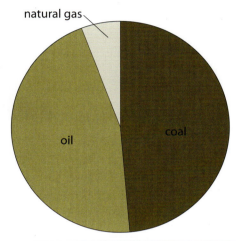

C Fossil fuel consumption in the UK in 1970.

? 6 Why does the government need to control the amount of pollution produced by power stations?

7 How would increasing the efficiency of power stations affect air quality? (Note: efficiency is the percentage of the energy in the fossil fuels that is turned into electricity. The rest of the energy becomes waste heat.)

Summary

Write a short article for a magazine explaining the ways in which air quality could be improved by changing the way electricity is produced.

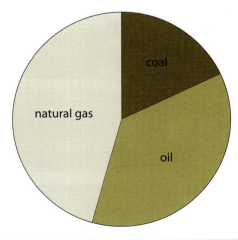

D Fossil fuel consumption in the UK in 2000.

Pollution and transport

How can pollutants in emissions from transport be reduced?

A Aircraft engines burn fossil fuels.

When we travel or when we buy goods that have travelled from somewhere else we contribute to poor air quality. We could stop all the travel but there are less drastic things that could be done to reduce pollution from most methods of transport, especially road vehicles.

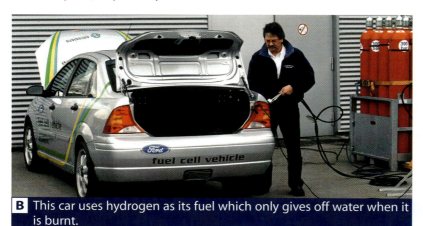

B This car uses hydrogen as its fuel which only gives off water when it is burnt.

D This vehicle charges its batteries by plugging into the electricity supply.

C Cars are charged for driving on these city streets. Perhaps it would be cheaper to leave the car at home and use public transport.

A Use less fuel for each kilometre travelled. Engines could be made more **efficient**, reducing the amount of energy that is wasted as heat. Vehicles could be smaller and lighter so that less energy is needed to move them.

B Remove sulfur. If the sulfur isn't in the fuel it cannot be burned to form sulfur dioxide. The sulfur is removed at the oil refinery and can be sold to make useful chemicals.

C Use vehicles with **catalytic converters** that encourage chemical reactions between the harmful pollutants (carbon monoxide, nitrogen oxide) to form harmless nitrogen and less harmful carbon dioxide.

D Use public transport, ride bicycles or walk. A train, tram or bus uses less energy per passenger than if the passengers had travelled in their own cars. Short journeys can be made almost as quickly on foot or by bicycle as by car. Increasing the cost of using cars would encourage people to think of other ways of travelling. **Tax** on fuel could be increased. There could be a fee for use of certain roads, or parking charges could be increased.

E Test vehicles to make sure that they obey the laws on **emissions** of pollutants. Cars and lorries have to pass the MOT test every year. If the vehicle fails the emissions test it must be repaired or scrapped. The laws could be made stricter to reduce air pollution.

F Develop engines that do not burn fossil fuels. For example, electric vehicles use electricity that could be generated by renewable resources.

E Modern public transport is quick, convenient and produces less pollution than cars.

?

1 A bus burns a litre of fuel every 2 km, while a car can travel 15 km on a litre of fuel. How does the bus improve air quality?

2 Draw a sketch to show the molecules entering and leaving a catalytic converter.

3 Explain why making an engine more efficient reduces pollution.

4 a Which of the suggestions on the left is likely to increase the cost of travelling?
   b Which suggestions may be unpopular to car drivers?
   c Which methods could be used to reduce the air pollution caused by aircraft?

5 Write down a plus, a minus and an interesting point about this statement: Electric cars are the answer to air pollution problems.

6 Look at table F.
   a What is the tax for each gram per kilometre of CO_2 in each band?
   b If a car in each band travels 10 000 km in a year, how much carbon dioxide is produced?

Maximum CO_2 emissions (g/km)	Road tax paid in 2005 (£)
150	115.00
165	135.00
185	160.00

F

Summary

Convert the suggestions given in this topic into a mind map. Put the words 'Reducing pollution from transport' in the centre.

Making choices about air quality

What decisions can be made to improve air quality?

A Decisions must be taken to improve air quality.

International choices

In the 1990s in Kyoto, Japan, world leaders met to find ways to reduce the amount of carbon dioxide and other pollutants released into the air from burning fossil fuels. The USA (the biggest user of fossil fuels), and other countries have failed to follow the plans suggested. As a result the Kyoto conference has had little effect.

National decisions

People who are ill as a result of air pollution may require medical treatment, may be unable to work and could cost a country a lot of money. If a government can improve the air quality then the health of the population will improve and costs will go down. To fund improvements in air quality the government may have to raise taxes or introduce charges such as the London congestion charge. New laws may be needed to make companies or individuals introduce methods of reducing air pollution. In a democracy like the UK, the government can only introduce these laws if a majority of the people are in favour of them.

?
1 Why might a government refuse to reduce the amount of fossil fuels it burns?

2 a What would be the effect of increasing taxes on fuels?
  b Why might this not be popular?

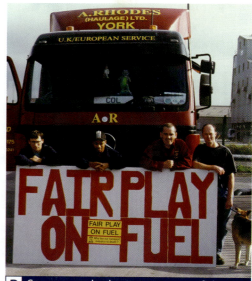

B Some people do not approve of the high tax on fuel in the UK.

Local decisions

We are most aware of the air quality in the place where we live. There are many local decisions that can change air quality. Local government can alter traffic patterns, encourage people to use public transport, and monitor pollution levels.

Groups of people can make choices that help decrease air pollution. For example, in some places parents have organised 'walking buses'. Instead of driving children to school in polluting cars, a parent supervises a group of children walking to school.

C A 'walking bus' saves energy, keeps the air cleaner and improves health.

And finally, ourselves

In a country of 60 million people, one person's decisions may seem unimportant, but lots of individual choices can be effective collectively. Each person can switch off lights or electrical equipment when not in use; insulate their home to require less heating; take public transport, cycle or walk instead of travelling in a private car. Think of all the things that you could do.

D In a city a cyclist can travel just as fast as a car and produces no pollution.

? 3 What are the benefits and problems associated with 'walking buses'?

4 What can a local government do to encourage people to cycle or walk instead of driving?

5 In some parts of the world air quality is becoming worse. Why is this so?

6 Various measures have been suggested to improve air quality. How can scientists and governments evaluate which ones are successful?

Summary

Draw four concentric circles. Label the inner circle 'Me', the next 'My city/town/village', the next 'My country' and the outer circle 'The Earth'. In each circle write things that could be done to reduce air pollution.

Looking at air quality

What do you know about air quality and how it can be improved?

Josh and Emily live in a small town. The streets in the town centre are clogged with traffic and Josh and Emily think that the air quality is poor. They have decided to do a project to investigate air quality in their town and find ways of improving it.

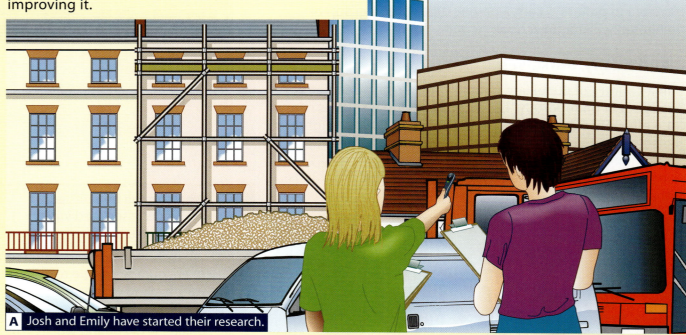

A Josh and Emily have started their research.

1 Emily and Josh have used sticky-backed cards to collect soot in the school grounds and near a busy road. Using a microscope they counted the number of soot particles collected in the millimetre squares marked on the cards.

Card location	Number of particles per mm²				
	1	2	3	4	5
school field	19	21	20	22	18
road side	33	29	20	32	30

B

   a Which measurement is probably an outlier?
   b What should Emily and Josh do with the results to reach valid conclusions?
   c What do the results indicate about the amount of soot in the air at the two locations?
   d Soot is found in the exhaust fumes of vehicles. Explain how it is formed.
   e What happens to the soot particles in the air?

2 Emily has found out that catalytic converters are fitted to cars. Catalytic converters convert some pollutants into less dangerous substances. Copy and complete table C to show how the amount of each substance is changed by the catalytic converter. Tick one box in each row. One has been done for you.

Substance	Increases	Decreases	Stays the same
carbon monoxide		✓	
carbon dioxide			
nitrogen oxides			
argon			
nitrogen			

C

3 Nitrogen oxides are air pollutants produced by vehicles burning fossil fuels. Josh has discovered that it is thought that the amount of nitrogen oxides in the air over the UK increased until the early 1990s. At this time catalytic converters were fitted to most cars and levels of nitrogen oxides have remained constant or fallen slightly since then. Josh wonders if nitrogen oxides are linked to cases of asthma.

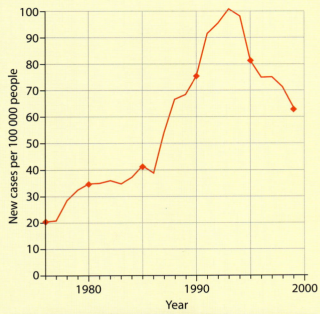

New asthma cases reported in the UK, 1976–2000.

a Why is accurate data on nitrogen oxide in the air only available for recent years?
b What evidence is there for a correlation between new cases of asthma and the amount of nitrogen oxide in the air?
c Explain why the correlation does not prove that nitrogen oxide causes asthma.
d Give two ways that air quality in cities could be improved to reduce the number of asthma cases.

4 Emily and Josh both know that sulfur dioxide is a common air pollutant. Table E shows the sources of sulfur dioxide emissions in one year.

Source	Sulfur dioxide (thousands of tonnes)
homes	69
industry	418
power stations	1318
oil refineries	123
road vehicles	38
railways	2
others	60
total	2028

E Sources of sulfur dioxide emissions in one year in the UK.

a How many oxygen atoms are combined with each sulfur atom in sulfur dioxide?
b What is the formula for sulfur dioxide?
c Many fossil fuels contain sulfur. How is sulfur dioxide formed?
d Which source is responsible for over 60% of the sulfur dioxide produced?
e What can be done to reduce the amount of sulfur dioxide produced by this source?
f What environmental problem is caused by releasing sulfur dioxide into the air?
g What evidence is there that using railways instead of road vehicles would improve air quality?

5 Josh has heard that the power station on the edge of town has been converted from burning coal to burning natural gas.
a List the pollutants produced by burning:
   i coal
   ii natural gas.
b Why is natural gas considered a cleaner fuel than coal?
c Suggest two ways of producing electricity that do not involve the burning of fossil fuels.

6 Emily and Josh would like to end their project with some suggestions on how to improve air quality in the centre of town. They think that one way would be to reduce the number of vehicles that use the streets in the town centre. Give Emily and Josh three ideas about how this could be done.

The Earth in the Universe

Where do you live?

A

You might have written an address like this at some time, but usually we stop at the postcode. We live on a **planet** that is one of nine in the **Solar System** that are orbiting our own special **star** – the Sun. Our Sun is just one of billions of stars that make up our **galaxy**, the **Milky Way**, and our galaxy is just one amongst the billions that can be seen looking deep into space using telescopes.

Here are some questions that you may have thought about:

- How old is the Earth?
- Why is it the way it is, with mountains in some places, plains in others and oceans in between?
- Is it a safe place to live?
- How long will it stay safe?
- What might threaten life on Earth?

Scientists study many things, including trying to answer questions like the ones above. We are interested in the answers, particularly if the answer is likely to affect us personally. We don't worry too much when we are told that the Sun will only burn for another five billion years, but when we read that a massive **meteorite** could smash into the Earth in 10 years time it seems to be a lot more important!

B

Bam Earthquake
Over 25 000 dead, over 100 000 homeless

Pinatubo erupts!
Thousands evacuated.

C

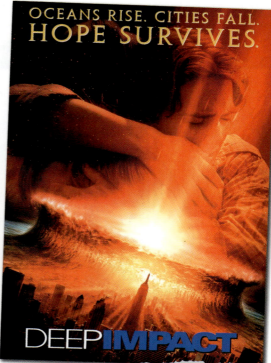

OCEANS RISE. CITIES FALL.
HOPE SURVIVES.

DEEP**IMPACT**

Hollywood hype or real risk?

If you were told that a meteorite could hit the Earth, you would need to ask more questions before you started to panic. You could ask:

How can scientists know this?
How certain are they that a disaster will happen?
What will it do to life on Earth?
Can we do anything to stop it happening?
Can we do anything to increase our chances of survival?

In this module we will look at what we know about the Earth, the forces that shaped it and its place in our Solar System. We will look at the different ideas suggested by scientists and other thinkers to explain why the Earth is the way it is, and test the different ideas and explanations to see which seem the most valid. Some of the things that we now accept as scientific facts were once thought not just to be wrong, but wicked or crazy!

?

1 a Put the following events in order of how often you think they happen, with most frequent first: meteorite impacts, earthquakes, volcanic eruptions.
  b How did you work out your answer to part **a**?

2 a Which type of event do you think is most dangerous?
  b Explain your answer to part **a**.
  c What other information would you need to give a better answer to this question?

3 a Are meteorite impacts with the Earth always dangerous?
  b What do you need to know to decide whether an impact is dangerous or not?

4 The *size* of earthquakes is measured using the Richter Scale, but this does not tell us how dangerous an earthquake is. What else do you need to know to judge how dangerous an earthquake is?

P1.2 # The face of the Earth

What is the structure of the Earth, and how is the Earth changing?

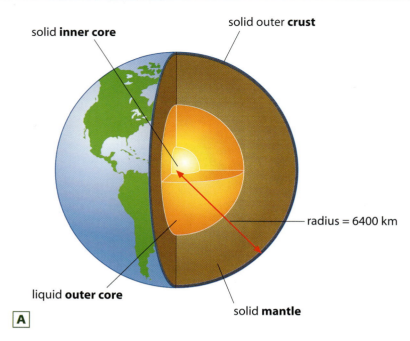

solid **inner core**

solid outer **crust**

radius = 6400 km

liquid **outer core**

solid **mantle**

A

The Earth is shaped like a sphere that is slightly squashed at the poles. The inside of the Earth is heated by the decay of radioactive elements. The solid surface that we live on is called the crust. The **crust** under the sea is called **oceanic crust**, and is made of denser rocks than the **continental crust**.

The photographs on these pages show some views of the Earth's crust as it is today. Scientists try to explain why the Earth's crust is divided into **continents** separated by oceans, and why some parts of the continents are flat and others have mountain ranges.

? **1** Describe the structure of the Earth.

B The Lyngen Peninsula in Norway.

C The ice in the glacier wears rocks away and carries the broken pieces downhill.

D These pinnacles in the Arizona desert have been worn away by the wind.

E The sea is gradually eroding the white cliffs of Dover, on the south coast of England.

Rocks are being **weathered** (broken down) all the time. Broken bits of rock can be carried away by water, ice or the wind. This process is called **erosion**.

The rate at which rocks are weathered depends on how hard the rocks are and the type of weathering taking place. Hard rocks take a very long time to wear down, but soft rocks are worn down more quickly.

Even very hard rocks like granite show wear after a hundred years or so. The oldest rocks on the Earth are about 4 billion years old, so the Earth must be older than this. If all the mountains had been made at the same time as the Earth they would have been worn away by wind and water by now. The Earth would not look like it does.

Worn bits of rocks are carried away in streams and rivers, and eventually deposited as **sediments**. Some sediments get buried and eventually become new rock. The processes of **sedimentation** and erosion can help us to understand past changes to the Earth.

Summary

Write notes for an introduction to a radio talk to explain why today's mountain ranges are younger than the age of the Earth.

?

2 Explain the difference between weathering and erosion.

3 Look at photo D. Explain how these rocks have been worn into these shapes.

4 Look at photo E. Explain how the sea can erode cliffs.

5 Why do scientists think that mountains must have been formed since the Earth was formed?

6 Think of a plus, a minus, and an interesting point about this statement: Rocks should not wear away.

7 **a** How can ice move bits of rock?
   b What evidence might geologists find to show that this has happened?
   c Do you think that there has always been the same amount of rock movement by ice in the world? Explain your answer.

Continental drift

What was Wegener's theory about mountain building?

A Fossils of sea creatures are sometimes found at the top of high mountains. This could only happen if mountains rose after the Earth was formed.

B Alfred Lothar Wegener.

In 1915 Alfred Wegener (1880–1930) published his theory of **continental drift**. Wegener thought that the continents of Africa and South America had once been joined together but had slowly drifted apart over millions of years. He gave the following evidence for his ideas:

• The shapes of the continents seem to fit together.
• Fossils of similar plants and animals are found in the two continents.
• There are similar rocks where the two continents may have been joined.

? 1 What evidence did Wegener have to support his idea that South America and Africa were once joined together?

2 Diagram C shows a land animal. Why would fossils of fish not be evidence for Wegener's ideas?

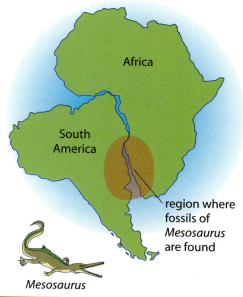

Africa

South America

region where fossils of *Mesosaurus* are found

Mesosaurus

C Evidence for continental drift.

Wegener also suggested that all the other land masses were once joined together in a 'supercontinent' called Pangaea. This broke up over 200 million years ago and the fragments drifted apart. He was not the first person to suggest that the continents had once been joined, but he was the first to provide evidence to support his ideas.

This idea suggested that mountains could have been formed when the huge masses of land crashed into each other and parts of them were slowly pushed upwards by the tremendous force of the collision. This would explain the folds that can be seen in the rocks in some mountains.

D Pangaea.

E Folds in the French Pyrennees.

Wegener's theory of continental drift was not accepted by most other scientists in his lifetime. There were several reasons for this:
- They did not see how great masses of rock could just drift around, ploughing through other great masses of rock, and no-one could detect the motion of the continents
- There were other explanations suggested for the similar fossil finds in Africa and South America.
- Wegener was not a geologist, and many thought that this was a very big idea with not enough evidence for it.

Summary

Write a short article for an on-line encyclopaedia to explain Wegener's ideas and the evidence for them.

?

3 a What was Pangaea?
b What happened to it?

4 How does Wegener's theory explain how mountains are formed?

5 Why wasn't Wegener's theory accepted in his lifetime?

6 An older theory of mountain building said that the Earth was hot when it was formed, and gradually shrank as it cooled.
a How would this explain the formation of mountains? (*Hint*: what might happen to the surface if the inside got smaller?)
b Why don't scientists agree with this idea today?

7 Coal is found in areas that have very cold climates today, and rocks in some tropical areas show marks left by glaciers. Explain how these pieces of evidence support Wegener's ideas.

Plate tectonics

What is the theory of plate tectonics?

More evidence

In 1948 an undersea survey discovered **oceanic ridges** (mountain ranges) that run down the middle of the oceans. They also discovered deep **oceanic trenches** in other parts of the oceans. **Radioactive dating** of rock samples showed that the rocks in the ocean floor were much younger than most of the rocks that formed the continents.

Evidence from rocks has shown scientists that the Earth's **magnetic field** changes direction several times in every million years. After lava or magma has cooled to form solid rock, iron-rich minerals in it become magnetised slightly, and the direction of the magnetism depends on where it is on the Earth and which way round the Earth's magnetic field is.

Other surveys of the ocean floors detected changing patterns of magnetism in the sea floor on each side of the oceanic ridges.

Plate tectonics

The theory of plate tectonics explains the results of these ocean floor surveys, as well as explaining all the observations that Wegener used to back up his theory. According to plate tectonic theory, the surface of the Earth is made up of large pieces, or **tectonic plates**, that can move around slowly. The plates consist of a part of the crust and the top part of the mantle beneath it (together called the **lithosphere**). There is a weak layer in the mantle

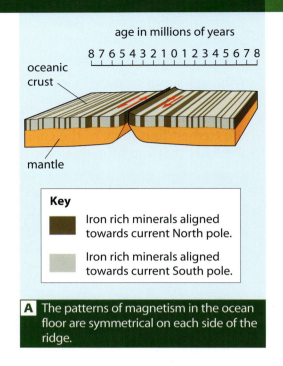

age in millions of years

8 7 6 5 4 3 2 1 0 1 2 3 4 5 6 7 8

oceanic crust

mantle

Key

Iron rich minerals aligned towards current North pole.

Iron rich minerals aligned towards current South pole.

A The patterns of magnetism in the ocean floor are symmetrical on each side of the ridge.

? **1** What is the difference between the crust and the lithosphere?

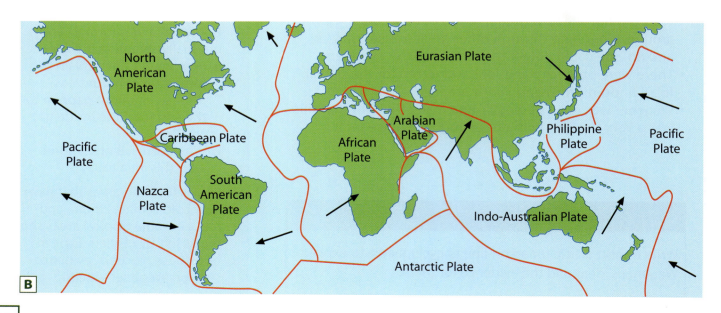

North American Plate

Eurasian Plate

Pacific Plate

Caribbean Plate

Arabian Plate

Philippine Plate

Pacific Plate

African Plate

Nazca Plate

South American Plate

Indo-Australian Plate

Antarctic Plate

B

beneath the lithosphere. The mantle is solid, but parts of it can move very slowly. Heat energy from the decay of radioactive elements sets up **convection currents** in the mantle which move the plates on the surface of the Earth.

Oceanic ridges are formed as two plates move away from each other at a **divergent plate boundary**. As the plates move, pressure on the mantle below is reduced. This allows part of it to melt and form a liquid rock called **magma**. This forces its way up to the surface where it cools and solidifies to form new rocks. The ocean gets wider by about 10 cm per year – this is called **seafloor spreading**.

If the floors of the oceans are spreading, then in other parts of the world the crust must be getting smaller. This happens at **convergent plate boundaries**. Diagrams D and E show what can happen when plates move towards each other.

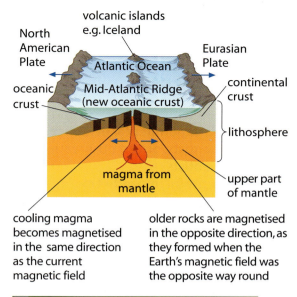

C Seafloor spreading in the Atlantic Ocean.

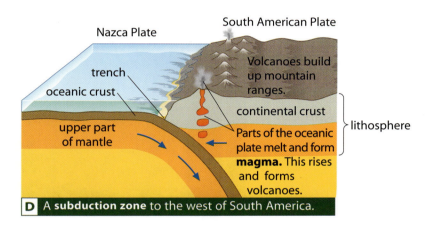

D A **subduction zone** to the west of South America.

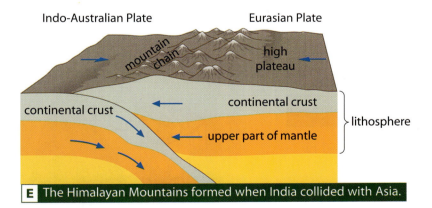

E The Himalayan Mountains formed when India collided with Asia.

Summary

Draw a concept map to summarise the ideas about plate tectonics.

2 What makes the plates on the surface of the Earth slowly drift about?

3 a Describe what happens at a divergent plate boundary.
   b Why are the magnetic 'stripes' in the sea floor symmetrical about the ridge?

4 Describe two different ways that mountain ranges can be built up.

5 Look at diagram E. Why is the oceanic crust subducted rather than the continental crust? (*Hint*: you may need to look back at page 62).

6 A mountain is not the same height as it was 10 years ago. Consider all the possible reasons for this statement.

7 Describe the differences between Wegener's theory of continental drift, and the theory of plate tectonics.

Weighing the evidence

Why are some theories accepted and not others?

For a theory to be accepted by other scientists it has to:
- fit in with known facts and not disagree with them
- use experimental evidence that is repeatable by other scientists, or use observations that are agreed by other scientists
- be useful in **predicting** new ideas or evidence.

If a scientific theory is able to do these things then it is likely to become accepted by other scientists. However, it may not be a complete and final answer to a problem. The discovery of new evidence can sometimes mean that accepted theories have to be changed.

Was Wegener right or wrong?

Wegener based his theory on his own observations and on evidence collected by other scientists. He used the evidence and his imagination to produce a theory that provided an explanation for the evidence that he had and linked together pieces of evidence that were previously thought to be unrelated.

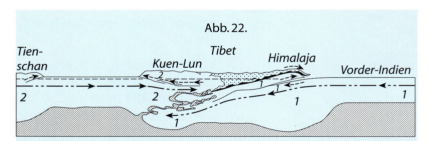

Abb. 22.

Tien- schan   Tibet   Himalaja

Kuen-Lun   Vorder-Indien

2   2   1   1

1

Meridianschnitt durch den lemurischen Zusammenschub, nach Argand.
1 = Lemurien (Indien); 2 = Asien.

B An illustration from Wegener's book about continental drift, first published in 1915.

Wegener's theory of continental drift was not accepted by most other scientists in his lifetime. They didn't necessarily disagree with his evidence, but they thought that there could be other explanations for it.

?
1 What does a good theory help other scientists to do?
2 Describe the evidence that Wegener used when formulating his theory. You may need to look back at page 64.

A This fossil tree fern is about 250 million years old. It is found on several continents.

C Some scientists said that 'land bridges' once existed between different continents.

D Map of the Mid-Atlantic Ridge.

E The submersible Alvin, which is used to study oceanic ridges.

The new theory

In 1930, towards the end of Wegener's life, new evidence about the structure of the Earth was discovered. By the late 1960s Wegener's ideas had been developed into the new theory of plate tectonics that scientists still use to explain many events, including volcanoes and earthquakes.

This theory is now accepted by most scientists because:
- there is a lot of evidence to **corroborate** it, from lots of different fields of science
- it explains *how* the plates can move.

New observations that agree with predictions increase confidence that a theory is a good explanation for what happens, but can never **prove** that it is correct. If observations do not agree with predictions then either the observation is wrong or the prediction is wrong. If several new observations do not agree with predictions, then scientists may change the theory to account for the new observations.

Summary

Write a letter from a scientist to a colleague in 1920, explaining why he (or she) does not agree with Wegener's ideas. Write another from a modern scientist explaining why the theory of plate tectonics *is* accepted.

?

3 **a** Which pieces of Wegener's evidence would 'land bridges' explain?
   b Which pieces of evidence does this idea *not* explain?
   c Why is the idea of land bridges not accepted today?

4 How do you think other scientists found out about Wegener's ideas?

5 What new evidence was discovered that led to the plate tectonics theory?

6 Why was the plate tectonics theory accepted when Wegener's theory had been rejected?

7 In some places on land, rocks are found that are magnetised in different directions. How does the theory of plate tectonics explain this observation?

Geohazards 1 – Volcanoes
How can we reduce the damage caused by volcanoes?

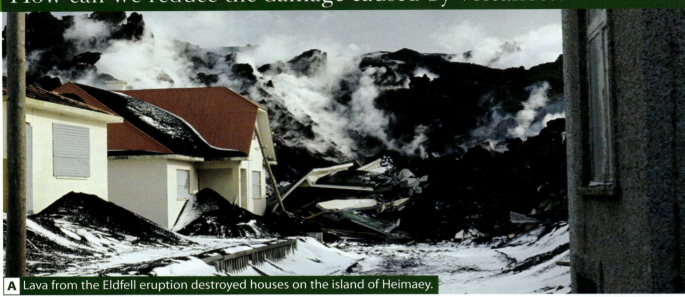

A Lava from the Eldfell eruption destroyed houses on the island of Heimaey.

Volcanoes and earthquakes are produced by enormous releases of energy, and they can cause massive destruction and loss of life. They are often referred to as **geohazards**. Records of these disasters show that they are most likely to happen along the boundaries of tectonic plates.

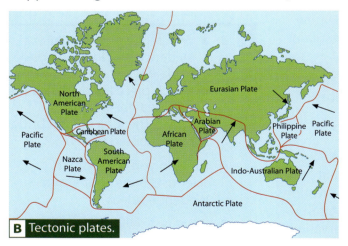

B Tectonic plates.

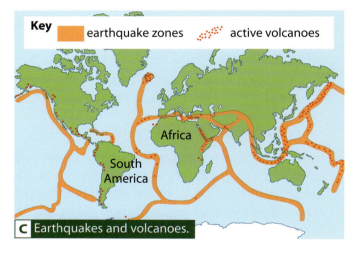

Key — earthquake zones — active volcanoes

C Earthquakes and volcanoes.

In a volcanic eruption, magma builds up in a chamber beneath the volcano. The pressure builds up until magma is forced out through cracks or **vents** in the volcano. Magma usually has bubbles of gas trapped within it. If the magma is runny, these bubbles can escape from the magma as it ascends, and when it reaches the surface it flows (as **lava**) down the mountain. However, some magma is more **viscous** and the gas bubbles cannot escape. The pressure from the gas builds up until the volcano erupts explosively, often shooting solidified bits of lava, ash and dust high into the air.

?
1 Why are volcanoes and earthquakes most likely to happen near the edges of tectonic plates?

2 Is an eruption of viscous magma more or less dangerous than one of runny magma? Explain your answer.

It is not just lava that can kill people. A **pyroclastic flow** is made up of a fast-moving cloud of hot gases, ash, dust and rock. An eruption often covers the surrounding land with thick layers of ash. If there is also heavy rainfall, or if a lake or river bursts its banks, the water and ash can form a swift mudflow, called a **lahar**. This can kill people and destroy farmland and property.

D Pyroclastic flows can move faster than cars and lorries!

E A lahar in Japan.

Scientists cannot stop volcanoes from erupting. However, they can help to reduce the damage by trying to predict when a volcano will erupt. **Public authorities** in areas near active volcanoes have plans to evacuate people when an eruption is predicted. Buildings can be strengthened to cope with ash falling on them.

On 15th June 1991, Mount Pinatubo in the Philippines erupted violently after lying **dormant** (not erupting) for over 500 years. Scientists had been monitoring the volcano carefully, and over 55 000 people were evacuated. The eruption killed around 400 people and left 400 000 people homeless. Damage continued after the eruption due to lahars caused by heavy rainfall.

?
3 Describe three different ways in which a volcanic eruption can damage property.

4 a What can scientists do to try to reduce the damage caused by volcanoes?
 b What can public authorities do?

5 Which is the odd one out: lava, magma, pyroclastic flow, lahar? Explain your answers.

6 Magma from the mantle in spreading regions tends to be less viscous than magma formed by melting part of a descending plate. Explain which kinds of eruptions you would expect in:
 a Iceland
 b the Andes.

Summary

Write a short fact sheet for someone intending to visit the Philippines, explaining how volcanoes form and the hazards they may face if an eruption occurs.

Geohazards 2 – Earthquakes

How can we limit the damage from earthquakes?

A Earthquake damage, San Francisco, 1989.

San Franciscans know that earthquakes are inevitable. This is because the city is built near the San Andreas Fault zone, which lies on a **conservative plate boundary** where two tectonic plates are trying to slide past each other.

Friction between the massive blocks of rock stops them moving smoothly. Force builds up until eventually something breaks and the rocks move suddenly. This sudden movement causes **seismic waves** to spread out. The place where an earthquake happens is called the **focus**, and the place on the surface immediately above is called the **epicentre**.

What can we do to protect people from earthquakes?

Throughout history major earthquakes have killed many thousands of people and destroyed towns and cities. Earthquakes are more common in some places than in others.

B The San Andreas Fault zone.

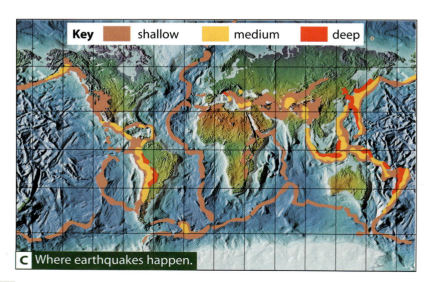

C Where earthquakes happen.

?

1 Describe the plate boundary that San Francisco is built on.

2 Why can an earthquake cause damage some distance from the epicentre?

3 **a** Explain why earthquakes occur mainly in certain areas of the world.

 b Central Africa and Australia do not experience large earthquakes. Suggest a reason for this.

Scientific knowledge can help us to reduce the number of people killed in earthquakes. One obvious precaution is not to live near plate boundaries, but this is not always possible. Some big cities grew up before people were aware of the risk.

Careful design of buildings can help them to withstand earthquakes without collapsing. New buildings can be built so that they can move to absorb the energy of an earthquake. Some buildings have flexible foundations, so the building does not move as much as the ground does.

D The Imperial Hotel, Tokyo, designed by architect Frank Lloyd Wright, successfully withstood the 1923 earthquake.

Predicting earthquakes can be more difficult than predicting volcanic eruptions. Scientists know *where* earthquakes are likely to happen. They can try to predict when the next earthquake will happen based on what has happened in the past, and on measurements of forces and small movements in the ground. However, there is often no warning.

?

4 Why shouldn't new towns be built near plate boundaries?

5 How can buildings in earthquake zones be made safer?

6 Look at the part of the map in diagram C that shows South America. Some earthquakes start deeper within the Earth than others. Suggest why the deep earthquakes are further from the coast than the shallow ones.

7 Look at diagram C on page 70. Suggest why the map shows more earthquake locations than volcanoes.

8 Tsunamis can cause death and destruction in coastal areas. Find out what tsunamis are and what causes them.

Summary

Design a poster for primary school children in California, explaining why earthquakes happen and how buildings are designed to be safe in an earthquake.

The Solar System

What is in the Solar System?

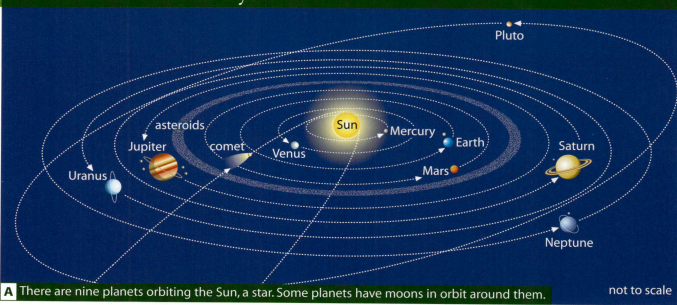

A There are nine planets orbiting the Sun, a star. Some planets have moons in orbit around them.

not to scale

The Sun, the planets and all the other objects that make up our Solar System were formed at roughly the same time. Matter was scattered across space when the Universe came into being. The matter cooled and was gradually pulled together by gravity, forming the Sun and the planets, about 5 billion years ago.

> **?**
> 1 **a** How did the Sun and planets form?
>   **b** How long ago did this happen?
>   **c** What is the evidence for this?
>
> 2 Where are the orbits of most of the asteroids?
>
> 3 What are the similarities and differences between asteroids, comets and moons in terms of:
>   **a** their composition
>   **b** their orbits?

B An artist's impression of the formation of the Solar System.

The Sun started to form about 5000 million years ago, and the Earth formed about 500 million years later. Evidence from meteorites and from rocks on the Moon and Mars support this estimate.

Asteroids are pieces of rock that orbit the Sun, but are too small to be considered planets. The smallest ones are only the size of a pebble, but the biggest (Ceres) is nearly one third of the diameter of our Moon.

Comets are largely made up of ice, frozen gases and a small amount of rock. They usually have very long, elliptical orbits. When they get close to the Sun, some of the water and gases evaporate and form the 'tail'.

Meteors and meteorites

Some asteroids move in irregular orbits that cross the orbit of the Earth. Asteroids the size of pebbles and small rocks frequently enter the Earth's atmosphere. Friction with the air heats them to very high temperatures and most of them burn up. A rock that completely burns up is referred to as a **meteor**. Larger pieces of rock may actually reach the ground, when they are called **meteorites**.

Once in a while the Earth is hit by a bigger piece of rock. These **impacts** from large, fast-moving objects leave **craters** when they hit the Earth. The bigger they are and the faster they move, the more energy they have and the more damage they cause.

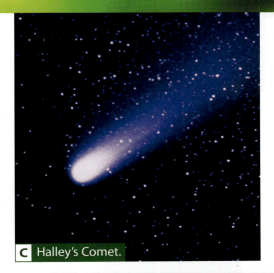

C Halley's Comet.

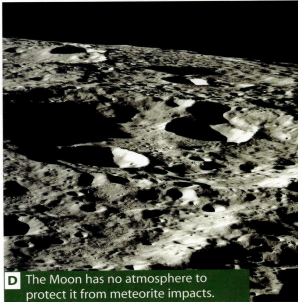

D The Moon has no atmosphere to protect it from meteorite impacts.

E This crater in Arizona, USA, was formed by a meteorite about 50 metres across and travelling at about 60 000 km/hour.

A How can you investigate the factors that affect the size of a crater?

Summary

Write short encyclopaedia entries for all the words in bold on these pages.

?

4 a What two factors determine how much energy a meteor or meteorite has?

b What is the relationship between the energy of a meteorite and the damage it could do?

5 There are many more craters visible on the Moon than on the Earth. Suggest as many reasons for this as you can.

6 There were many more meteor impacts when the Earth was young than there are now. Suggest a reason for this.

Asteroid impact!

Could life be destroyed by an asteroid?

edge of crater

centre of crater

A The hills in the distance are part of an impact crater 3.8 km in diameter.

Meteors larger than about 50 metres could reach the surface of the Earth before they burn up. The impact of an asteroid 2 km across could throw enough dust into the atmosphere to cool the Earth for several years and cause great food shortages.

Astronomers are trying to locate as many asteroids as they can and work out their orbits. If we have enough warning, we may be able to destroy or deflect an asteroid that is going to hit the Earth.

An asteroid big enough to cause a global disaster hits the Earth on average once or twice in every million years. You have a 1 in 20 000 chance of being killed by an asteroid impact – about the same as your chances of dying in an air crash! However, this is not a very helpful statistic, because it doesn't tell you *when* the next big impact will happen.

?
1 a Why is it important to find all the asteroids in the Solar System?
  b Why is it most important to find the ones that are bigger than 50 m across?

2 How could a large impact cause food shortages?

B An artist's impression of a large asteroid strike.

C Artist's impression of pieces of a comet that hit Jupiter in 1994. It would have had devastating consequences if it had hit the Earth.

The extinction of the dinosaurs

There is evidence that the Earth has been hit by very large meteorites several times in its history. One of these impacts occurred about 65 million years ago, at about the same time as the dinosaurs and many other species became **extinct**. Some scientists have a theory that the impact may have caused climate changes that killed off the dinosaurs.

Most scientists accept that there was a large impact about 65 million years ago. However, there is evidence that some species of dinosaur had died out at least 20 million years before the impact. There are also many other theories about the cause of the extinctions.

D An artist's impression of the crater formed by the impact that may have killed the dinosaurs. The actual crater is now beneath the sea and the jungle in Central America.

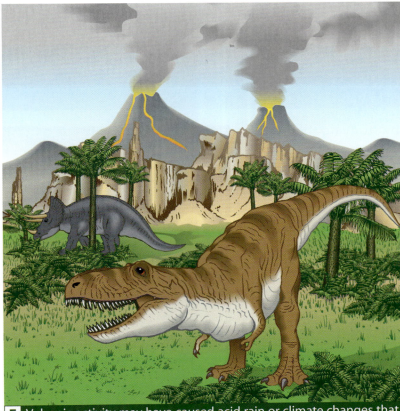

E Volcanic activity may have caused acid rain or climate changes that killed off the dinosaurs.

?

3 a How could a meteorite impact have killed off the dinosaurs?
  b What are the arguments against this idea?

4 Only about 150 meteorite impact sites have been discovered on the Earth. Does this mean that only about 150 meteors have ever hit the Earth? Explain your answer in as much detail as you can.

5 What problems do you think scientists will have to overcome if they need to destroy or deflect an asteroid?

6 A large asteroid impact happens far less frequently than air crashes, so why are your chances of dying similar in each case?

Summary

Write a short paragraph to answer the question at the top of page 76.

Studying the stars

How do we find out about the stars?

A These telescopes detect radio waves produced by stars.

Scientists learn about stars and galaxies by studying the radiation they give out.

Large telescopes on the Earth are usually built on high mountains so they are above most of the clouds and dust in the atmosphere. They need to be away from towns and cities, because **light pollution** interferes with observations.

The stars are a long way from the Earth. Because the distances are so big, astronomers use a unit called a **light year**, which is the distance that light travels in one year. Light travels at 300 000 km/s.

Proxima Centauri is 4.3 light years away, and is the nearest star to our Solar System. This means that we are seeing light that left the star 4.3 years ago. For a star 5000 light years away, we are seeing it as it was 5000 years ago.

B The Hubble Space Telescope has cameras that can detect visible light and infrared (heat) radiation.

?

1 Write down three different kinds of radiation produced by stars.

2 How is studying the stars different to studying the structure of the Earth?

3 **a** Describe the best location for a telescope on the Earth.
   b Describe some advantages and disadvantages of having a telescope in orbit around the Earth.

4 **a** What is a light year?
   b Why do astronomers use light years?

5 Why can we never see stars as they are now?

Some stars seem to change position very slightly at different times of the year. This is called **parallax**, and happens because stars are at different distances from us. Astronomers can work out the distances to nearby stars by carefully measuring the angle of the star at different times of year compared with the background of more distant stars. The change in the angles is very small, so measurements have to be very accurate. This way of measuring distances only works for nearby stars.

The **apparent magnitude** of a star is a number that describes how bright it appears when viewed from Earth. The brightness depends on how bright the star really is (its **absolute magnitude**), and on how far away it is. There are some kinds of stars (called Cepheid variables) that vary in brightness regularly. Astronomers have discovered that the length of time it takes for a Cepheid variable to change brightness is linked to its absolute magnitude. By comparing the absolute magnitude to the apparent magnitude, they can work out how far away the star is. These measurements have to be very accurate, because a small mistake could make a big difference in the distance calculated.

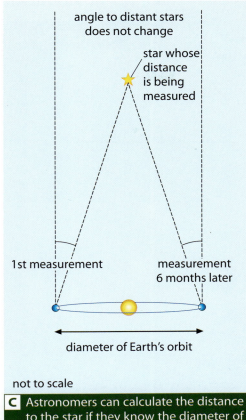

angle to distant stars does not change

star whose distance is being measured

1st measurement

measurement 6 months later

diameter of Earth's orbit

not to scale

C Astronomers can calculate the distance to the star if they know the diameter of the Earth's orbit and the two angles.

D Henrietta Leavitt, who discovered the relationship between brightness and period for Cepheid variables in 1912.

6 a What is the difference between apparent magnitude and absolute magnitude?
  b Why is it important to know the absolute magnitude of a star to be able to work out its distance?

7 Why is the parallax method less accurate for more distant stars?

8 How far is a light year in metres?

Summary

Write an encyclopaedia entry on how the distances to stars are measured.

The Sun and other stars

Are there other Solar Systems in the Universe?

A This is the Eagle Nebula, one of the places where new stars are forming in our galaxy.

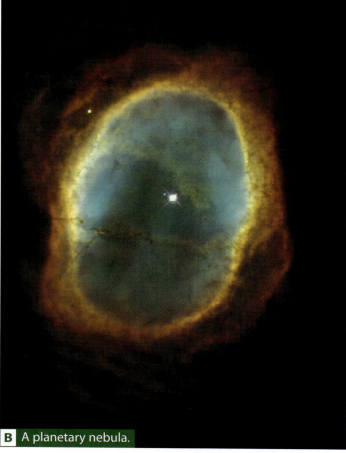

B A planetary nebula.

Atoms consist of a central **nucleus**, surrounded by tiny particles called **electrons**. If the pressure and temperature are high enough, the nuclei of atoms can join together to form new elements in a process called **fusion**. The Sun formed about 5 billion years ago when a cloud of mainly hydrogen gas was pulled together by gravity. The pressures and temperatures inside the Sun eventually became high enough to force hydrogen nuclei to fuse to form helium.

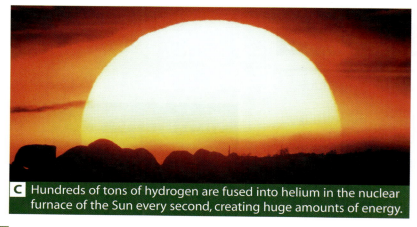

C Hundreds of tons of hydrogen are fused into helium in the nuclear furnace of the Sun every second, creating huge amounts of energy.

In about 5 billion years the Sun will have used up most of its hydrogen fuel. The core of the Sun will collapse, but its outward layers will expand to form a **red giant** star. The Sun will remain a red giant for about 1 billion years. After this it will eject a shell of gas and dust called a **planetary nebula** (although it has nothing to do with planets!). The rest of the star will shrink to form a small, hot **white dwarf** star. No further nuclear reactions take place in a white dwarf, and it gradually cools over about 1 billion years.

All stars of about the same size as the Sun have a similar **life cycle**. However, larger stars may explode at the end of their life cycle. When this happens, nuclear reactions in the exploding star form new elements. All the elements in the Solar System except hydrogen and helium were made in stars that existed before the Solar System was formed.

Evidence for life?

As far as we know, Earth is the only planet in the Solar System with life on it. Spacecraft have looked for signs of life on other planets, but so far there is no evidence of life now, or life that existed in the past.

Astronomers have detected planets orbiting around other stars. Even if only a small proportion of stars have planets, there are so many stars in the Universe that scientists think that it is likely that life exists somewhere besides Earth.

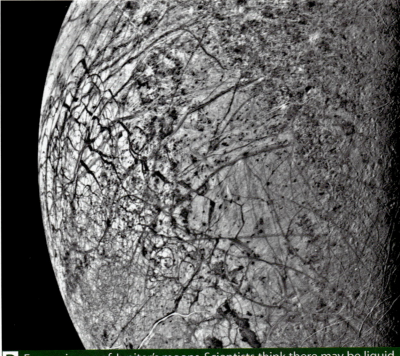

D Europa is one of Jupiter's moons. Scientists think there may be liquid water below its icy surface, and it is possible that there may be life there.

?

1 a What 'fuel' does the Sun use?
  b What happens to this fuel inside the Sun?
2 a What changes will take place in the Sun when it becomes a red giant?
  b What effect do you think this will have on the Earth?

3 Our bodies contain a lot of carbon and oxygen. Where did these elements come from?

4 a Why do scientists think there may be life on Europa?
  b Why do scientists think it is likely that life exists elsewhere in the Universe?

5 Which is the odd one out: galaxy, nebula, star? Explain your answers.

6 About 90% of Jupiter is hydrogen. Suggest why nuclear fusion does not happen inside Jupiter.

Summary

Write a set of points to be covered in a short TV article entitled 'Stars, planets and life.'

The Universe

How did the Universe begin, and how will it end?

A On a very clear night you may see a band of stars stretching across the sky. These stars are part of the Milky Way.

B The Andromeda galaxy is the nearest large galaxy to the Milky Way. It is about 2 or 3 million light years away.

Our Sun is just one of more than 200 billion stars that make up the Milky Way – our galaxy. The Milky Way is just one of billions of galaxies in the Universe. It is about 100 000 light years across.

The expanding Universe

In 1929 an American astronomer called Edwin Hubble discovered that distant galaxies are moving away from us. The further away the galaxy is, the faster it is moving. Scientists have explained this fact by suggesting that space itself is expanding.

If the Universe is expanding now, then in the past it must have been smaller. Most scientists think that the Universe began in a **Big Bang**, which happened about 14 billion years ago. By about 12 billion years ago the matter spreading out from the Big Bang had clumped together into stars and galaxies.

?
1 Why do astronomers need very powerful telescopes to look at other galaxies?

2 Why is the size of the Milky Way given as 'about' 100 000 light years? You may need to look back at page 79.

3 a What did Hubble discover about other galaxies in the Universe?
 b How do scientists explain this?

The future of the Universe

Gravity is a force that pulls matter together. The future of the Universe depends on how much mass there is in the Universe. If there is more than a certain **critical mass**, then gravitational forces will gradually slow down the expansion of the Universe, and will eventually pull all the matter back together again. The Universe could end in a **Big Crunch**.

If there is exactly the critical mass of matter in the Universe, it may reach a certain size and then stop expanding. If the mass is less than the critical mass, the Universe may just continue to expand forever.

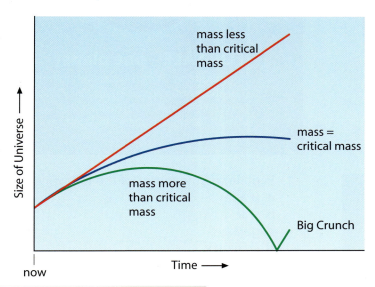

D Possible futures for the Universe.

Scientists do not know what will happen. Estimates of the mass of matter in the Universe change continually as better instruments are developed, or better theories are suggested to work out the mass of distant galaxies from observations we can make from Earth.

C Edwin Hubble (1889–1953).

?

4 How old is the Universe compared with
  a the Earth
  b the Sun
  c the Milky Way?

5 **a** What are the three different possibilities for the future of the Universe?
  b What determines which option will happen?

6 Why is the future of the Universe uncertain?

7 Find out how the 'steady state' theory explained the expansion of the Universe and why this theory is no longer accepted by most scientists.

Summary

The Astronomy department at your local college is holding an Open Day. Make a poster for them explaining what we know about the start and the end of the Universe.

Planet for sale!

What do you know about the Earth?

A

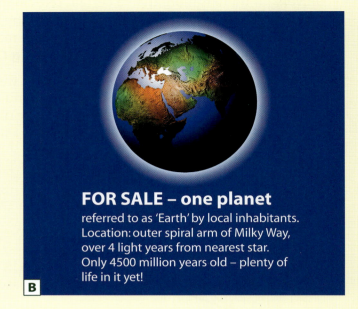

FOR SALE – one planet
referred to as 'Earth' by local inhabitants.
Location: outer spiral arm of Milky Way,
over 4 light years from nearest star.
Only 4500 million years old – plenty of
life in it yet!

B

Attractive scenery –
mountain ranges, oceans, rivers and plains

C

1 Explain the meanings of the following words:
   a planet
   b star
   c galaxy
   d Universe

2 a How did the Solar System form?
   b About how long ago did this happen?
   c What 'fuel' does the Sun use?
   d How does this fuel release energy?
   e What will happen to the Sun in the future?
   f How do scientists know what will happen
   to the Sun?

3 a What is a light year, and why is it used?
   b How can astronomers measure the
   distances to stars?
   c Why can't we see stars as they are now?

4 The Solar System is part of the Universe.
   a How do scientists think the Universe began?
   b What evidence do they have for this idea?
   c Describe three possible ways that the
   Universe might end.
   d What determines which possibility will
   happen?

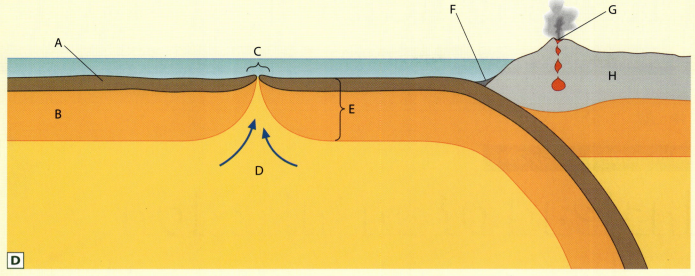

D

5 Name the parts labelled A to H in diagram D.

6 Alfred Wegener suggested the theory of continental drift.
   a What was Wegener's theory?
   b What evidence did Wegener have for his theory?
   c What did other scientists think about Wegener's theory?

Some minor geohazards, but nothing to worry about!

E

7 How does the theory of plate tectonics explain:
   a the formation of mountains
   b seafloor spreading
   c the pattern in magnetised rocks on the ocean floors?

8 a What causes earthquakes?
   b What can public authorities do to protect people against earthquakes?

9 a Why do most volcanoes occur near the edges of the tectonic plates?
   b Describe three different dangers from volcanoes.

10 The Solar System includes asteroids and comets as well as planets and their moons.
   a What happens to very small pieces of rock if they enter the Earth's atmosphere?
   b What could happen if a large asteroid entered the Earth's atmosphere?
   c How can we try to prevent this happening? Explain in as much detail as you can.

11 Most scientists agree that a large asteroid hit the Earth about 65 million years ago, at about the same time as the dinosaurs became extinct.
   a How could the asteroid have killed off the dinosaurs?
   b Why do many scientists disagree with this idea?

Health matters, 2 May 2015

Instead of an injection have a banana!!

Scientists have developed the world's first edible **vaccine** against a virus that causes severe diarrhoea.

Would you prefer this …

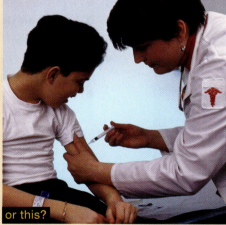
or this?

The vaccine has taken many years to develop and has cost a lot of money. Scientists added genes from the virus to banana plants. The bananas were fed to laboratory mice, to find out if the vaccine protected them against the virus, and to see if there were any side-effects. The vaccine was then tested on human volunteers in clinical trials in Mexico.

The World Health Organisation says that the new vaccine will help to reduce the number of deaths of young children in the developing world. Only 80% of the world's children are vaccinated against diphtheria, whooping cough, polio, measles and tetanus because it is expensive to transport and store the vaccines, and trained medical staff are needed to give the injections. Fruit containing edible vaccines could be grown locally, which would cut transport and storage costs and, without needles, the risk of infection would also be removed.

A health worker transporting vaccines.

A vaccine is an injection containing weakened microorganisms. It may be injected into your body so that you make antibodies that kill the microorganisms. If you are infected by this microorganism again you will not become ill. Children are given vaccines to protect them against many different diseases. However, not everyone agrees that children should be **vaccinated**. They believe that vaccines can cause harmful side-effects, but they don't want to risk their children's health. On the other hand scientists are excited about the possibilities of developing new vaccines against the virus that causes AIDS and against 'superbugs' which are difficult to control with other drugs.

Scientists are discovering more about how diseases affect our bodies. As new evidence is reported, the message on how to stay healthy can change. The way of vaccinating against diseases described in the report *could* happen in the future.

However, just because we *can* vaccinate people against diseases, doesn't mean that it *should* be done. Should we encourage people to have vaccines or let them make their own decisions? To do this they need to know something about the microorganisms that cause disease, the effects of these microorganisms on their body and how vaccines work. Decisions like these are called **ethical decisions**.

A This dangerous bacterium is a 'superbug' (magnification ×10 000).

B Parents need to decide whether or not to have their children vaccinated.

?

1 Explain how vaccines work.

2 Vaccines can be developed in different ways. Describe the stages in the development of the new vaccine mentioned in the health report.

3 What are the advantages of the edible vaccine described in the report?

4 Write down some arguments against using vaccines.

5 Do you think that all children should be vaccinated against diseases?

6 What do you need to find out so that you can answer these questions better?

7 Describe some other ways of protecting ourselves from disease.

8 Note down any words on these pages that you don't understand and try to find out their meanings.

Microorganisms and disease

What causes diseases?

A **microorganism**, or microbe for short, is any organism that you can only see clearly with a microscope. The air around us is full of microorganisms and your body is covered in them. Most microorganisms are harmless and do not affect us, but some can cause **infectious diseases** in humans and plants. If these harmful microorganisms get inside your body they quickly grow in number and make you feel ill. Some species of microorganisms can produce 10^{21} offspring from a single individual in just 24 hours!

There are three main types of microorganisms.

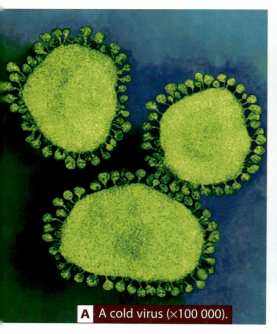

A | A cold virus (×100 000).

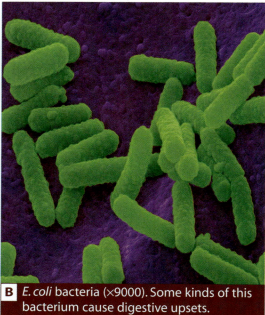

B | *E. coli* bacteria (×9000). Some kinds of this bacterium cause digestive upsets.

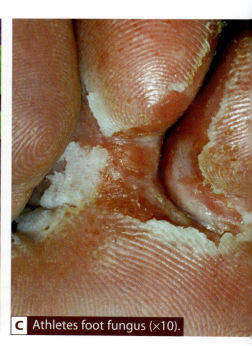

C | Athletes foot fungus (×10).

Viruses can be seen with very powerful microscopes. They cannot reproduce on their own. Viruses take over living cells and force them to make more viruses.

Bacteria are bigger than viruses. You could fit about 1000 medium sized ones on this full stop. A bacterium is a single cell with a cell wall, but no nucleus.

Fungus cells are between 10 and 100 times bigger than bacterial cells. Some fungi grow on skin and release chemicals that digest skin cells. These can make the skin red and sore.

Bacteria and fungi can reproduce on their own.

?

1 Ben says that the definition of a microorganism is 'a small organism that causes disease'. Is he right? Explain your answer.

2 Draw up a table that summarises the key features of each type of microorganism.

How do microorganisms affect you?

Harmful microorganisms can cause disease in two ways:
- They can destroy body cells, for example tuberculosis viruses can destroy lung tissue.
- They can release poisonous chemicals called **toxins**, for example clostridium bacteria make a toxin that gives you one kind of food poisoning.

The effects that microorganisms have on your body are called **symptoms**.

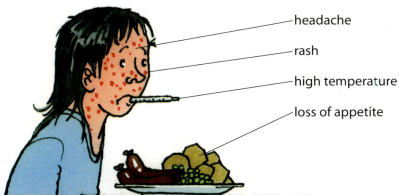

- headache
- rash
- high temperature
- loss of appetite

E Symptoms are caused by your body trying to fight the invading microorganisms.

Disease	Microorganism responsible	Symptoms	How long symptoms last
diphtheria	bacteria	severe fever; can also damage the heart	a few weeks, but damage to the heart can last a lifetime
ringworm	fungus	itchy skin rashes	a few weeks
rubella (German measles)	virus	red rash, swollen glands	2 weeks; can be fatal in babies and can harm unborn babies if the mother catches it

F Some common diseases and their symptoms.

?
3 Explain how harmful microorganisms cause disease.

4 What does the word symptom mean?

5 How could a doctor on the telephone diagnose that you have rubella?

6 Which is the odd one out: bacterium, virus, fungus? Explain your answers.

7 Imagine that scientists have found out how to kill every single type of microorganism on the planet. List as many effects that this would have on our lives as you can.

A How can you show there are bacteria on your skin?

D

Summary

Write an article for a magazine describing the causes and symptoms of some diseases. Add labelled diagrams to illustrate your descriptions.

Body defences

How do our bodies keep harmful microorganisms out?

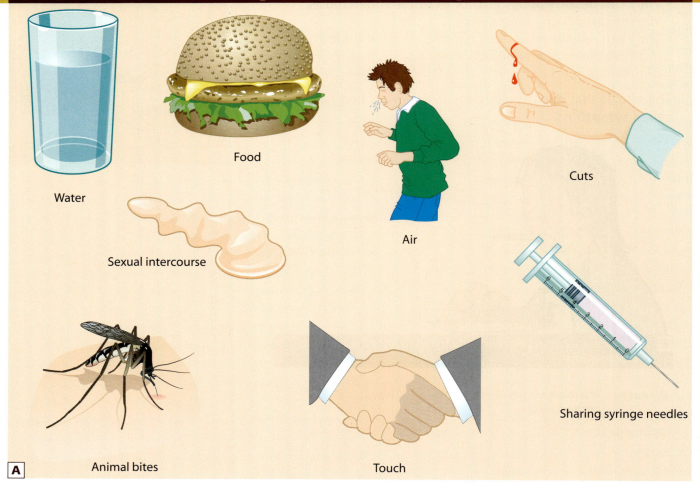

Water

Food

Sexual intercourse

Air

Cuts

Sharing syringe needles

Animal bites

Touch

A

Picture A shows how microorganisms can get into your body.

What happens if microorganisms get inside you?

If harmful microorganisms get inside your body they start to reproduce quickly. They damage cells in your body or release poisonous chemicals called toxins. You don't start to feel ill until a lot of cells are damaged or a lot of toxins have built up.

?

1 Draw up a table to show the ways that diseases can be spread. Give suggestions on how each method of spreading can be prevented.

2 Write down diseases that you or your friends have caught in the past. How do you think you caught these diseases?

3 When microorganisms get inside your body why don't you feel ill straight away?

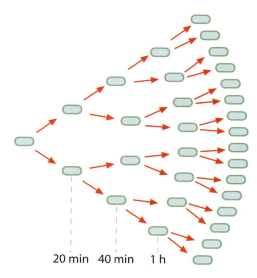

20 min   40 min   1 h

B When conditions are right bacterial cells can divide into two new cells every 20 minutes.

Keeping microorganisms out

Our bodies are very good at keeping harmful microorganisms out. Diagram C shows the body's defences.

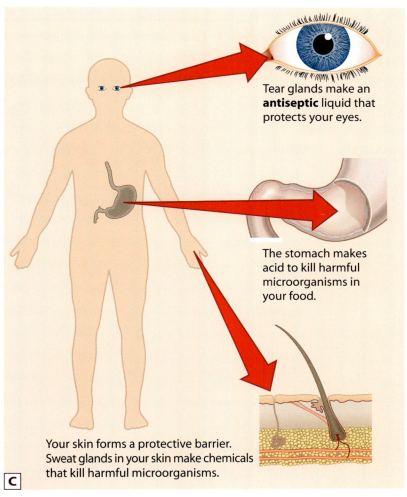

Tear glands make an **antiseptic** liquid that protects your eyes.

The stomach makes acid to kill harmful microorganisms in your food.

Your skin forms a protective barrier. Sweat glands in your skin make chemicals that kill harmful microorganisms.

C

?

4 **a** Draw up a table of the physical and chemical barriers to infection. Explain how these barriers stop microorganisms getting in.
   b Explain how these barriers might fail and what happens if they do.

5 Survey your class and find out who has had flu, measles, chicken pox, mumps and colds. For each disease find out:
   a how many people have had the disease once
   b how many people have had the disease more than once.

6 What do your answers to question **5** tell you about each disease?

7 Which is the odd one out: food, animal bite, dirty needle? Explain your answers.

8 Suggest two reasons why your lungs need to be protected from infection.

Summary

Summarise in not more than three sentences how the body protects itself against harmful microorganisms.

Fighting off infection

How do our bodies kill microorganisms?

Once harmful microorganisms get inside your body, they are killed by white blood cells that are part of your **immune system**. These cells protect us against infection by:

- **engulfing** or swallowing the microorganisms and digesting them with enzymes
- making **antibodies** – these may kill the harmful microorganisms directly or make them clump together, which makes it easier for other white blood cells to engulf them (see diagram A)
- destroying the toxins that the harmful microorganisms make.

?
1 Describe three ways that white blood cells protect the body.

2 If you have cowpox antibodies in your blood:
   a why won't you be protected against rubella
   b why will you be protected against smallpox?

3 What is the difference between an antibody and an antigen?

Becoming immune

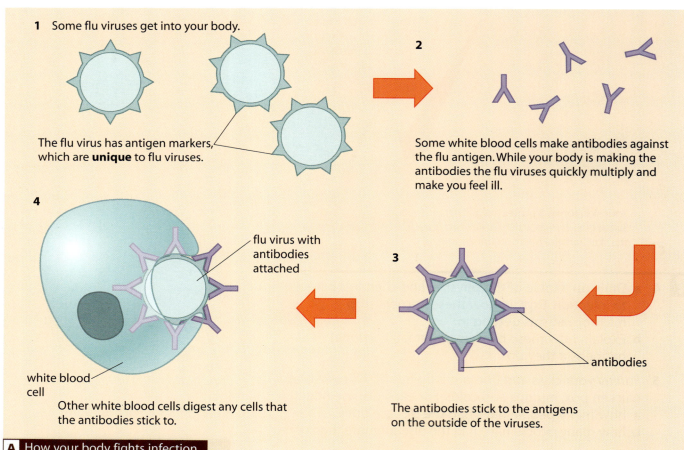

1 Some flu viruses get into your body.

The flu virus has antigen markers, which are **unique** to flu viruses.

2 Some white blood cells make antibodies against the flu antigen. While your body is making the antibodies the flu viruses quickly multiply and make you feel ill.

4 flu virus with antibodies attached

white blood cell

Other white blood cells digest any cells that the antibodies stick to.

3 antibodies

The antibodies stick to the antigens on the outside of the viruses.

A How your body fights infection.

All cells have **antigen** markers on the outside. Cells from different species have different antigens. Antibodies made against a particular antigen are **specific**, so antibodies made against one kind of microorganism will usually only attack that kind. There are some exceptions to this, for example cowpox antibodies will attack smallpox viruses.

When your body makes an antibody it also makes **memory cells** that keep a pattern of the antibody after the infection has gone. If the microorganism gets into your body again, the memory cells will recognise it and start to make the right antibodies to kill the microorganisms before you get ill. This means you are now **immune** to that disease. Immunity that you get after an infection like this is called **active immunity**.

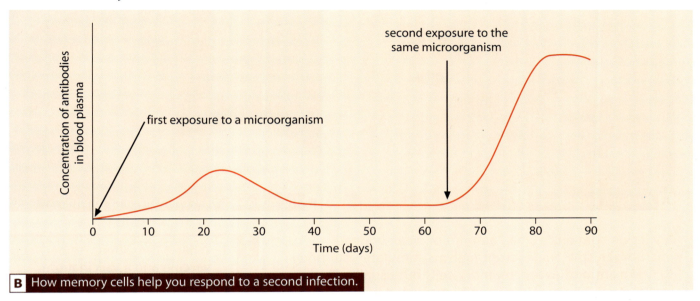

B How memory cells help you respond to a second infection.

Babies can get antibodies from their mother without having to be infected. This is called **passive immunity** and protects babies in the first few months of life. Antibodies can also be made artificially in laboratory animals to give you passive immunity to fast-acting microorganisms such as the tetanus bacterium. Your body does not make memory cells in this case and you will lose your immunity, so another injection will be needed if you are infected again.

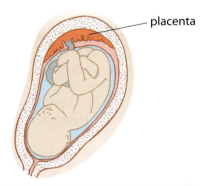

placenta

C Antibodies pass from the mother to her baby through the placenta.

D Antibodies pass from the mother to her baby in breast milk.

?

4 What does being immune mean?

5 Look at graph B. Explain what is happening to the concentration of antibodies in the bloodstream.

6 Explain the similarities and differences between active immunity and passive immunity.

7 Sketch a graph to show the level of antibodies in a baby who has not been vaccinated when they are exposed to whooping cough at 6 months and 12 months old. Write a paragraph to explain your graph.

Summary

Design a cartoon strip for a children's science magazine showing how antibodies destroy harmful microorganisms.

How do vaccines work?

Doctors can give you immunity to a disease without you having to catch the disease first. They do this by vaccination.

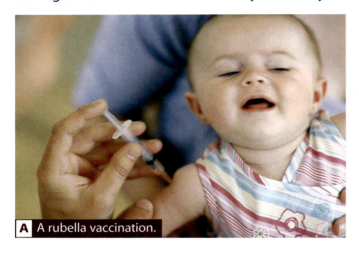

A A rubella vaccination.

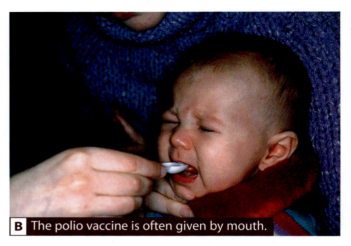

B The polio vaccine is often given by mouth.

A vaccine contains a small amount of weak or dead microorganisms. The microorganisms stimulate your body to make antibodies and memory cells but usually do not make you ill. The active immunity produced by vaccinations can protect you for many years, although you may need **booster** vaccinations occasionally to keep up the level of memory cells in your blood.

Vaccines can have **side-effects** after the vaccine has been given. These are usually mild, such as a slight rash or feeling 'off colour' for a few days. Sometimes the side-effects can be more serious and cause the symptoms of the disease the person has been vaccinated against. On very rare occasions they cause permanent harm.

?
1. What is the difference between a vaccine and a vaccination?

2. Describe how a vaccine can prevent you catching an infection.

3. Explain why vaccines which contain live microorganisms do not usually make you ill.

4. How do booster vaccinations help maintain a person's immunity to disease.

?

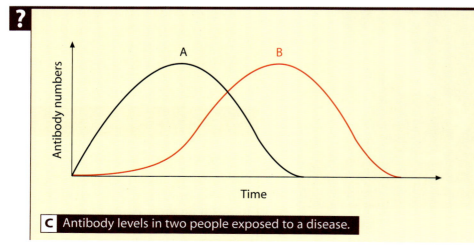

C Antibody levels in two people exposed to a disease.

5. Graph C shows the levels of antibodies in two people exposed to a disease.
   a Which person has had the disease before? How can you tell?
   b Person C has been vaccinated against the disease. Would a graph of their antibody numbers resemble A or B? Explain your answer.

The problem with influenza and AIDS

Influenza (or flu) is caused by a virus which reproduces rapidly. Its DNA changes or **mutates** often and each year new forms or **strains** of the flu virus appear, with different antigens on the surface of the virus. Sometimes the changes are small, so having influenza one year may leave you with immunity against infection from the next strain. But every so often a big change in the virus takes place. This causes a major outbreak known as an **epidemic**, because nobody has immunity. Each of these major strains needs its own vaccine, because other flu vaccines will not cause your body to make the right antibodies. Flu vaccines are usually given to older people or those who do not have effective immune systems.

AIDS is caused by the **HIV** virus, which damages the immune system itself, making it harder for the infected person to fight off all kinds of infections. So far we don't have a vaccine against HIV because, like the influenza virus, it mutates very quickly. By the time a vaccine had been fully tested it would be out of date.

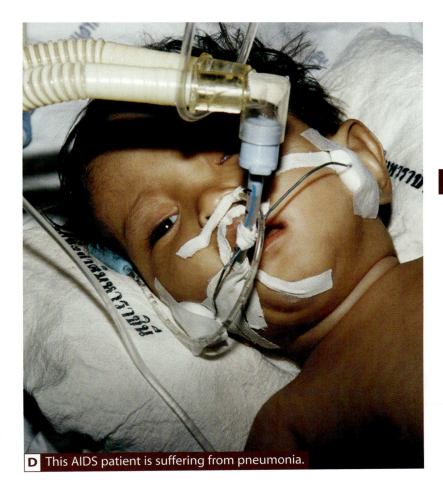

D This AIDS patient is suffering from pneumonia.

?

6 Explain why a vaccine can never be totally safe.

7 Explain why influenza and AIDS are difficult to control by vaccination.

8 Scientists cannot make vaccines against every disease. Which diseases do you think that they should try to make vaccines against? Explain your answer.

Summary

List the pros and cons of vaccination.

The good and bad side of vaccination

Why are we encouraged to have vaccinations?

A Polio can cause permanent damage.

B Mumps.

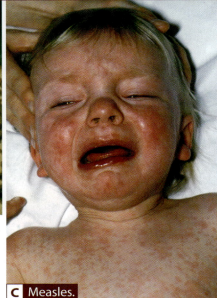

C Measles.

Many diseases, such as measles, mumps, polio and whooping cough, are highly infectious and can cause death or serious permanent harm. Without vaccination many hundreds of children in the UK each year could be harmed.

Whooping cough used to be a common illness in children in the UK. It causes a wracking cough with characteristic 'whoops' and it may last for 2–3 months. It can lead to a serious lung disease and may also cause brain damage in young babies.

Vaccination against whooping cough started in the 1950s. Before then about 100 000 cases were reported in the UK each year. By 1973 more than 80% of the population had been vaccinated and the number of cases of whooping cough had dropped dramatically.

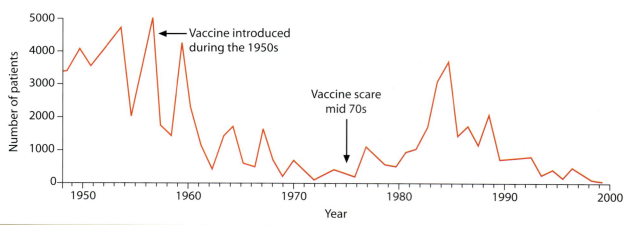

D Number of cases of whooping cough in the UK since 1948.

?

1 Look at graph D:
   a What are the variables in the graph?
   b Describe and explain the shape of the graph up to 1972.

Some children suffer mild side-effects from the whooping cough vaccine such as fever and headache. More severe side-effects are shown in table E.

Harm caused	Caused by the whooping cough vaccine (per 100 000 vaccinations)	Caused by whooping cough (per 100 000 cases)
death	0.2	4000
permanent brain damage	0.6	2000
swelling of the brain	3.0	4000
fits	90	8000

E

If a large proportion of the population is vaccinated, and so is immune to a disease, then the chances of the disease being spread to the few people who haven't been vaccinated is quite small. This means that vaccinating a large proportion of the population can prevent an epidemic. If the proportion that isn't vaccinated increases because people are worried about side-effects, then the risk of an epidemic increases too.

Parents have to decide whether the risk of their child catching whooping cough is less than the chances of their child suffering severe side-effects from the vaccine.

? 2 Look again at graph D.
  a What does the graph show happening in the mid 1970s?
  b What effect did this have?

3 How does the risk of harm from the vaccination against whooping cough compare with the risk of harm from catching the disease?

4 Think of a plus, a minus and an interesting point about this statement: All babies should be vaccinated against whooping cough.

? 5 Imagine you are a parent. Would you have your child vaccinated against whooping cough? Explain your answer.

6 Changes in vaccination have led to decreases in infection and death from measles as shown in table F.
Imagine you are a parent with a young child.

	1983–1987	2000
Scotland	25 453 cases 6 deaths	3 cases 0 deaths

F

  a How would the data for 1983–1987 affect your decision whether or not to have your child vaccinated? Explain your answer.
  b Does the data for 2000 change your decision? Explain your answer.

Summary

Produce an information leaflet for parents, giving information on the benefits and risks of the whooping cough vaccination.

How do I make decisions about vaccinations?

In Britain, **mass vaccination** programmes for diseases like measles, mumps and whooping cough mean that very few people will catch the diseases. Governments encourage all parents to have their children vaccinated at an early age, but it is not compulsory. Governments realise that people have:

• the right for public protection (i.e. a large proportion of the population needs to be vaccinated)
• the right of personal choice, because there is a slight risk from the side-effects of a vaccination.

For society as a whole, vaccination is the best choice. But for each individual it is a difficult choice for their own child. People need clear and unbiased information to help them make their decision.

Most people in this country have never seen a case of diphtheria, whooping cough or polio. They do not realise how much damage these diseases can cause. Some people believe these illnesses are a thing of the past and that there is no need to have their child vaccinated. These diseases are now rare *because* of improved vaccination services and the availability of improved vaccines.

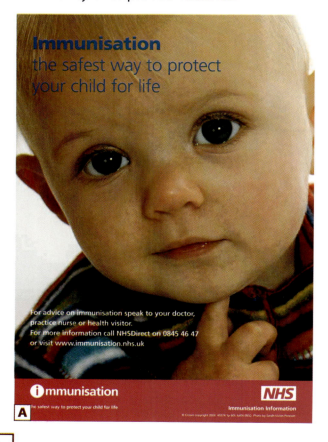

Immunisation
the safest way to protect
your child for life

For advice on immunisation speak to your doctor,
practice nurse or health visitor.
For more information call NHSDirect on 0845 46 47
or visit www.immunisation.nhs.uk

i mmunisation **NHS**

A he safest way to protect your child for life
Immunisation Information

? 1 **a** Why would Governments like everyone to be vaccinated against diseases like whooping cough?
b Explain why it is not compulsory to have children vaccinated.

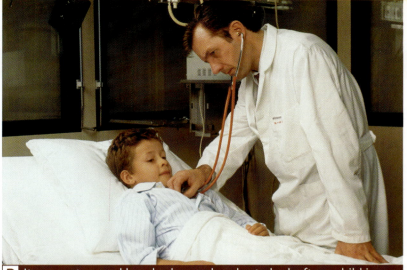

B It can cost several hundred pounds a day to look after a child in hospital.

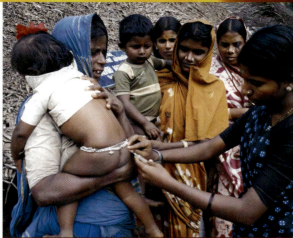

C People in developing countries may make different decisions compared to people in rich countries. In some countries, 1 in 5 children die from infections before their fifth birthday.

There are benefits and drawbacks to being vaccinated, and there are also benefits and drawbacks if you are not vaccinated! Some of these apply to parents and children, and some to the government.

Table D shows some of the benefits and drawbacks of having a child vaccinated against whooping cough.

	Vaccinated child	**Government**
Benefits	Will not catch the disease and so no risk of being harmed by it.	Saves money on hospital treatment.
Drawbacks	Slight risk of side-effects for a few days after vaccination, and a *very* small chance of harm from the vaccine.	Costs about £4.00 for each vaccination. If vaccination causes permanent damage, it will cost a lot of money to look after the person for the rest of their life.

D Benefits and drawbacks of vaccination.

?

2 a Give three different points of view parents may have about giving their child the whooping cough vaccine.

b For each of these points of view, list the main benefits and drawbacks for all the people involved.

3 Why might it be easier for a mother of a child in a poor country to make the decision to have her child vaccinated?

4 Consider all the possible explanations for this statement: There is an epidemic of whooping cough.

5 You are a government minister and you have to decide which vaccines should be given free of charge and which should be paid for. Make a list of all of the information that you would need to make your decision and explain why you would need to know it.

Summary

Design a poster for a doctor's waiting room to encourage parents to have their child vaccinated against whooping cough.

What are antibiotics?

Some microorganisms that enter our bodies can cause illness or even death before our immune system can destroy them. We can use **antibiotics** to kill these microorganisms. Antibiotics are chemicals that can be used to treat diseases caused by bacteria and fungi. They save millions of lives each year.

Penicillin was the world's first antibiotic and was developed during the Second World War. Nowadays there are many kinds of antibiotic that doctors can prescribe to treat diseases.

Antibiotics work in different ways. Some antibiotics weaken the cell walls of bacteria and fungi so that they burst and die. Others interfere with chemical processes inside these cells. Human cells are different so antibiotics do not kill them. Antibiotics also do not kill viruses because they are not proper cells and do not work in the same way.

Antibiotic resistance

Genes in all cells may occasionally mutate. Some mutations in bacteria and fungi may stop them being killed by antibiotics. They become **antibiotic resistant**. If you treat an infection with an antibiotic, it will kill the non-resistant bacteria. This will leave more space and food for resistant bacteria so they can increase rapidly in number.

A By 1944 enough penicillin was being produced to treat all the British and American casualties in the war.

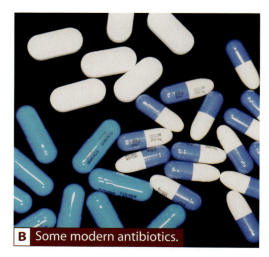

B Some modern antibiotics.

A How can you find out which antibiotics work the best?

C

?
1 Describe how antibiotics work.
2 Explain why your doctor won't prescribe antibiotics for diseases like colds or 'flu'.

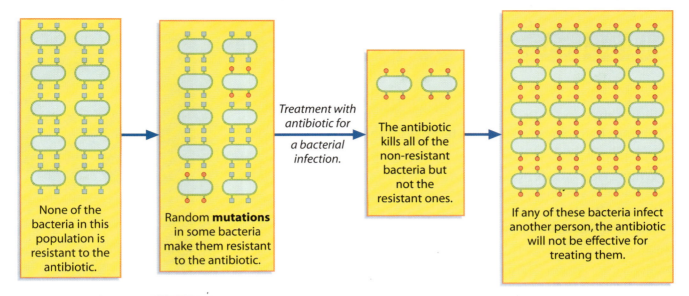

D How antibiotic resistance can cause a problem.

None of the bacteria in this population is resistant to the antibiotic.

Random **mutations** in some bacteria make them resistant to the antibiotic.

Treatment with antibiotic for a bacterial infection.

The antibiotic kills all of the non-resistant bacteria but not the resistant ones.

If any of these bacteria infect another person, the antibiotic will not be effective for treating them.

When a doctor prescribes antibiotics you are told that you should always complete the course. This is because it reduces the risk of resistant bacteria developing. If you only take the antibiotics until you feel well again, and don't finish the course, there is a much greater chance that resistant bacteria will develop and spread to other people.

You can reduce the spread of antibiotic resistant microorganisms by:
- not using antibiotics when you don't need them, such as when you have a viral infection
- always finishing a course of antibiotics
- practising good hygiene in hospitals, such as cleaning hands before touching a patient to prevent the spread of infections.

E Completing your course of antibiotics will help reduce the spread of antibiotic resistance.

?

3 What does antibiotic resistance mean?

4 Explain how antibiotic resistance occurs.

5 Why is antibiotic resistance a problem?

6 **a** Describe two ways to reduce the risk of bacteria developing antibiotic resistance.
 b Explain why each method helps.

7 In the 1960s American soldiers were treated for syphilis with the antibiotic penicillin. Some of the syphilis bacteria became resistant to the penicillin. Explain how this could have happened.

8 A major problem in hospitals is the existence of bacteria which are resistant to many different kinds of antibiotic. Describe how these bacteria have arisen and explain why they are a particular problem in hospitals.

Summary

Write an encyclopaedia entry for penicillin, explaining why it is no longer effective in treating many bacterial infections.

Testing treatments

How are new medicines tested?

Medicines are chemicals that make you better when you are ill, but they can cause different side-effects in different people. Medicines must be tested before they can be prescribed by doctors.

When scientists design a new medicine they start by looking at what causes the disease in the first place and how it affects the body. This gives clues about what chemicals to use to prevent or treat the disease.

New medicines are tested first on **cultures** of human cells (a collection of cells grown in the laboratory). Successful medicines are then tested on animals to make sure that they are safe.

Human trials are first carried out on healthy volunteers to study how the medicine affects the body and to make sure it is safe. Then there are **clinical trials** on patients who have the disease that the medicine is to treat. Trials last for 3–5 years to test thoroughly how the medicine works.

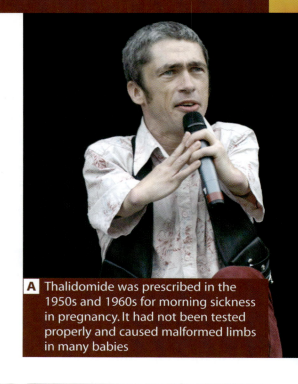

A Thalidomide was prescribed in the 1950s and 1960s for morning sickness in pregnancy. It had not been tested properly and caused malformed limbs in many babies

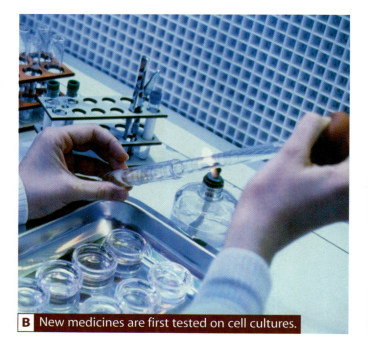

B New medicines are first tested on cell cultures.

C New medicines may be tested on animals to make sure they are safe.

?

1 Write down two reasons why new drugs should be tested before they are used.

2 Why are new medicines tested on animals before they are tested on humans?

The patients are divided into groups. Some groups are given different doses of the new medicine and one group may have a **placebo** (a 'dummy pill' that doesn't contain any medicine). It is considered unethical to use placebos when there is already a treatment for a disease – the new medicine needs to be tested against the old treatment to see if it is better.

In a **blind trial** the patients do not know which group they are in. In a **double blind trial** even the doctor does not know which group is getting which dose. This stops **bias** creeping into the results because the patients and doctor might expect certain results and report them even if they were not present.

Developing a new medicine is a long and slow process, and can cost a drug company a lot of money. Before it is developed the company needs to be sure that:
- there is a need for the treatment
- it can manufacture the medicine
- enough people need the medicine so it will sell enough to get back the money it spent and make a profit.

D Drug companies advertise their medicines to try to get doctors to prescribe them.

Summary

Draw up a table showing the similarities and differences between the two types of human drug trials.

? 3 Draw a flow chart showing the stages in the development of a new medicine.

4 **a** The patients taking the placebo are acting as a control. Explain what this means.
  b Why is it unethical to give someone a placebo if there is already an effective treatment?

5 **a** Explain the difference between a double blind trial and a blind trial.
  b Why is a double blind trial the best way of testing drugs?

6 Suggest reasons why:
  a developing countries cannot afford new drugs
  b major drugs companies do not spend money on researching cures for diseases such as malaria.

The testing debate

Is it ethical to test new drugs on animals or people?

Most people agree that it is wrong to make animals suffer. Many also agree that there are some circumstances in which the interests of humans are more important than the interests of animals, such as using animals to test new medicines. Many people find nothing wrong with this as long as everything is done to minimise the pain and suffering of the animal. However, other people believe that the use of animals to test medicines is wrong whatever the benefit.

If we didn't test medicines on animals we wouldn't have most of the medicines we use today. It would be very difficult to find better treatments in the future.

Dr McCue

We should find alternatives to animal testing. If we must use animals, they must be protected from pain and suffering.

Tina

There are no good reasons for experimenting on animals whatever the benefits. It's cruel.

Jeff

Human trials

Many clinical trials take part in countries in the developing world where poor people are willing to be paid to take part because they need the money so badly. The fee should be large enough to compensate for the inconvenience of taking part in the trial but not so large that poor people are tempted to take part in something they would rather not do.

?

1 List the advantages and disadvantages of testing medicines on animals.

2 Why are some people against testing medicines on animals?

3 Which of the views above is closest to your own view? Explain your answer.

4 Is it logical for someone who eats meat and wears leather shoes to object to the use of animals in medicine testing? Explain your answer.

Medical ethics committees decide if the possible benefits of a clinical trial are worth the risk to the health of the volunteers. They make sure that volunteers are carefully chosen so that only suitable volunteers take part. They should not be:

• poor people who are desperate for money
• people who have recently taken other medicines which might interact with the medicine being tested
• people who are not capable of understanding the possible risks of the trial.

People make their own decisions about whether to take part in clinical trials.

Mr Bushe

I don't really want to do it but my family needs the money.

Sheela

If people in rich countries don't want to take part in clinical trials then it's OK for people in poor countries to do it if they want to.

Dr Griffiths

Taking part in clinical trials is an easy way to earn some money.

Kosey

?
5 Most clinical trials are carried out in developing countries. Suggest reasons why this is the case.

6 Is it ethical to pay people in poor countries if companies cannot get volunteers to take part? Explain your answer.

7 Describe three different viewpoints people may have about testing new drugs on animals. Give evidence that supports each of these different viewpoints.

Summary

Write an article for a newspaper, giving the arguments for and against testing drugs on animals as well as humans.

Heart disease

How can we prevent heart disease?

Coronary heart disease, including heart attacks, causes more than 120 000 deaths a year in the UK. It is a major cause of death in developed countries and is becoming more common in developing countries.

Your heart pumps blood around your body through arteries, capillaries and veins. Diagram B shows how the structure of the blood vessels is related to their function. Healthy arteries have smooth walls and allow the blood to flow through easily.

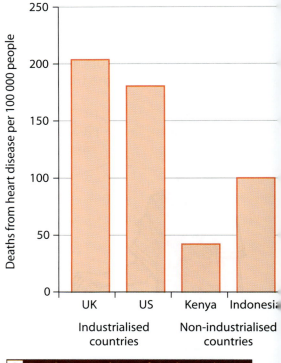

A Death rate each year from heart disease in the UK, US, Kenya and Indonesia

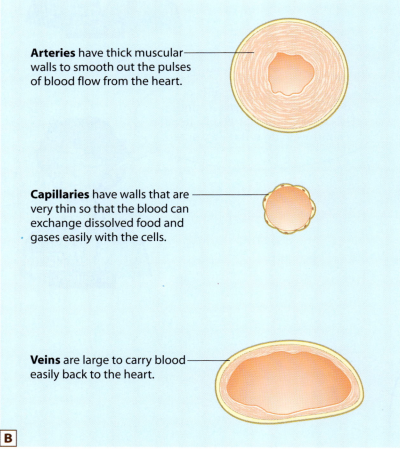

Arteries have thick muscular walls to smooth out the pulses of blood flow from the heart.

Capillaries have walls that are very thin so that the blood can exchange dissolved food and gases easily with the cells.

Veins are large to carry blood easily back to the heart.

B

?

1 a How many people die from heart disease each year in the UK per 100 000 people?
b What does the graph in A suggest about the death rates in industrialised and non-industrialised countries.

2 What is the most important role of blood in the body?

Your heart muscles also need food and oxygen to keep working. The **coronary arteries** carry these to the cells in the heart muscle. If a coronary artery becomes partly blocked it can cause chest pains because the heart muscle is not getting enough food and oxygen. This is called **angina**. A total blockage in a coronary artery can cause a **heart attack** when the heart stops beating altogether.

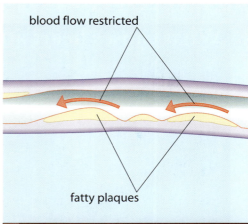

D Fatty **plaques** on the inside of a coronary artery can cause heart attacks.

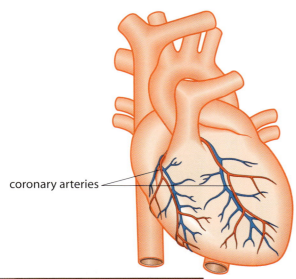

coronary arteries

C The heart and coronary arteries.

Heart disease is usually caused by **lifestyle** or genetic factors. Only very occasionally is it caused by microorganisms. The factors which most increase the risk of a heart attack are shown in table E.

Genetic factors	Lifestyle factors
• being male • inheriting genes which make you more likely to have a heart attack	• being overweight • eating a poor diet • smoking • drinking too much alcohol • being unfit • stress

E Factors linked to heart disease.

Regular exercise that makes your heart pump harder makes you fitter and reduces stress, so you are less likely to have a heart attack. It also helps your heart recover more quickly if you do have a heart attack.

Summary

Design a poster for a doctor's waiting room which summarises in 250 words the key points about the factors that increase the risk of a heart attack. Include two or three diagrams.

?

3 Explain why fatty plaques in arteries are so dangerous.

4 a Which of the lifestyle factors do you think would be most difficult to change? Explain your answer.
   b Which of these factors do you think would be easiest to change? Explain your answer.

5 Describe the advice a doctor would give to a man with a family history of heart disease to help him reduce the risk of having a heart attack.

6 It is often said that 'prevention is better than cure'.
   a What are the advantages of changing lifestyle factors to prevent heart disease, rather than curing it by an operation after it has happened?
   b What might be the disadvantages?

7 Think of a plus, a minus and an interesting point about this statement: Alcohol should be banned.

8 Explain how people can find out whether they are at a high risk of getting heart disease.

Finding the cause

What causes heart attacks?

A

Scientists have tried to find out what causes heart attacks so that they can work out how to reduce the problem. There have been many **epidemiological studies** where groups of people have been studied for many factors, including lifestyle, and whether or not they have had heart attacks.

Comparing people who have had heart attacks with those who haven't shows **correlations** between some factors and heart attacks. A correlation is when a change in one factor shows a similar pattern to a change in another factor.

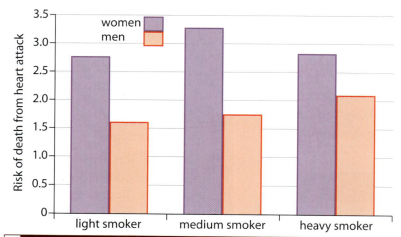

B Death rate from heart attack for smokers compared with non-smokers. A male light smoker is 1½ times as likely to have a heart attack as a man who has never smoked.

?

1 Name some of the lifestyle factors that would have been included in studies on heart attacks.

2 When comparing groups of people, the data is first grouped by other factors such as sex. Why do you think this is so?

3 Look at graph B.
   a Why does the graph suggest a correlation between smoking and heart disease?
   b What does the graph suggest about differences between men and women who smoke?

The data for graph B came from a study in Copenhagen, Denmark. The study took about 12 years and included 11 472 women and 13 191 men. This was a **reliable** study because it was made over a long time and studied many people.

Just because there is a correlation between two factors, such as smoking and heart disease, does not prove that one *causes* the other. For example, being overweight is correlated with heart disease, but it may not be weight that is the cause. It could be something else such as lack of exercise that could cause both obesity and heart disease.

To say that smoking is a **cause** of heart disease, we need to show that there is a possible way that it may lead to the result. Studies have shown that smoking increases the amount of fatty material in the blood. This fatty material makes plaques on the inside of arteries and so can cause heart attacks.

Every cigarette we smoke makes fatty deposits stick in our arteries.

We'll help you give up before you clog up completely. bhf.org.uk

C

Quitting smoking reduces the risk of heart attack to nearly the same as someone who has never smoked.

D Quote from World Health Organisation advice on smoking.

?

4 Jodie's grandfather has smoked heavily since he was young, but he is now 83 and still healthy. Jodie thinks that there is no correlation between smoking and heart disease. Suggest how she is wrong.

5 Results from many other long-term studies have also shown a correlation between smoking and heart disease. Why is it important that many reliable studies are done?

6 Explain how smoking can lead to a heart attack.

7 Governments in many developed countries spend lots of money on health campaigns about smoking, eating, exercise and alcohol. What effect are they trying to have?

8 How would you choose members for two groups to find out whether smoking increased the risk of heart attacks? What would you want to keep the same in both groups?

Summary

Write an encyclopaedia entry for 'epidemiological study', using research into the causes of heart disease as an example.

A doctor's day

How can we keep healthy?

A Doctors have to know a lot about how diseases are caused so that they know how to cure them.

1 Draw up a table to summarise the differences and similarities between a virus, a bacterium and a fungus.

2 Give three ways microorganisms can spread from one person to another.

3 Why is there is a period in an infection when you don't show symptoms?

4 Look at graph B, which shows a patient's temperature after infection with a bacterial disease.

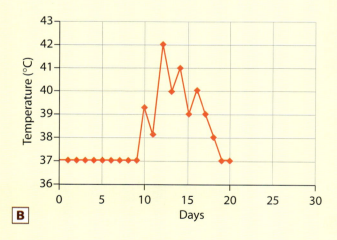

B

a What symptom of the disease does the graph show?
b How long does the illness last for?

I think I might have flu.

C Sarah is feeling unwell.

5 Sarah is off school with the flu.
  a What group of microorganisms caused the disease?
  b Can Sarah take anything to get rid of the disease? Give a reason for your answer.

6 a What does it mean when you are immune to a disease?
  b Describe two ways that you can become immune to a disease.

I want to know if I should have Jatinder vaccinated against measles.

D Mrs Patel has brought Jatinder for a vaccination.

7 a What is a vaccine?
  b How does a vaccine protect you from an infection?
  c What are the benefits and drawbacks of getting Jatinder vaccinated against measles, from Jatinder's point of view and from the government's point of view?

8 Explain why it is important for women to be vaccinated against German measles before they have babies.

9 What is active immunity? Draw a flow chart to explain your answer.

How do I know these pills are safe?

E Mrs Fraser is worried about taking a new medicine.

10 Scientists think that a chemical may be useful in treating hay fever.
  a Draw a flow chart to describe how the chemical will be tested before it is used in human trials.
  b Write down two reasons why new medicines need to be tested.

11 List the advantages of double blind trials.

12 One artery in diagram F is narrowed where a fatty deposit has formed. Explain how the artery could become completely blocked.

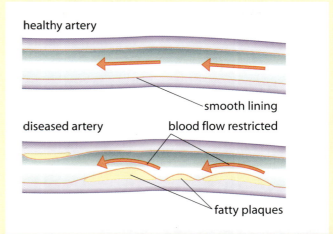

healthy artery

smooth lining

diseased artery   blood flow restricted

fatty plaques

F Diagram showing lengthways section of a healthy artery and a diseased artery.

13 What are the causes and symptoms of angina?

14 What is a heart attack and how is it caused?

15 List three factors that increase your chance of having a heart attack:
  a that you can do nothing about
  b that you can do something about.

16 Look at table G.
  a Work out the percentages of men in each category who took regular exercise.
  b How would you expect heart attack rate to change with exercise? Explain your answer.
  c Do the results support what you expected?
  d How could the study have been improved?

Age (years)	Number of men who have had one heart attack			Number of men who have not had heart attacks (control group)		
	Little or no exercise	Regular exercise	Total	Little or no exercise	Regular exercise	Total
40–49	59	9	68	98	28	126
50–59	109	14	123	174	56	230
60–64	25	5	30	48	12	60

G Effect of exercise on risk of heart attacks.

Material choices

What are the different materials that we use?

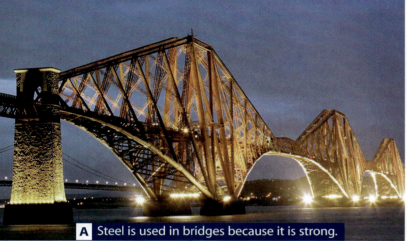

A Steel is used in bridges because it is strong.

B An alloy of aluminium is used in the bodies of aircraft because it is strong but light.

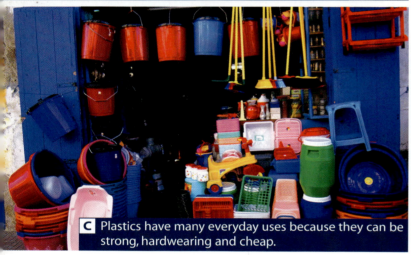

C Plastics have many everyday uses because they can be strong, hardwearing and cheap.

D Ceramics can be moulded into various shapes.

Substances may be solids, liquids or gases. Many of the materials you can see and use are solids. You are probably sitting on a solid material, and wearing some as well. This book is made of a solid material. All materials are made of **particles** and materials such as wood, rubber and wool are built from **molecules**. There are 90 or so naturally occurring **elements** but the materials we use are rarely pure elements. Most materials are **mixtures** of two or more different elements, or **compounds**. Compounds are substances in which elements are chemically joined together.

How we use a material depends on its properties.

Many of the materials we use are **natural**, although they are often changed or processed to make them more useful. For instance, wool from sheep is washed, spun and dyed before being knitted or woven into jumpers or carpets.

?

1 What properties should the materials have that are used in these objects?
   a a saucepan and its handle
   b a car windscreen
   c a mountain-climber's rope

2 What materials are used to make
   a containers for drinks
   b clothes?

3 Give reasons why the materials in question **2** are used.

Other materials are **synthetic** or artificial. This means that they have been manufactured from raw materials which are unlike the final product. For example, the material used to make your pen is made from substances found in crude oil. Obtaining all these materials can have a harmful effect on the environment. We will be considering how some materials are manufactured and the environmental effects of this.

When objects are no longer useful we throw them away. We need to consider the effects on the environment of disposing of materials and whether alternative materials and methods need to be found.

F Why do most materials end up being thrown away?

E Some materials are made from plants, such as cotton.

? **4** Which of the following materials do you think are natural and which are synthetic? Explain your answer.

nylon leather wood cotton polythene Lycra wool

5 What environmental problems may be the result of manufacturing the following materials?
  a A cotton shirt – the cotton plant is grown on large farms that often use pesticides.
  b A glass window – glass is made from materials dug from the ground.

6 Which is the odd one out: PVC, nylon, leather? Explain your answers.

7 Make a list of the questions you need to ask about a material in order to decide:
  a what its uses may be
  b how harmful it could be to the environment.

Fit for the job

How can we pick a suitable material for a particular product or task?

A How do we know the rope is strong enough?

B How can we compare the properties of these materials?

To find out if a material is suitable for a job, its properties must be measured. Instruments are used to make measurements. Each measurement will have an **uncertainty**, that is it will be slightly different to the true value, for the following reasons:

- The instrument may not be set up properly (diagram C).
- The data may be read incorrectly (diagram D).
- The measuring instrument may not be precise or accurate (diagram E).
- The conditions may have changed while the readings were being taken.

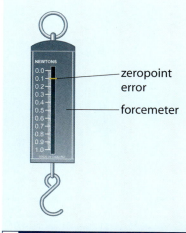

zeropoint error

forcemeter

C Every reading taken with this forcemeter will be inaccurate

D Both these clocks are showing the same time but the angle from which the face is viewed makes the time appear different.

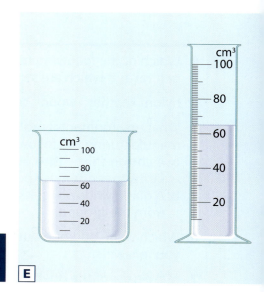

E

? **1** Which instrument in diagram E should be used to measure out 65 cm³ of water? Explain your answer.

Each reading should be taken a number of times. Readings that appear different from the others are **outliers** and can be discarded. The **best estimate** of the true value is the mean of a set of results. The **range** is the highest and lowest results in a set once the outliers have been discarded. Differences between two sets of data may not be real if each best estimate lies within the other's range.

A How accurate are measurements made with simple instruments?

F

?

2 Sarah tried to measure out 10 g of a powder on a balance near an open window.
   a Why might her readings be inaccurate?
   b What should she do to improve the accuracy?

3 The forcemeter in diagram C was used to weigh an object three times. The readings were 0.5 N, 0.7 N and 0.6 N. What is the best estimate of the weight? Explain how you worked out your answer.

4 The following data was collected for the mass (in grams) of an object.
   20.1 20.3 20.2 21.8 20.2
   a Which result is an outlier? Give your reason.
   b What are the mean and range of the data?

?

5 The volumes of two mugs were measured. The best estimates and ranges were calculated. Mug A: 254 cm³, range 250–258 cm³; Mug B: 256 cm³, range 253–259 cm³. Is there a real difference between them? Explain your answer.

6 Jed and Sophie wanted to know the length of an elastic band before it was stretched. Jed measured the length five times with a ruler. His readings were:
   14.2 cm   14.4 cm   13.5 cm   14.1 cm   14.3 cm
   a Which of the measurements is an outlier?
   b What is the best estimate of the length of the elastic band? Show how you worked out the answer.
   Then Sophie did the same thing. Her measurements were:
   14.6 cm   14.3 cm   14.4 cm   14.5 cm   14.3 cm
   c Was Sophie measuring the same or a different elastic band? Explain your answer.

Summary

Describe how you would obtain the best estimate for the mass of a roll of bubble wrap, and explain how uncertainties may arise.

Comparing properties

How do the properties of different materials compare?

We can compare materials by looking at different properties.

Melting point

A cooking dish that is put into an oven must be able to withstand high temperatures. Solid materials chosen for a job must remain solid at the working temperature, so we must know their **melting point**.

Pure substances melt at a precise temperature. For example, ice melts at 0 °C and copper melts at 1083 °C. Mixtures soften over a range of temperatures before becoming liquid. Some compounds **decompose**, or if they are in air will start to burn, before they melt.

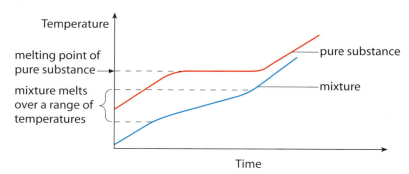

B Melting curves for a pure substance and a mixture.

A An oven dish needs to keep its shape up to about 300 °C.

C Tools used to handle molten steel must be able to withstand temperatures up to 1500 °C.

?

1 A solid material begins to melt when the temperature is 154 °C. It is not completely liquid until the temperature is 160 °C. Is the material a pure substance? Explain your answer.

2 Look at table D. Which of these materials is suitable for making a food container for use in a microwave oven? Explain your answer. (*Hint*: microwaves cook by heating water in the food to boiling point.)

Material	Temperature at which material starts to soften (°C)
polypropene	80
PVC	60
polythene	65
nylon	185

D

3 A murderer used an ice dagger to kill his victim. What does this tell you about the temperature of the surroundings at the time of the murder?

Density

The **density** of a material is the mass of a specific volume of the material.

$$\text{density (g/cm}^3) = \frac{\text{mass of material (g)}}{\text{volume of material (cm}^3)}$$

Mass can be measured in kilograms or grams and volume in cubic metres or cubic centimetres. The units of density are kg/m^3 or g/cm^3.

An object made out of a dense material will have a larger mass than one of the same size made from a material with a lower density.

The density of a material needs to be considered if the object to be made from it is to be moved or lifted. For example, plastic bottles are lighter than glass bottles of the same volume.

A How can you find:
- the melting point of chocolate
- the density of chocolate?

F

Summary

Describe how you would measure the melting point and density of a new material and explain why this information would be useful.

E How does plastic make marathon running easier?

?

4 Glass is denser than polythene. Why can a lorry carry more 2 litre polythene bottles filled with mineral water than 2 litre glass bottles?

5 What instruments are needed to measure the density of a lump of solid material?

6 Think of a plus, a minus and an interesting point about this statement: Different plastics soften at temperatures from 60°C to over 300°C.

7 Raj and Mina wanted to find the density of a piece of rubber. Table G shows the data they collected. Determine the best estimate and the range of the density.

	Readings				
	1	2	3	4	5
mass (g)	50.0	50.1	49.8	49.9	51.5
volume (cm³)	39	41	48	40	39

G

More properties

How do the properties of different materials compare?

Words like hard, strong, stiff and tough have particular meanings in science.

The **strength** or breaking force of a material is the force needed to break a specific thickness of the material when it is put under **tension** (a stretching force), or **compression** (a squashing force). Metals are strong under tension but crumple when compressed. Brick and glass are strong when compressed but snap easily if stretched.

A **tough** material is strong but does not change shape or **deform** when lightly stretched or compressed. However, it will deform before it finally breaks. Steel is a tough material. A **brittle** material such as glass does not deform much before breaking. Brittle materials shatter. Plasticine is not tough because it can be deformed easily. Tough materials are more likely to be **durable** (last a long time in use).

Materials that can be squeezed into new shapes are **malleable** and those that can be drawn into wires or fibres are **ductile**. Many materials become more malleable or ductile when they are warmed. Steel can be moulded into sheets, pipes and rods when it is red hot. A material is **elastic** when it returns to its original shape when a force is removed from it but **plastic** if it keeps a new shape once it has been deformed.

A The sails of these yachts are made from Kevlar, a material which is strong in tension.

?

1 Why is Kevlar used in sails and bulletproof vests?

2 How do you think Plasticine got its name?

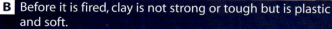

B Before it is fired, clay is not strong or tough but is plastic and soft.

C After it has been fired clay is stiff, hard and brittle.

Stiffness or **flexibility** is a measure of the force needed to bend a piece of the material with a particular cross-sectional area. Tough materials are usually stiff. Brittle materials are often not flexible and snap when bent.

The **hardness** of a material is determined by how easily it can be scratched or cut. Diamond is the hardest naturally occurring material. Materials which are not hard are described as soft. Hard materials may be tough or brittle. Steel and glass are both hard materials.

E Cars are made from many different materials.

3 Why are paperclips made from steel?

4 Why are drill bits used for cutting through concrete given a coating of diamond?

5 You are looking for a suitable material for a new design of case for a mobile phone. What properties should the material have?

6 Which is the odd one out: flexible, malleable, ductile, elastic? Explain your answers.

7 Look at photo E. List the parts of the car shown and describe the most important properties for each part.

8 Find out what materials are used for car bodies, how the properties of these materials compare and what advantages and disadvantages each has.

A How can we test the properties of materials?

D

Summary

Look back at the work you have done in Topics C2.2 to C2.4. Draw a concept map for properties of materials, making sure you include all the bold words in the topics.

A Polythene containers can be found on many supermarket shelves.

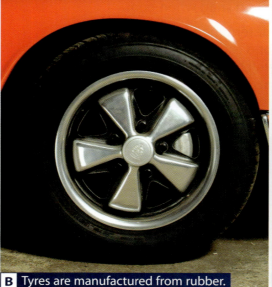

B Tyres are manufactured from rubber.

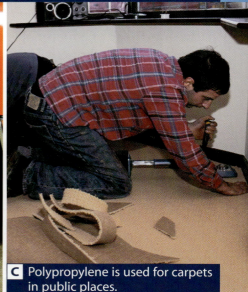

C Polypropylene is used for carpets in public places.

Many of the materials that we use are made from substances obtained from animals and plants such as cellulose (wood, paper and cotton), rubber, wool and silk. Today we also have synthetic materials such as polythene, nylon, polycarbonate and artificial rubbers.

Natural and synthetic materials have a wide variety of properties but they can be classed as three types:

- **Plastics** are materials that can be moulded into various shapes, either when they are made or when they are warmed up. When they become cool they retain the shape they were given but become tougher and stronger. Lots of synthetic materials are plastics; some examples are polythene, nylon, PVC, polypropylene and polycarbonate.

- **Rubbers** are waterproof, elastic materials. Natural rubber is obtained as liquid latex from rubber trees. It only becomes tough and elastic when heated with sulfur in a process called vulcanising. Today we have many synthetic materials which mimic natural rubber but have a wide variety of properties.

- **Fibres** are materials that can be woven, knitted or twisted into ropes. Wool, cotton and silk are natural fibres. Synthetic fibres are made by pushing warm, soft plastics through tiny holes called spinnerets. The fibre cools and becomes stronger, tougher and harder, but stays flexible and elastic. Materials such as nylon, polypropylene, polyester and Kevlar can be drawn into fibres. Woven materials have gaps which allow air or water to pass through.

?

1 Why are many consumer goods packed in polythene containers?

2 Why did inflatable rubber tyres replace steel rims for wheels?

3 Look at photo C. What properties do you think polypropylene fibres must have?

A How can we investigate the properties of plastics, rubbers and fibres?

D

A material needs the correct range of properties to suit a purpose. Cost often needs to be considered also. Natural materials are still used for many purposes but are often more expensive than their synthetic alternatives.

E Neoprene is a synthetic rubber used for wetsuits.

Summary

Draw up a table listing the different types of material, examples of each, their properties and uses.

?

4 Which type of material is needed for the following applications? Explain your answers.
 a a 'bungee' rope
 b the soles of a pair of boots
 c the casing of a computer
 d a fishing net

5 What properties does Neoprene have that makes it good for wetsuits?

6 Why are cotton, wool and silk still used in clothes?

7 Many natural materials have been replaced by synthetic alternatives. Think of as many different reasons as you can to explain this statement.

8 A Formula 1 racing car has its tyres changed at least once during a race while a normal car driver would expect to use the same tyres for several years. What differences in properties do you think racing and normal tyres have?

Synthetic materials

What are synthetic materials made from?

From natural to synthetic

Until the 20th century all plastics, rubbers and fibres were obtained from plants and animals. Cotton fibres and wood are made of plant cellulose while wool and silk are animal proteins. However, there were limits in the supply and it was difficult to modify natural materials to give them new properties. The plastic age began in the 1930s when synthetic materials started to take the place of natural materials and new uses were found for them.

Living cells build materials, such as cellulose, from simple chemicals. Scientists discovered that they could build synthetic materials starting from the simple substances found in **crude oil**. In the early 20th century crude oil was already a valuable source of fuels. It soon became an important resource for the chemical industry.

Crude oil is a thick, black liquid found in the Earth's crust. It is formed from dead plants and animals that were trapped in sediment at the bottom of oceans. Over millions of years the remains of the organisms were changed by heat and pressure into crude oil.

A Cellulose from cotton plants supplied the textile industry in the 19th century.

Molecules large and small

Crude oil is a mixture of thousands of different compounds. Most of these compounds are **hydrocarbons** – compounds made up only of carbon and hydrogen. In hydrocarbon molecules carbon atoms form the links in a chain, which varies in length from one carbon atom to hundreds of carbon atoms.

?

1 Why was the textile industry interested in new synthetic fibres?

2 Why did owners of oil wells become rich early in the 20th century?

3 Why is crude oil not a renewable resource?

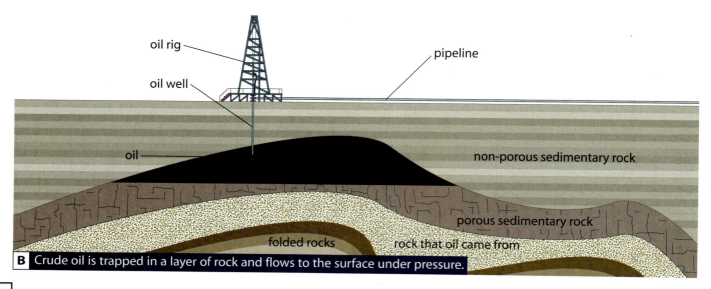

B Crude oil is trapped in a layer of rock and flows to the surface under pressure.

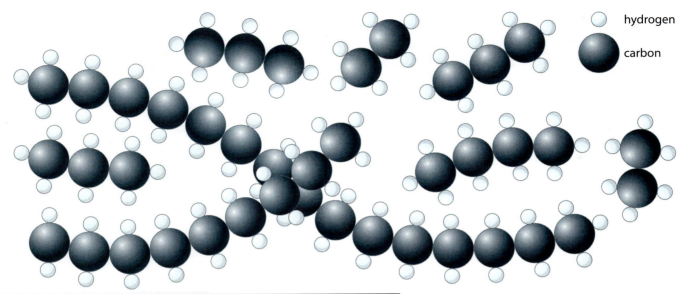

hydrogen

carbon

C Crude oil is a mixture of hydrocarbons with many sizes of molecule.

The melting and boiling points of hydrocarbons depend on the size of the molecules.

Number of carbon atoms in molecule	Boiling point (°C)
1–4	Up to 25
5–7	40–100
8–11	100–150
11–14	150–250
15–19	220–340
20–30	over 350
Over 30	over 400

D

?

4 Which of the following molecules are hydrocarbons?
methane CH_4, ethanol C_2H_6O, ethene C_2H_4,
carbon dioxide CO_2, octane C_8H_{18}

5 If a hydrocarbon boils at 120 °C, approximately how many carbon atoms does it have in a molecule?

6 Some people say 'synthetic materials are made from chemicals, but wool and cotton are natural'. Explain why this statement does not make scientific sense.

7 **a** What evidence shows that crude oil is a mixture of different substances?
   b Find out what other properties change as the length of the hydrocarbon chain increases.

Summary

Write sentences to explain the difference between:
A natural and synthetic materials
B crude oil and a hydrocarbon
C a hydrocarbon with a boiling point of 1 °C and one with a boiling point of 216 °C.

Refining oil

How are raw materials obtained from crude oil?

The compounds in crude oil are separated by a process called **refining**. The first stage divides the crude oil up into **fractions**. Each fraction is itself a mixture of many hydrocarbons which boil within a range of temperatures.

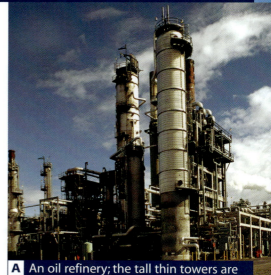

A An oil refinery; the tall thin towers are the fractionating columns.

Fractional distillation

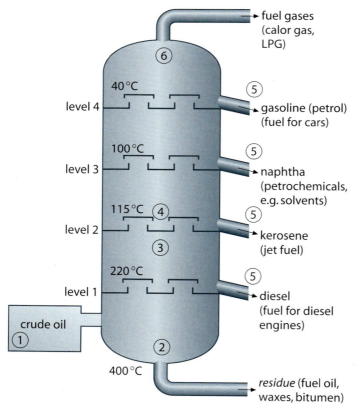

Some of the fractions, particularly the **naphtha** fraction, are taken to other fractionating columns and separated further until pure compounds are collected on each tray.

6 Some hydrocarbons stay as gases right at the top of the column where the temperature is normal.

5 The liquids are piped off from the trays.

4 Each compound condenses at its boiling point and the liquid is trapped in trays. The trays are placed at the appropriate heights in the column to collect all the hydrocarbons that have boiling points between certain ranges.

3 The vapours rise and cool. The larger molecules with the higher boiling points condense first. Smaller molecules remain as gases and rise further up to the cooler parts of the column.

2 The vapour, at a temperature of about 500 °C, is passed into the **fractionating column**.

1 The crude oil is heated until it boils.

B Crude oil is separated into fractions by the process of **fractional distillation**.

?

1 What is the relationship between the size of a hydrocarbon molecule and its boiling point?

2 How does the temperature vary as you go up the fractionating column?

3 In what state are the hydrocarbons put into the fractionating column?

4 Do hydrocarbons with small or large molecules reach the top of the column?

Using the fractions

Most of the fractions of crude oil are used as fuels in transport and industry. The smaller molecules with low boiling points are also used by the chemical industry to make synthetic materials and other useful compounds. These hydrocarbons make up just a small part of crude oil.

Name of fraction	Number of carbon atoms in molecule	Uses
fuel gases	1–4	bottled gas for houses, caravans
gasoline (petrol)	5–7	fuel for cars
naphtha	8–11	synthetic materials and other chemicals
kerosene	11–14	aircraft fuel
diesel	15–19	fuel for cars, lorries
mineral oils	20–30	lubricating oils
fuel oil	30–40	fuel for ships, power stations
bitumen	over 40	tar for roads

C

 A How can we separate the substances in crude oil?

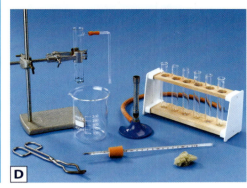

D

?

5 Which fraction of crude oil is used to make synthetic materials?

6 What are most of the fractions of crude oil used for?

7 Think of a plus, a minus and an interesting point about this statement: Crude oil is too valuable as a raw material for it to be burnt as fuel.

8 Describe how the chemicals in the naphtha fraction are separated. Suggest the temperatures that would be needed at the top and bottom of the column.

Summary

Describe what happens to a molecule of a hydrocarbon in crude oil as it passes through the oil refinery.

Making polymers

How are polymers made?

Synthetic materials are substances called **polymers**. The raw materials used to make polymers are small molecules called **monomers**. A polymer molecule is a chain of many small monomers joined together.

An example of a monomer is the hydrocarbon ethene, C_2H_4. When ethene is heated and compressed, the molecules begin to join together to form a chain.

More molecules join the chain until it contains thousands of carbon atoms linked together. The large molecule is a polymer called poly(ethene) or, more simply, polythene. The reaction is called **polymerisation**.

Polymer chains formed in this reaction are of different lengths so a polymer is not a pure compound. This means that a polymer does not melt at a precise temperature but softens over a range of temperatures.

Each different polymer starts with a different monomer. Most monomer molecules are a little more complex than ethene and produce polymers with short chains of atoms attached to the main long chain. Polymer chemists are able to decide which monomers to use to make polymers with the properties they are seeking. Table C shows the properties of some different polymers.

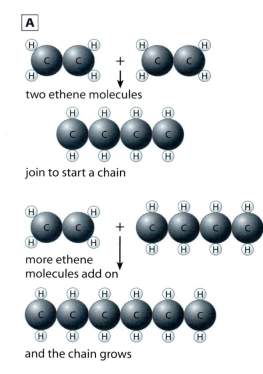

A

two ethene molecules

join to start a chain

more ethene molecules add on

and the chain grows

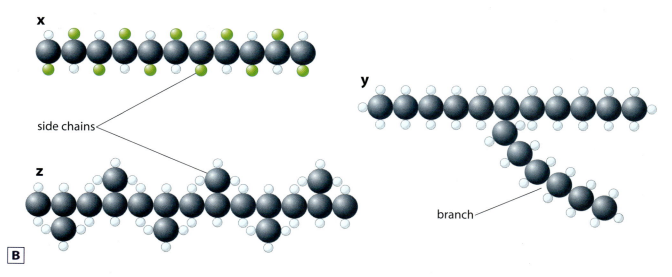

x

side chains

y

z

branch

B

?

1 What is the difference between a monomer and a polymer?

2 What is the name of the monomer used to make poly(propene)?

Polymer	Properties	Uses
poly(ethene)	flexible, cheap	bags, containers
poly(propene)	tough (doesn't break easily), can be drawn into fibres	buckets, bowls, carpets
Teflon	tough, slippery	non-stick coatings
Perspex	tough, hard, clear	unbreakable windows
polystyrene	tough, hard, can be moulded into complex shapes or 'blown' into foams	disposable cups, packaging, car dashboards
PVC	tough, hard, long-lasting	window frames, pipes
polyamide, nylon	tough, elastic, ductile	clothes, carpets

C Polymers and their uses.

Cork or plastic?

Corks have been used to seal wine bottles for centuries. Cork is a material obtained from certain trees. It is waterproof and airtight but is sometimes attacked by microorganisms. When this happens the cork can make the wine bad.

A polymer has been made that looks and behaves like cork, is cheap, and is not attacked by microorganisms. Many wine producers now use 'corks' made from the polymer to seal their wine bottles.

?
5 Which polymer would you use to make:
   a a coating for cloth which stops dust from sticking to it
   b the casing for an MP3 player
   c unbreakable tumblers for a café
   d rope for a sailing boat?
   Give reasons for your choices.

6 **a** Draw a table to list the advantages and disadvantages of cork and polymer for sealing wine bottles.
   b What reasons may people have for not approving of synthetic corks?

7 Monomers with side chains can be represented as shown in diagram F. Match them up with the polymers in diagram B. Explain how you made each match.

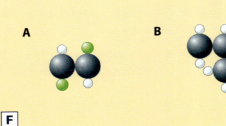

F

?
3 How do we know that polymers are not pure compounds?

4 Nylon is made from two different monomers that add on to the chain alternately. Copy and complete diagram C to show a nylon polymer chain.

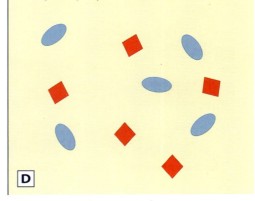

D

E Natural or synthetic; which is best?

Summary

Copy diagram A. Add labels explaining the terms monomer, polymer, polymerisation. Add some examples of polymers and their uses.

Inside polymers

Why do polymers behave as they do?

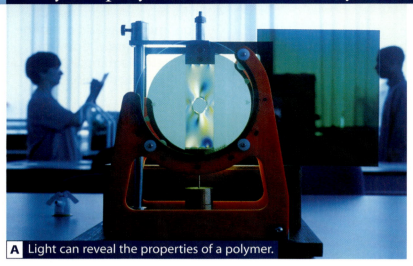

A Light can reveal the properties of a polymer.

Polymer scientists cannot see the molecules in a polymer but they can measure the properties of polymers. The data they collect is used to test theories about their structure. Scientists use successful theories about how the polymer molecules behave to predict the properties of new materials.

Sticking together

Temperature is related to the average energy possessed by each molecule. To make a solid melt or a liquid boil we must provide heat, giving the molecules extra energy to move or separate. Similarly, we need energy to pull on the ends of a piece of solid until it breaks or to stir a viscous liquid such as tar. Energy is required to pull the molecules apart or make them move into new positions. This energy is needed to overcome forces between the molecules.

Scientists have proposed the theory that there are forces that attract molecules together. The more atoms there are in a molecule, the stronger the force between molecules. The force is stronger when the molecules are closer together.

Ethene is a gas at room temperature. The forces between ethene molecules are weak. It has low melting and boiling points because not much energy is needed to pull molecules of ethene apart.

Polythene is a solid at room temperature. A sheet of polythene requires quite a lot of force to pull it apart. The forces between polythene molecules must be quite strong.

Polythene is lots of ethene molecules joined together, so the differences between ethene and polythene must be due to the size of their molecules.

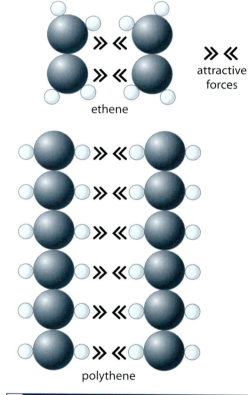

ethene

attractive forces

polythene

B The forces between large molecules are greater than the forces between small molecules.

?
1 Explain why polythene is a solid at room temperature.

2 a How would you check the proposals made by the theory about forces in polymers?
  b Why is a successful theory useful?

C

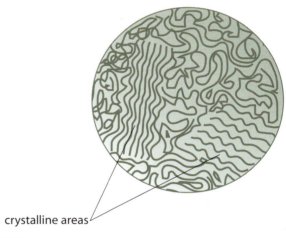

crystalline areas

D

The arrangement of particles in a metal or lump of salt resembles a pile of cans in a supermarket. They are arranged in regular layers, one on top of another. A regular arrangement of particles in a solid is called a **crystal lattice**. Many polymers are like a bowl of cooked spaghetti with their long molecules all jumbled up. In parts of a polymer, some of the molecules may line up together like dry spaghetti in a packet. This part of the polymer is said to be **crystalline**.

In the crystalline parts of the polymer the molecules are closer together than in the jumbled up bits so the forces between the molecules are stronger in these areas. More crystallinity makes a polymer stronger and increases its melting point.

 3 Describe the arrangement of particles in a crystal.

4 How do you think the melting point of a highly crystalline polymer would compare with that of a polymer with lower crystallinity?

5 How does the correlation between the boiling points of the fractions of crude oil and the number of carbon atoms in the molecules support the theory of forces between molecules?

Summary

Sketch a diagram of part of a polymer. Label the crystalline areas and note where the forces between molecules are strong and weak.

Changing polymers

How can the properties of polymers be modified?

A successful theory makes predictions that are accurate. Scientists are able to design new polymers with properties predicted by the theory of forces between polymer chains discussed in the last topic. We now have polymers designed for many different purposes.

Changing the forces

The forces holding polymer molecules together can be changed by making small differences to the molecules.

- **Longer molecules:** By increasing the length of the polymer chains, chemists can make the force between the polymer molecules larger. More energy will be needed to pull the molecules apart so the polymer will be stronger and tougher and soften at a higher temperature.

- **Increasing crystallinity:** Polymer molecules can be designed to make it easier for them to lie alongside one another. This increases the amount of crystallinity in the polymer. The more crystalline areas, the stronger the polymer. Unfortunately, increased crystallinity stops the polymer molecules moving so the polymer can become stiff and brittle. When polymers are drawn into a fibre they are pulled into a more regular arrangement, so polymer fibres are highly crystalline.

- **Cross-linking:** It is possible to link atoms in one polymer molecule directly with atoms in another molecule. This can be done by using special monomers in the chain that form cross-links, or by adding reactive substances to the polymer that link the chains together. Cross-links are very strong and give the polymer a high melting point and high strength.

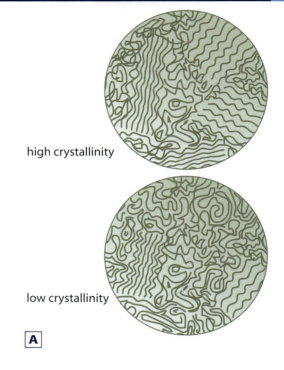

high crystallinity

low crystallinity

A

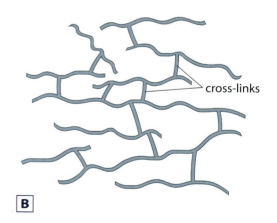

cross-links

B

?

1 Why are nylon fibres stronger than a lump of nylon?

2 Latex from rubber trees is a viscous liquid. It is mixed with sulfur and heated to make the tough, solid rubber we are familiar with. How has the sulfur modified the rubber polymer molecules?

- **Adding plasticiser:** Plasticisers are small molecules that fit between the polymer molecules. They keep the polymer molecules apart and so weaken the forces holding them together. This helps the polymer molecules move and makes the polymer flexible and soft.

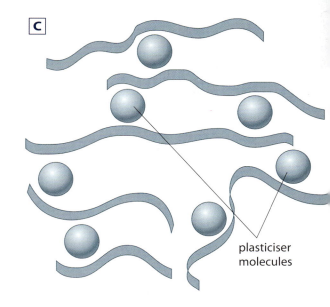

C

plasticiser molecules

melamine – cross-linked

PVC – plasticiser

high density poly(ethene) – longer molecules

polystyrene – more crystalline

D

A How can we compare different polymers?

E

Summary

Draw a mind map with 'polymer' at the centre and branches to the different types of polymer describing how their properties are modified.

?

3 Which of the following increases the force between polymer molecules?
increasing chain length, increasing crystallinity, cross-linking, adding plasticiser

4 Unplasticised PVC is used for window frames, while plasticised PVC is used to make waterproof coats. Compare the properties of the two types of PVC and explain their uses.

5 Why is crystallinity sometimes not required in a polymer?

6 Why is the theory of the structure of polymers considered to be a successful theory?

7 Polymers have a wide variety of uses. Consider all the possible reasons for this statement.

8 a The side groups on some polymer chains have atoms which are strongly attracted to side groups on other chains. What effect do you think this has on the properties of these polymers?
b The side groups on Teflon repel other atoms. What property does this give to Teflon?

Life cycle of a polymer

What is the 'life cycle' of a polymer?

We use synthetic polymers for many products – from clothes to carpets and mobile phones to packaging. When choosing a polymer, we should consider which material is best for the job and we should also ask about the effect of using the material on the environment. We need to look at the whole **life cycle** of the product, that is:
* the raw materials that are used to make it
* how much energy is needed
* how much waste is produced
* how the packaging and the product are disposed of after use.

Disposing of polymers

A

Natural polymers will rot, but bacteria cannot digest most synthetic polymers. They are said to be **non-biodegradable**. There are three ways of disposing of waste.

* **Landfill:** Most plastic rubbish is dumped in the ground and buried under soil. This is cheap but we are running out of suitable sites. New biodegradable polymers could be developed which would decompose, but the resources used to make the polymer would still be lost.

* **Incineration:** Most polymers burn well if they are heated to a high temperature. The energy released could be used to generate electricity, but unless the combustion is controlled very carefully, poisonous gases are given off.

?
1 Disposable cups are made from paper or a synthetic polymer.
   a What are the raw materials from which each is made?
   b What effect does obtaining these raw materials have on the environment?
   c The cups are used all over the world. What effects does transporting the cups from the factory where they are made have on the environment?

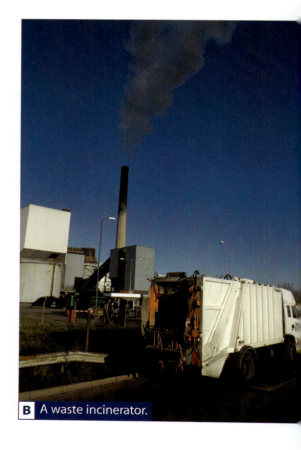

B A waste incinerator.

- **Recycling:** Many polymers can be melted and reused. Most polymers look very similar and sorting them is time-consuming. Polymer products are stamped with a symbol saying what polymer the object is made from but sorting relies on people to do the job.

Local councils are responsible for collecting and disposing of waste. The government sets targets for the amount of waste to be recycled.

PET
(polyethylene terephthalate)
e.g. plastic bottles, meat packaging

HDPE
(high density polyethylene)
e.g. milk bottles, detergent bottles, oil bottles, toys, plastic bags

V
(polyvinyl chloride)
e.g. vegetable oil bottles, blister packaging

LDPE
(low density polyethylene)
e.g. plastic bags, shrink-wrap

PP
(polypropylene)
e.g. margarine containers, yoghurt containers

PS
(polystyrene)
e.g. egg cartons, fast food trays

OTHER
(all other resins)
e.g. multi-resin containers, microelectronic components

C Polymer recycling symbols.

? 2 Which method of disposal:
  a produces useful energy
  b has the most beneficial effects for the environment?

3 Synthetic polymers were invented by scientists. What benefits and undesirable effects have they had?

D Polymers sorted for recycling.

? 4 Fresh food sold in supermarkets often comes with two or three layers of plastic packaging.
  a Who benefits from the packaging? Explain your answer.
  b Who is harmed by the packaging? Explain your answer.

5 Some of the ways of getting rid of plastic waste are cheaper and easier to do than others.
  a Which methods of disposal can we use without much change to our way of life?
  b Which methods would require us to make changes in the way we use polymers? Explain your answers.

6 Synthetic polymers are used in supermarket carrier bags and in bags for storing blood for patients needing transfusions.
  a Does one product have a greater benefit than the other? Explain your answer.
  b How does this affect the choices we have to make about using polymers?

Summary

A Make a list of the ways that using polymers affect the environment.
B Draw a table to show the advantages and disadvantages of the different methods of disposing of polymer waste.

Polymer decisions

What is a Life Cycle Assessment?

A Habitats are destroyed by logging and can only recover if similar new trees are planted.

B Crude oil is toxic and harms the environment if leaks occur.

C These products make money for the workers and factory owner, but at what cost to the environment?

A **Life Cycle Assessment** (**LCA**) considers all the ways that a product has an impact on the environment throughout its life. The outcome of an LCA depends on the applications of the material being considered.

The main features of a LCA are:
- *sustainability* of the raw materials – a sustainable resource can be replaced in a relatively short period of time and using it does little damage to the environment
- *preparing* the natural resources – leaks of harmful materials can damage the environment; transport produces air and noise pollution
- *manufacturing* the product – factories replace natural habitats and produce waste
- *using* the product – delivery and use creates pollution and waste

- *disposing* of the product
- *energy input* – energy is used at every stage in the life cycle of the product
- *costs* – the expenses of making the product and coping with the environmental problems that it causes
- *alternatives* – could a different material be used that has less impact on the environment?

As people become better off, the demand for new products increases. Scientists can use LCAs to identify problems and suggest changes to practices, such as encouraging sustainable development to cause as little lasting damage to the environment as possible. We may lack the technological expertise or the willingness to spend the money for some solutions such as recycling polymers.

Some people experience the benefits of materials while others suffer from the drawbacks. For example, the people who live near logging operations experience the damage to the environment while the rest of us benefit from the wood products.

Solutions to the problems depend on social and economic factors. In a developing country it may be cheaper to sort and recycle polymers by hand than in a developed country, where workers are expensive.

Some questions cannot be answered by scientists. An example is: 'who should pay for disposing of waste polymers?' Questions like these must be answered by governments and citizens.

D Many things can be re-used before they are recycled.

?

1. Which of the following are sustainable resources? Explain your answer.
   crude oil   rubber trees
   cotton plants   wool from sheep

2. How might the following processes harm the environment?
   a felling trees for wood
   b drilling for oil

3. Most manufacturing processes use electricity as a source of energy. Electricity is often made by burning fuels obtained from crude oil. How does burning fuels harm the environment?

4. Monomers for biodegradable synthetic polymers are made by certain bacteria that feed on plant material. What benefits does this have?

5. Which of the following questions cannot be answered by scientists?
   A How much energy is needed to make a polymer?
   B How can we encourage people to recycle packaging materials?
   C How does burning polymers change the environment?
   Explain your answer.

6. Clothes designers use a new fibre that resists dirt. What information do you need to work out the impact that clothes made from these fibres will have on the environment?

Summary

Carry out an LCA on a product of your choice and explain each part of the assessment.

A shopping trip
What's in the packaging?

Ragiv and Alex have been shopping in their local supermarket. They noticed that various materials were used as containers for the things that they bought.

Ragiv and Alex's shopping included a can of baked beans, a jar of peanut butter, a plastic bottle of toilet cleaner and a plastic bottle of water.

A

1 Choose from the following words to write a sentence describing the properties of the metal used in the can of baked beans.
  tough   brittle   malleable   stiff
  strong   hard   soft   plastic

2 Rajiv thought that the jar of peanut butter was heavy because it was made of glass. He decided to find out the density of the glass when all the peanut butter was removed.
  a What quantities must Ragiv measure to work out the density?
  b What is the formula for working out density?

3 Alex says, 'The bottle containing the toilet cleaner is tougher than the bottle containing the water'.
  a What does Alex mean when she says one bottle is tougher than the other?
  b Why do you think the toilet cleaner is stored in the tougher bottle?

Ragiv and Alex notice that the supermarket is offering paper bags as well as polythene bags for packing goods. They wonder which is best to use. Help them decide by answering the following questions.

B

Ragiv wonders which bag is the strongest. He tests five paper bags and five polythene bags. He hangs each bag from a hook and adds apples until the handles break. He records the number of apples in the bag at that moment.

Bag	Number of apples in each bag				
	1	2	3	4	5
paper	17	18	17	17	19
polythene	20	16	21	19	20

C

4 a Ragiv noticed that the handles of the polythene bag stretched when he put the apples in it and they didn't go back to their original length when he took the apples out. Which word best describes this property of the polythene?

 b Which measurement was probably an outlier? State the material and number of the bag and explain your answer.

 c Calculate the best estimate and the range for each bag.

 d Which was the strongest bag?

 e Was there a real difference in strength? Explain your answer.

Alex knows that paper is made from wood and has found that the raw material for the polythene is crude oil. She has some questions about how the plastic is made.

5 a Crude oil is a mixture of hydrocarbon molecules. What are hydrocarbons?

 b The hydrocarbon molecules have different numbers of carbon atoms. How does the boiling point of a hydrocarbon with two carbon atoms differ from one with eight?

6 a The hydrocarbons in crude oil are separated by factional distillation. Describe how this is done.

 b Only a small part of the crude oil is used to make chemicals such as polymers. What are most of the fractions of crude oil used for?

7 Ragiv has discovered that polythene is made from ethene molecules. Ethene is a monomer.

 a What is a monomer?

 b What is the name of the process which turns ethene into a polymer?

8 a Describe two ways that the polythene used in the bags could be made stronger. Explain your answers. (You can draw diagrams to help you.)

D

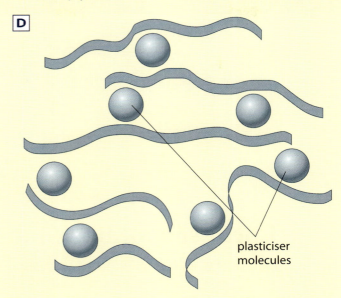

plasticiser molecules

Diagram D shows a polymer that has been modified by adding a plasticiser.

 b How do the plasticiser molecules affect the polymer molecules?

 c What effect does this have on the properties of the polymer material?

9 Which of the bags is made from a sustainable resource. Explain your answer.

10 The carrier bags will probably end up in a landfill site. What will happen to the paper and polythene bags?

11 Twice as much energy is required to make 1 kg of paper as 1 kg of polythene. The bags are the same size but the paper bag has a mass of 10 g and the polythene bag is 15 g. Which bag took the most energy to manufacture?

12 Ragiv and Alex used the answers to all the questions they had asked to write out a Life Cycle Assessment (LCA) on the bags.

 a What does an LCA show?

 b What can an LCA be used for?

Radiation and life

Is radiation useful or harmful?

This summer choose

SLOWTAN
Sun Cream

Why burn
when you can tan?

Slowtan sun cream helps protect against the harmful effects of ultraviolet radiation. Using Slowtan lets you stay in the sun longer without burning.

A Over exposure to ultraviolet radiation may cause skin cancer

Local school bans mobile phones

Dangerfields Secondary School has banned students from carrying mobile phones. The Headteacher said, "We don't really know yet if there are risks from the microwave radiation that these phones give out. I have a duty to protect all students at the school – how could I forgive myself if in ten years time mobile phones were found to be unsafe and I had allowed innocent children to be exposed to this radiation?"

B

This week's Poll

Is Dangerfields right to ban mobile phones? Vote by telephoning the numbers below

Yes: 01234 8912
No: 01234 89

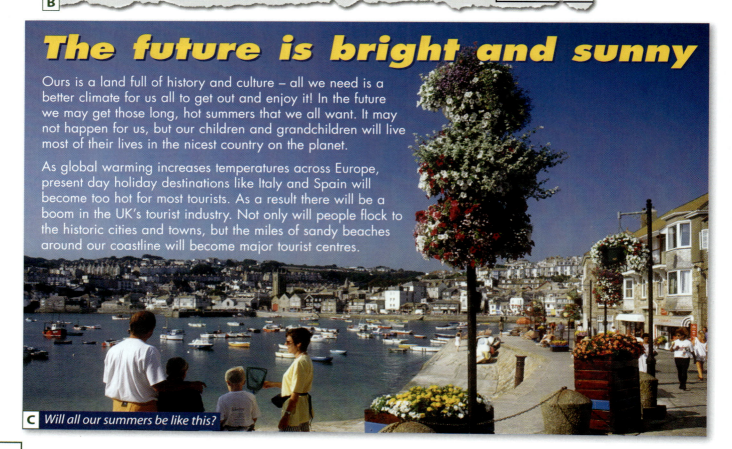

The future is bright and sunny

Ours is a land full of history and culture – all we need is a better climate for us all to get out and enjoy it! In the future we may get those long, hot summers that we all want. It may not happen for us, but our children and grandchildren will live most of their lives in the nicest country on the planet.

As global warming increases temperatures across Europe, present day holiday destinations like Italy and Spain will become too hot for most tourists. As a result there will be a boom in the UK's tourist industry. Not only will people flock to the historic cities and towns, but the miles of sandy beaches around our coastline will become major tourist centres.

C Will all our summers be like this?

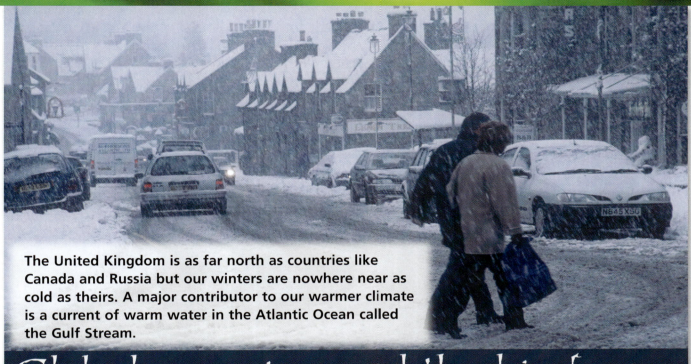

The United Kingdom is as far north as countries like Canada and Russia but our winters are nowhere near as cold as theirs. A major contributor to our warmer climate is a current of warm water in the Atlantic Ocean called the Gulf Stream.

Global warming and the big freeze

D

Global warming is melting the ice caps and disrupting the flow of the Gulf Stream. Scientific research suggests that before too long the Gulf Stream will cease to flow and the UK will no longer receive the additional heat energy it provides. Global warming could lead to a big freeze across the United Kingdom. Predictions suggest that temperatures could regularly fall to –20 °C or even colder, and the sea around our coastline will freeze during winter.

?

1 a Describe three ways of protecting yourself from sunburn.
   b Why do you need to do this?

2 a Do you think mobile phones should be banned in schools? Give reasons for your answer.
   b Write a list of the things you would need to find out to give a better answer to this question.

3 What causes global warming? Explain in as much detail as you can.

4 The two magazine articles predict opposite effects from global warming. Why do you think this is? Suggest as many reasons as you can.

5 a Should we try to stop global warming getting worse?
   b How could we do this? Explain in as much detail as you can.
   c Write a list of the things you need to find out to give a better answer to this question.

The electromagnetic spectrum

What types of radiation are there?

increasing energy

A Refraction inside raindrops splits up white light into the colours of the visible spectrum.

Visible light is **electromagnetic radiation** that we can see. Electromagnetic radiation delivers energy in 'packets' called **photons**. The photons of different colours of light deliver different amounts of energy.

Visible light is **emitted** by **sources** such as light bulbs and candle flames. The light travels from the source to our eyes, which act as **detectors**.

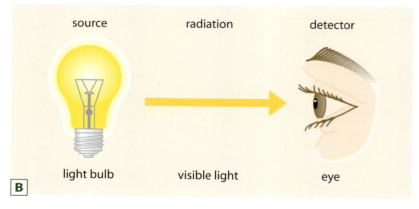

source   radiation   detector

light bulb   visible light   eye

B

The visible spectrum is only a small part of the much larger **electromagnetic spectrum**. Table C shows the different kinds of radiation that make up the electromagnetic spectrum.

?

1 Which colour in the visible spectrum has the lowest energy photons?

2 Suggest why the parts of the spectrum next to visible light have the names they do.

	Type of Radiation	Notes
lowest energy photons	**radio waves** 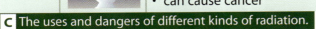	• emitted by radio and TV transmitters • used to send radio and TV programmes • detected by aerials and radios/TVs
	microwaves	• emitted by radio transmitters, mobile phones and microwave cookers • used to carry information and to cook food • can damage living tissue by heating the water in it • detected by aerials and radios/mobile phones
	infrared (IR)	• emitted by warm and hot objects, and by TV remote controls or car locks • detected by skin and thermometers • too much infrared can burn the skin
	visible	• emitted by hot objects • detected by eyes and photographic film
	ultraviolet (UV)	• emitted from very hot objects including the Sun • causes human skin to tan but can also cause skin cancer • detected by photographic film
	X-rays	• go through flesh but not bone • used to look at bones inside the body • regular exposure can cause cancer • detected by photographic film
highest energy photons	**gamma rays**	• emitted from radioactive substances • used to sterilise medical instruments • can penetrate deep inside the body • can cause cancer

C The uses and dangers of different kinds of radiation.

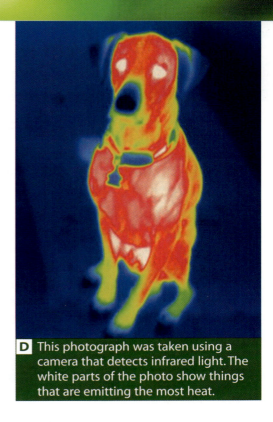

D This photograph was taken using a camera that detects infrared light. The white parts of the photo show things that are emitting the most heat.

?

3 Write down three types of radiation that can:
   a be detected by photographic film
   b cause cancer.

4 Look at photograph D and explain what it is showing.

5 Look at diagram B. Draw similar labelled diagrams to show:
   a how you can feel the warmth of the Sun
   b a photo of a flower taken in ultraviolet light
   c X-rays being used to find a broken bone.

6 Which is the odd one out: radio waves, microwaves, infrared, ultraviolet? Explain your answers.

7 Do you think there is a link between the energy of electromagnetic radiation and its ability to cause cancer? Explain your answer.

Summary

Write down the types of electromagnetic radiation in order, and add two or three key facts about each type.

Heating with radiation

What happens when radiation hits an object?

The particles in all objects vibrate slightly and emit infrared radiation. The hotter an object, the faster the vibration of its particles and the more infrared radiation it emits. We can feel infrared radiation, but we cannot see it.

The Sun produces most of the electromagnetic radiation we are exposed to. When infrared rays from the Sun fall on an object, some of their energy is **absorbed** and converted to heat energy. Some radiation is **transmitted** by the object (the radiation passes through it), and some is **reflected** from its surface. The amount of energy transmitted, absorbed or radiated depends on the colour and transparency of the material and how shiny it is.

A If an object is hot enough it will also emit visible light.

Infrared radiation from the Sun.

Some radiation is transmitted through the parasol.

Some radiation is reflected.

The man absorbs some of the radiation and gets warmer.

B

The amount of heating depends on the **intensity** of the radiation and its **duration**. The intensity is the amount of energy that falls on a certain area each second. The energy transmitted by a beam of radiation depends on how many photons arrive each second and how much energy each photon carries.

A How can you show that different colours absorb different amounts of radiation?
- What will you use as an infrared source?
- What will you use as a detector?
- How will you make your test fair?

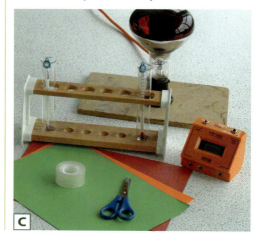

C

? **1** How does the energy of photons of infrared radiation compare with those of visible light?

2 Why is it not totally dark on a day with 100% cloud cover?

? **3** Look at photograph B. If you covered the parasol with silver foil, explain how this would change:
a the amount of radiation reflected by the parasol
b the intensity of the radiation hitting the man
c how warm he feels.

Cooking with radiation

Food can be cooked using infrared or microwave radiation. A grill emits infrared radiation; this is absorbed by the food which heats up. Microwaves can be used to cook moist food because water molecules in the food absorb the microwaves and vibrate faster. The energy carried by the microwaves is converted to heat energy.

Microwaves can be harmful to the human body, which contains a lot of water. Microwaves are reflected by metal but they can pass through glass so microwave ovens have a metal case and a metal screen on the door. The holes in the metal screen are too small for the microwaves to pass through, but allow visible light through.

D Using infrared radiation to cook food.

screen

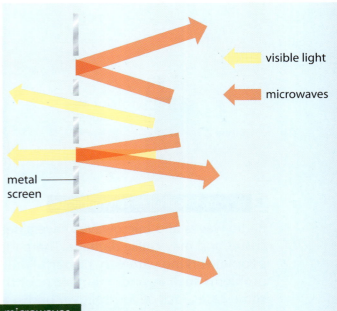

visible light

microwaves

metal screen

E The screen on a microwave oven door protects us from harm by the microwaves.

?

4 How is food cooked:
   a under a grill
   b in a microwave oven?

5 Describe two ways you can increase the amount of energy absorbed by food under a grill.

6 **a** What could microwaves do to the human body?
   b Suggest why you can see through the door of a microwave oven, but microwaves cannot pass through it.

7 Explain why the intensity of radiation from the Sun is highest at noon in the summer. Draw a diagram to illustrate your answer.

Summary

Write two short encyclopaedia entries, one for infrared radiation and one for microwaves.

Mobile phones and microwaves

Should people use mobile phones?

A mobile phone sends and receives microwave signals whenever it is switched on, so the network knows where the phone is and can make it ring if the phone's number is dialled.

The microwaves used for mobile phones have photon energies between radio waves and the microwaves used for cooking.

A

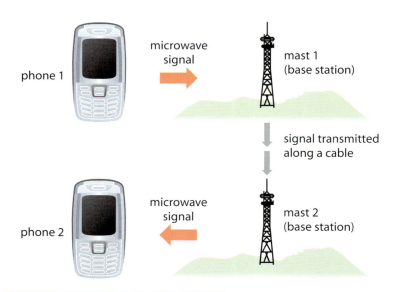

phone 1 — microwave signal → mast 1 (base station)

signal transmitted along a cable

mast 2 (base station) → microwave signal — phone 2

B How mobile phones communicate.

Radio waves and microwaves have a heating effect on living tissue, and may cause damage. There is some evidence that people working with very powerful radio waves experience problems such as poor memory, poor thinking skills and, in some cases, lack of control over body movement. This has led some people to think that there may also be risks associated with mobile phone use.

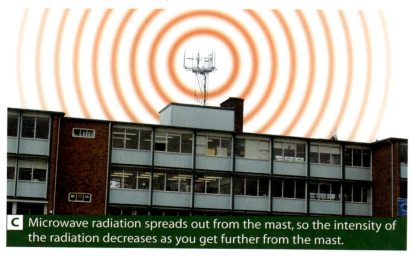

C Microwave radiation spreads out from the mast, so the intensity of the radiation decreases as you get further from the mast.

?

1 Why are microwaves transmitted by a mobile phone that is switched on even when you are not talking on the phone?

2 Describe the similarities and differences between the microwaves used for cooking and the ones used for mobile phones.

3 a Why do people think there may be a risk from mobile phone use?
 b Suggest why someone may not agree with this idea.

4 Why might you be at more at risk from microwave radiation if you live close to a mast compared to someone who lives further away?

Some scientists believe that the microwaves from mobile phone networks can heat up parts of the body and damage them, and some research shows that mobile phone users are twice as likely to develop cancers in areas of the brain close to the ear. Other scientists argue that the microwaves used are not powerful enough to damage tissue, and there is no evidence that the slight heating effect could cause cancer. At present there is not enough evidence to say this is definitely linked to using mobile phones.

Children may be more at risk because their brains are still developing, and their skulls are thinner. Some people think we should apply the **precautionary principle** (or 'better safe than sorry') and only allow children to use mobile phones in an emergency.

A Do you agree with these statements? Discuss reasons for and against each statement.

Mobile phones should be made illegal until we definitely know they are safe to use.

If you ban mobile phones you should ban cars.

D

?
5 Suggest reasons why scientists are not sure that mobile phones are responsible for cancers near the ears.

6 How would you use the precautionary principle to decide whether or not to put a new mast on top of a school building?

7 Satellites are used to transmit telephone signals over long distances. Draw a diagram to show how you could talk to a friend in the USA using mobile phones.

Summary

A mobile telephone company has applied for permission to build a new mast in your village which will improve reception on your phone. Write two letters to your local paper – one giving reasons supporting the new mast, and one giving reasons why it should not be built.

Ionising radiation

How does ionising radiation damage the human body?

Gamma rays, X-rays and ultraviolet light are forms of **ionising radiation**. They have enough energy to change atoms into charged particles called **ions**. Ionised molecules are more likely to react chemically, and these reactions can damage human cells and may lead to cancer. The more ionising radiation a person is exposed to, the higher their chances of getting cancer.

A This person has been exposed to too much ultraviolet radiation.

X-rays

X-rays can cause cancer, but they are still used in hospitals to scan for broken bones and look at teeth. The benefits of using X-rays for these purposes are greater than the possible risk. However, hospital workers need to reduce the risks to themselves as far as possible, by ensuring that the exposure to radiation is as low as possible. They only use enough X-ray radiation to get a good picture, only take X-ray pictures when absolutely necessary, and usually leave the room while the X-ray is being taken.

This approach to safety is often called the **ALARA principle**, which stands for **A**s **L**ow **A**s **R**easonably **A**chievable.

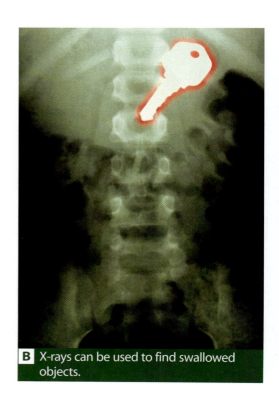

B X-rays can be used to find swallowed objects.

?
1 **a** Which forms of radiation can ionise atoms?
   b How does ionising radiation damage cells?

2 Explain all the measures an X-ray worker would take when following the ALARA principle.

Ultraviolet radiation

You cannot see or feel ultraviolet radiation, so by the time you realise you have been sunburnt, it is too late and your skin has already been damaged. If your skin is repeatedly damaged by ultraviolet radiation, you may get skin cancer.

A **perceived risk** is the amount of risk a person thinks they are exposed to. For example, many people think there is no risk of exposure to ultraviolet radiation if the weather is cloudy or they are sitting in the shade. However there is a risk, as ultraviolet radiation can be transmitted through clouds, and can also be reflected by water, sand, snow and other surfaces. In this case, the **actual risk** is greater than the perceived risk.

The actual risk of skin cancer from exposure to ultraviolet radiation is difficult to work out because some people's skin is more susceptible to damage than others, and some people's immune system may help to destroy cancerous cells.

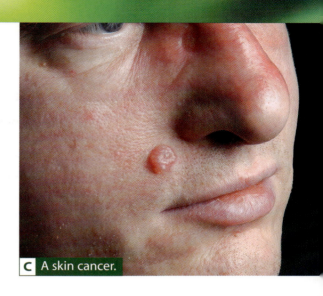
C A skin cancer.

?

3 Why is the perceived risk not always the same as the actual risk?

4 Diagram E shows the Tanner family on their summer holiday.

E

a List the names in the correct order starting with the person with the highest actual risk of exposure to ultraviolet radiation, and explain your answer.
b Who probably perceives their risk as less than it actually is?

5 Think of a plus, a minus and an interesting point about this statement: People should never sunbathe.

6 X-ray film is now more sensitive than it used to be. Explain how this can help to implement the ALARA principle.

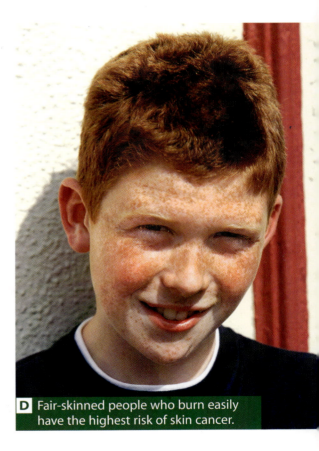
D Fair-skinned people who burn easily have the highest risk of skin cancer.

Summary

Draw a mind map to summarise what you know about ionising radiation, risks and safety.

The Earth is surrounded by a thin layer of atmosphere that lets radiation pass through. It contains oxygen molecules, consisting of two atoms of oxygen bonded together.

Ozone is a form of oxygen with three atoms. Most ozone is found in the **ozone layer**, between 25 to 30 kilometres above ground level. It is not a solid layer, but just a part of the atmosphere where ozone molecules are more concentrated.

When ultraviolet light strikes a molecule of oxygen, the molecule absorbs the energy and breaks up to form two single oxygen atoms. These atoms can join with other oxygen molecules to form ozone.

Ozone itself also absorbs energy from ultraviolet radiation, and splits up to form an oxygen molecule and a free oxygen atom. This atom can join up with an oxygen molecule to form ozone again. This cycle continually absorbs much of the ultraviolet radiation reaching the Earth, and so protects living organisms.

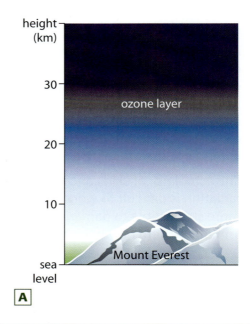

A

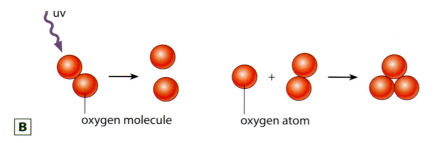

B

    oxygen molecule   oxygen atom   ozone molecule

? **1** Describe two ways in which ultraviolet radiation is absorbed in the atmosphere.

The amount of ozone in the atmosphere changes with the seasons. However, in the 1970s scientists discovered that the amount of ozone over the Antarctic each spring was getting less. This decrease in the amount of ozone is sometimes called a 'hole' in the ozone layer. The amount of ozone over the rest of the world has also decreased, but not as much. Ozone levels recover over the summer, but the depletion happens again the following spring. The amount of ozone over the rest of the world has also decreased, but not as much.

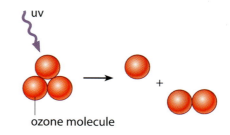

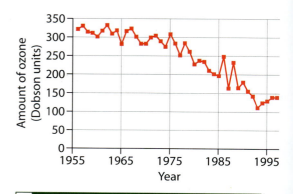

C The amount of ozone over the Antarctic is decreasing, as measured at the same time every year.

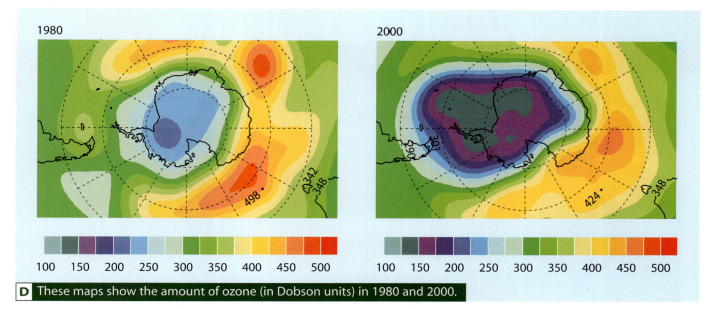

1980   2000

| 100 | 150 | 200 | 250 | 300 | 350 | 400 | 450 | 500 |

D These maps show the amount of ozone (in Dobson units) in 1980 and 2000.

When the hole in the ozone layer was first discovered, there was a public health campaign in Australia to try to cut down the amount of ultraviolet radiation that people received. Diagram E shows a poster from this campaign.

Chlorofluorocarbons (CFCs) are gases that were used in aerosol sprays, in refrigerators, and in foam packaging. Scientists think that the ozone hole was caused by these gases being released into the atmosphere. The gases react with ozone and destroy it. In 1987 an international agreement called the Montreal Protocol was signed, which set out how countries around the world would cut down on the production of CFC gases. This should eventually allow the ozone layer to recover.

SLIP
on a shirt

SLOP
on the suncream

SLAP
on a hat

E You can also stay in the shade to protect yourself against ultraviolet radiation, particularly in the middle of the day.

? 2 Describe the changes that have taken place in the ozone layer since 1980.

3 There is a greater risk of skin cancer in Australia than in the UK. Suggest as many reasons for this as you can.

4 Explain how you would apply the ALARA principle to your exposure to ultraviolet radiation.

5 Why are CFC gases no longer used in refrigerators?

6 Suggest how scientists may have found out that CFCs were responsible for the ozone 'hole'.

7 Find out more about the Montreal Protocol.

Summary

Design a poster or a leaflet to explain to people why ozone is important, but that it does not stop all ultraviolet radiation so other precautions have to be taken.

Photosynthesis

How does radiation make life on Earth possible?

A The Sun provides energy so crops can grow.

The Earth would be a very dark and cold place without the Sun. Radiation from the Sun passes through the atmosphere and provides the heat and light energy that most plants and animals need to survive.

Plants use visible light from the Sun to supply the energy for **photosynthesis**. Plants take in water through their roots and the leaves absorb carbon dioxide from the atmosphere. A green pigment in the leaves called **chlorophyll** absorbs light energy from the Sun.

The plant uses the carbon dioxide, water and energy to make glucose (a sugar) and oxygen. The oxygen is released into the atmosphere. Some of the sugar is used for energy, and the rest is converted to starch and stored by the plant for later use.

B Plankton are tiny plants that float near the surface of the sea. They are responsible for about half the photosynthesis that happens on the Earth.

E

$$\text{carbon dioxide} + \text{water} \xrightarrow[\text{chlorophyll}]{\text{light}} \text{sugar} + \text{oxygen}$$

Animals and plants use oxygen from the air for **respiration**. Respiration releases energy from food that is needed by the organism for growth, repair and movement.

E

$$\text{glucose} + \text{oxygen} \longrightarrow \text{carbon dioxide} + \text{water} (+ \text{energy})$$

?

1 **a** What are the reactants for the photosynthesis reaction?
   b What are the products?

2 Josie puts one plant in a sunny spot, and puts a similar plant in a dark corner. Which one would produce the most oxygen? Explain your answer.

Plants recycle carbon dioxide back into the glucose and oxygen that all organisms need for respiration.

Plants will be very important if humans ever live in space for long periods. Diagram C shows a dome that people might live in on the Moon.

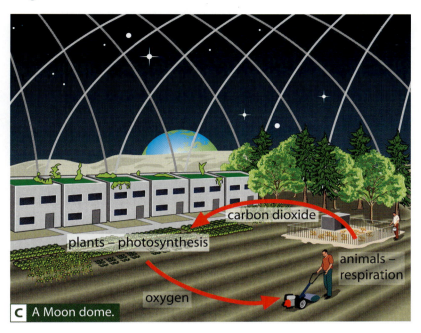

carbon dioxide

plants – photosynthesis

animals – respiration

oxygen

C A Moon dome.

The amounts of oxygen and carbon dioxide in the atmosphere depend on how much respiration and photosynthesis is happening. Graph D shows how the concentration of carbon dioxide in the atmosphere varies in the northern hemisphere.

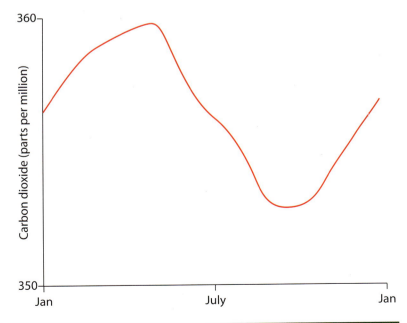

Carbon dioxide (parts per million)

360

350

Jan   July   Jan

D Changes in carbon dioxide concentration in the northern hemisphere.

? 3 a How do living things add carbon dioxide to the atmosphere?
b How is carbon dioxide removed from the atmosphere?

4 Look at diagram C.
a Why are plants needed in the dome?
b Why should the dome be made of glass or clear plastic?
c If the dome had to be made of metal, what would the people need to do to make the plants grow?

5 a Explain the shape of graph D. (*Hint*: photosynthesis happens faster when it is warm and when there is more light.)
b Sketch a graph to show how you would expect the concentration of oxygen to change over a year at the same place.
c How would you expect graph D to be different if it was for a place in the southern hemisphere? Explain your answer.

6 A plant was moved from a windowsill to a shady place in the house. Explain why its leaves might turn from light green to dark green.

Summary

Describe what might happen if half the plants on Earth were destroyed, and explain your predictions. You should write about 250 words.

The carbon cycle

How is the amount of carbon dioxide in the atmosphere changing?

Carbon dioxide is added to the atmosphere by:
- respiration of plants, animals, and **decomposers**
- **combustion** (burning) of **fuels**.

> **?** **1** List the ways in which carbon dioxide is added to and removed from the atmosphere.

The movement of carbon is called the **carbon cycle**.

For thousands of years the amount of carbon dioxide in the atmosphere has remained roughly constant. The amount added to the atmosphere by respiration and combustion of wood was balanced by the amount taken out by photosynthesis.

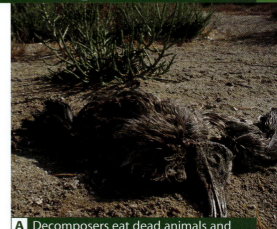

A Decomposers eat dead animals and plants.

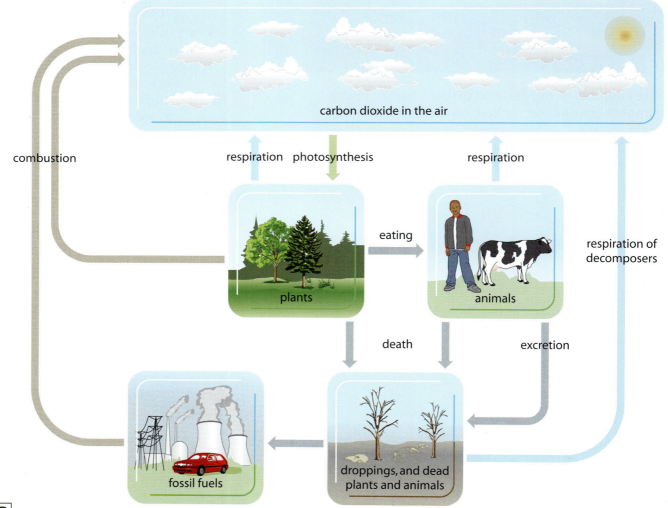

carbon dioxide in the air

combustion respiration photosynthesis respiration respiration of decomposers

plants eating animals

death excretion

fossil fuels droppings, and dead plants and animals

B

Graph D shows how the amount of carbon dioxide in the air has changed over the last 250 years. The increase is due to humans:
• burning increasing amounts of fossil fuels to make electricity, for transport and for heating and cooking
• burning forests to clear land.

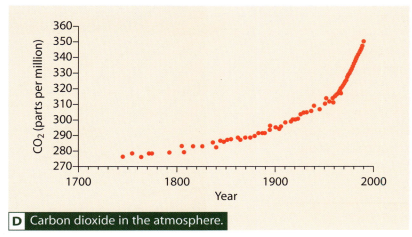

D Carbon dioxide in the atmosphere.

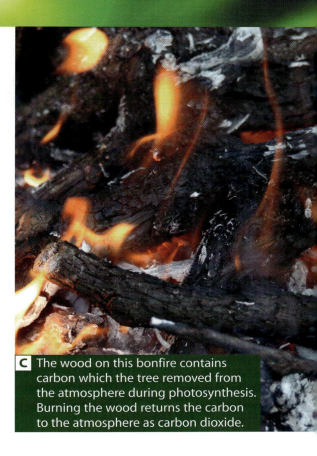

C The wood on this bonfire contains carbon which the tree removed from the atmosphere during photosynthesis. Burning the wood returns the carbon to the atmosphere as carbon dioxide.

Fossil fuels are made from the remains of plants and animals that lived millions of years ago. The carbon in them was originally taken out of the atmosphere, and when we burn them we are returning this carbon to the atmosphere as carbon dioxide. The problem is with the timescales – it took many thousands of years to extract the carbon dioxide from the atmosphere that eventually became fossil fuels, but we put a lot of it back into the atmosphere at once when we burn them.

A similar problem occurs when we burn forests, although the timescales are much shorter. Many trees take between 50 and 100 years to grow to full size, and they take carbon dioxide out of the atmosphere while they are growing. When we burn forests, we are putting all that carbon dioxide back into the air very quickly. However, the land cleared by burning forests is often used to grow crop plants, which will remove carbon dioxide from the atmosphere again.

?
2 a Sketch a graph representing carbon dioxide in the atmosphere from 1400 to the present day.
  b Explain the shape of your graph.

3 Burning fossil fuels and burning forests both affect the level of carbon dioxide in the atmosphere. What are the similarities and differences between the two?

Summary

Draw a diagram showing the carbon cycle, and add labels to explain each process in more detail.

?
4 Planting cleared land with crops allows carbon dioxide to be removed from the atmosphere.
  a What will happen to the carbon in the crop plants?
  b How will growing crop plants affect carbon dioxide levels over 10 years?

5 Which is the odd one out: coal, tree, horse? Explain your answers.

6 Look at graph D. A graph showing world population for the same years would have a very similar shape. Explain why the two things are likely to be connected.

7 Consider the motion of the Earth in its orbit around the Sun. Suggest two things other than the greenhouse effect that could cause the average temperature of the Earth to rise.

The greenhouse effect

What is the greenhouse effect?

The Earth and its atmosphere are surrounded by empty space. The temperature of the Earth depends on the amount of radiation it receives from the Sun and the amount of radiation it emits into space. If it emits as much radiation as it receives, it stays at a constant temperature.

Certain gases in the atmosphere help to trap heat in the Earth's atmosphere. A greenhouse traps heat in a similar way, which is why this is called the **greenhouse effect**. **Greenhouse gases** include carbon dioxide, methane and water vapour. Without these gases the average temperature of the Earth would be about −20 °C instead of the present value of 15 °C.

?
1 Why are greenhouse gases essential to life on Earth?
2 Why is infrared radiation from the Earth absorbed by greenhouse gases, but not infrared radiation from the Sun?

A If the Earth emitted more radiation than it received from the Sun it would cool down and become a very cold planet.

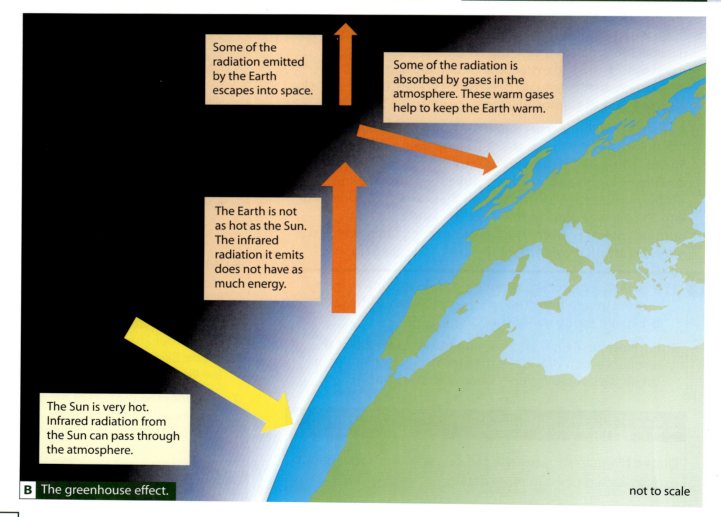

Some of the radiation emitted by the Earth escapes into space.

Some of the radiation is absorbed by gases in the atmosphere. These warm gases help to keep the Earth warm.

The Earth is not as hot as the Sun. The infrared radiation it emits does not have as much energy.

The Sun is very hot. Infrared radiation from the Sun can pass through the atmosphere.

B The greenhouse effect.

not to scale

Gas	% of atmosphere	Major sources
water vapour	1–4	evaporation from rivers, oceans and plants
carbon dioxide	0.035	burning, respiration and decay
methane	0.002	animal digestion, decaying vegetation, rice growing, sewage and landfill sites

C Greenhouse gases.

As more carbon dioxide and methane are added to the atmosphere the Earth gets a little warmer. Diagram D shows how this happens. This rise in the Earth's temperature is called **global warming**.

? **3** Look at Table C.
  a Why does the percentage of water vapour have such a large range compared to the other gases?
  b Why do you think that most people only mention carbon dioxide when discussing the greenhouse effect?

4 Look at diagram D. Explain why the temperature of the Earth does not continue to rise when the percentage of greenhouse gases is increased.

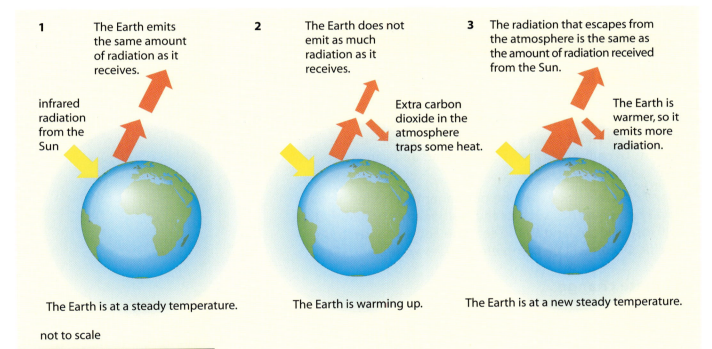

1 The Earth emits the same amount of radiation as it receives.

infrared radiation from the Sun

The Earth is at a steady temperature.

2 The Earth does not emit as much radiation as it receives.

Extra carbon dioxide in the atmosphere traps some heat.

The Earth is warming up.

3 The radiation that escapes from the atmosphere is the same as the amount of radiation received from the Sun.

The Earth is warmer, so it emits more radiation.

The Earth is at a new steady temperature.

not to scale

D How global warming happens.

Scientists use computer models to try to work out what will happen to the Earth's climate if global warming continues. However, there are so many different factors to take into account that there is still a lot of disagreement about what will happen.

? **5** Which is the odd one out: oxygen, carbon dioxide, nitrogen? Explain your answers.

6 The concentrations of gases in the atmosphere are often given in parts per million (ppm). Convert the percentages in Table C into ppm.

Summary

Draw two diagrams of the Earth: one with an atmosphere and one without. Add notes to explain why one would be a colder planet than the other.

What will happen if global warming continues?

Polar bears extinct!

Bumper crop of oranges in Greenland.

Ten more Pacific islands now completely under water.

A Some of the possible consequences of global warming.

Rising sea levels

Global warming will cause ice in glaciers and the ice cap at the South Pole to melt. The extra water flowing into the oceans will cause sea levels to rise. If the water in the oceans becomes warmer it will expand and cause a further rise in sea levels.

Many coastal regions will be permanently flooded. Some low-lying countries such as the Netherlands or Bangladesh will lose a lot of land to the sea, and some islands in the Pacific Ocean will be completely under water.

Climate change

Global warming will increase the amount of water vapour in the air, and so increase the cloud cover. Increased cloud cover could result in more radiation being reflected back into space. Some computer models predict that this might stop the Earth warming up any further. However, the extra water vapour could also tend to increase global warming.

B Over half of Bangladesh would be under water if sea levels rose by 5 metres.

? 1 a Give two reasons why global warming could cause sea levels to rise.
  b How could rising sea levels affect humans? Suggest as many ways as you can.

2 a Why will global warming increase the amount of water vapour in the air?
  b How might this increase global warming?
  c How might clouds stop global warming?

D If the Earth gets warmer, storms like this could become more common.

C Flooding like this could happen more often.

Weather patterns could also change, so some areas may get less rainfall than they do now and others may get more. Changing weather patterns could also cause stronger winds.

Effects on living organisms

Food crops are grown in the places where conditions suit them. Changes in climate could mean that we have to grow different crops. In some places, drier conditions may make it impossible to grow crops at all.

E Droughts could become more common in some parts of the world.

Warmer temperatures could also change the type and number of insects that live in a region. This may increase the spread of diseases that are carried by insects.

Some animals may be able to migrate to cooler regions, but many will not be able to and may become extinct. Many plants could also die out.

?

3 What effect would increased rain have on rivers around the world?

4 What effect would stronger winds have on:
   a houses
   b waves on the sea
   c cliffs around the coastline?

5 Explain the three headlines in diagram A.

6 a Why is global warming likely to have more serious effects on the developing world than on richer countries?
   b What do you think the richer countries should do to help the developing world?

7 What could be the economic effects of global warming? Consider both the rich countries and the developing world. You could consider crops, tourism, weather and flood defences and damage, health, etc.

Summary

Write a list of bullet points outlining the possible consequences of global warming.

The global warming debate

Are greenhouse gases responsible for global warming?

Scientists often look for **correlations** between factors when they are investigating something. Graphs A and B show that there is a correlation between the average global temperature and the concentration of carbon dioxide in the atmosphere. However, this does not necessarily mean that the increase in carbon dioxide has caused the increase in temperature – the correlation could just be a coincidence.

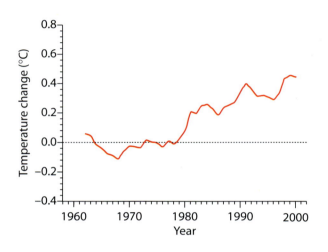

A The change in global temperature between 1960 and 2000.

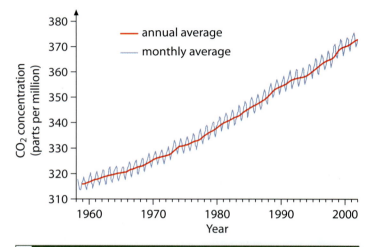

B The amount of carbon dioxide in the atmosphere between 1960 and 2000. A graph of methane levels over the same period shows a similar shape.

Graph C shows the results of estimates of the temperature of the Earth and carbon dioxide concentrations for the last 200 000 years.

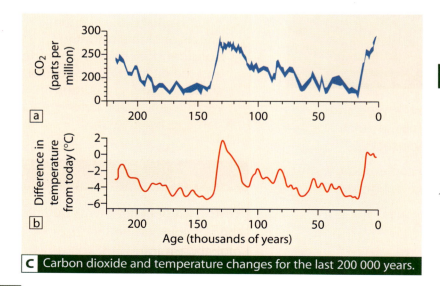

C Carbon dioxide and temperature changes for the last 200 000 years.

?

1 Why doesn't the correlation between graphs A and B *prove* that carbon dioxide causes global warming?

2 a Why does graph C provide better evidence that there may be a link between carbon dioxide levels and temperature?

b Why doesn't it prove that carbon dioxide causes global warming?

D Scientists can use bubbles of air trapped in ice to find out how much carbon dioxide there was in the air thousands of years ago.

The graphs in C show good correlation between carbon dioxide and temperature over thousands of years, which means that the correlation is less likely to be a coincidence. However, this still does not prove that carbon dioxide *causes* global warming. There could be some other factor that affects both temperature and carbon dioxide levels.

Scientists have carried out laboratory experiments with different gases, and they have shown that carbon dioxide and methane absorb infrared radiation. In fact, methane absorbs much more infrared radiation than carbon dioxide. Scientists therefore have a theory which explains why these gases could cause global warming. Today most scientists agree that the extra greenhouse gases in the atmosphere are making the Earth warm up.

If extra greenhouse gases *are* causing global warming, then we could try to reduce the warming effect by reducing **emissions** of carbon dioxide. We could do this by burning less fossil fuels for transport or electricity generation, and reducing the amount of methane produced by landfills, domestic livestock and rice paddies. We could also plant more forests to use up carbon dioxide.

?

3 Suggest why most scientists agree that greenhouse gases cause global warming.

4 a Why are scientists concerned about methane, when there is a far higher percentage of carbon dioxide in the atmosphere?
   b Suggest how we could reduce methane emissions. (*Hint:* you may need to look back at page 155.)
   c What problems might there be in implementing these suggestions?

5 The River Thames has not frozen for more than 50 years.
   a Explain why some people would say this is evidence for global warming,
   b Why might other people disagree with them?

6 What are the arguments for and against burning garden waste rather than letting it rot on a landfill site?

Summary

Write a short script for a radio programme, explaining why most scientists accept that rising levels of greenhouse gases are causing global warming.

The way forward

What should we do about global warming?

Not everyone agrees on the risk of global warming or what should be done about it.

Our country is still developing. We need to clear the forests for new homes. We also need to build power stations for our new industries.

Mrs Sanchez

Mr Blake

We could easily cut carbon dioxide emissions by using public transport – 20 people on a bus use less fuel than 20 cars! And if we insulated our houses better we would use up less fuel for heating – we would save money as well as reducing global warming!

Mr Patel

Spend money on a wind farm or a hospital – I know which I'd choose!

Mr Bushton

Not all scientists agree that burning less fossil fuels would solve the problem. It will cost us a lot of money to convert to renewable resources for generating electricity.

Mrs McDuff

It won't make much difference to me, but I would like my grandchildren to have a nice world to live in, without all these storms and droughts they are talking about.

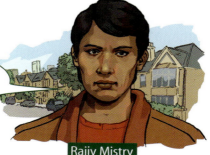

Rajiv Mistry

Stopping people cutting down the rainforests will also help wildlife.

Susie Reddish

Better safe than sorry, that's what I say! Anyway – we also need oil for making plastics and there isn't an alternative to that. Oil will run out eventually, so it makes sense to cut down the amount we burn.

Ms Jeffries: I would use the bus if I could, but there is only one bus a day to my village!

Mrs Mboto: Climate change could lead to mass starvation. We cannot afford to take the risk.

Mr Penh: Each person in the USA emits over 50 times as much carbon dioxide as a person in my country. They are the ones who should change!

Miss Linton: If it gets hotter, more clouds will form. They will reflect heat from the Sun, and the Earth will cool down again. No problem!

A Discuss the different opinions on this page.
- Who thinks we should follow the precautionary principle?
- What reasons are there for not reducing carbon dioxide emissions?
- What problems could there be in trying to reduce the global emissions of carbon dioxide?
- How might we solve these problems?

?

1 Write down five ways of reducing greenhouse gas emissions.

2 a Write down two reasons why people might not want to cut emissions.
  b Write down two reasons for cutting emissions.

3 Which people think we should follow the precautionary principle? (You may need to look back at page 145.)

4 a What do you think developing countries should do to reduce the risk of global warming?
  b What should developed countries be doing?
  c Do you think that developed countries should help poorer countries? Explain your answer.

Summary

Write a letter to your MP, stating how the government can help people in this country to cut emissions, and how the government should be helping developing countries to cut their emissions.

never using a mobile phone

Stay safe!

never using microwave cookers

staying away from mobile phone masts

Radiation is all around us – we cannot avoid it. It can damage tissues in your body, and even cause cancer.

You can stay safe by:

A

always covering up with clothing if you have to go outside

staying out of the Sun as much as you can

1 Visible light is part of the electromagnetic spectrum.
  a List the other types of radiation in the electromagnetic spectrum in order, starting with the type with the lowest energy photons.
  b Write down one source of each type of radiation.
  c Which of these types of radiation are ionising radiations?
  d How can ionising radiations harm the body?

2 Microwaves can be used to cook food.
  a How do microwaves cook food?
  b Describe two features of microwave ovens that stop microwaves escaping from the oven.
  c Explain how these safety features work.

3 Mobile phones communicate using microwaves.
  a Why will you receive microwave radiation from a mobile phone whenever it is switched on, even if you are not phoning someone?
  b Why do people think that mobile phones might prove to be a health risk?
  c Why might the health risk be greater for children?

4 a Why doesn't everyone agree on the risk from mobile phones?
  b What is the 'precautionary principle'?
  c What does ALARA stand for?
  d Jenny needs to use a mobile phone for her job. If you followed the ALARA principle, what advice would you give her?

5 a Why does the safety poster advise people to stay out of the Sun?
   b Explain how part of our atmosphere provides some protection against ultraviolet radiation.
   c Explain what 'actual risk' and 'perceived risk' are, and how they can apply to exposure to ultraviolet radiation.

Most scientists agree that the increasing quantities of greenhouse gases in the atmosphere are making the Earth warmer.

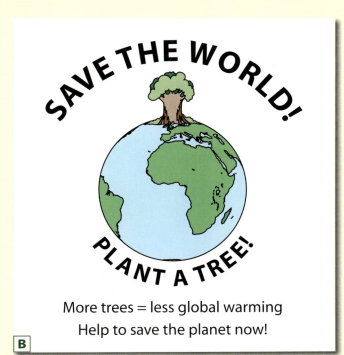

SAVE THE WORLD!
PLANT A TREE!

More trees = less global warming
Help to save the planet now!

B

6 a Write down three ways in which carbon dioxide is added to the atmosphere.
   b Write a word equation for photosynthesis.
   c Explain why photosynthesis is essential to life on this planet.
   d Methane is also a greenhouse gas. State three sources of methane

7 The amount of carbon dioxide in the atmosphere remained fairly constant for thousands of years.
   a Why did the amount of carbon dioxide remain constant?
   b Why has the amount of carbon dioxide in the atmosphere increased in the last 200 years?
   c How might planting more trees help to stop carbon dioxide levels rising further?
   d Describe how using less electricity could cut carbon dioxide emissions.
   e How does walking instead of using a car help to cut emissions?

8 a How does carbon dioxide in the atmosphere help to keep the Earth warm?
   b Why do some scientists think that extra carbon dioxide is causing global warming? Use the word 'correlation' in your answer.
   c Describe three possible effects of global warming.
   d Why don't all scientists agree what will happen if the Earth gets warmer?

9 There are lots of different opinions concerning what we should do about global warming, or even whether we should do anything at all. Give one reason why someone might think we should:
   a not try to do anything about it
   b cut emissions to try to reduce global warming.

Life on Earth

What is happening to life on Earth?

It is the year 2020 AD and the following communication has been received on Earth from the Intergalactic Federation.

Earth!!

Delete Reply Reply All Forward Print

From: Intergalactic Federation   Date: 1st October 2076
Subject: Earth!!   To: Humans of Earth!

Humans of Earth! Prepare to stand trial for the extinction of millions of species of other Earth life forms.

There has been life on your planet for over 3500 million years. During that time there have been millions of different species. Changes to conditions on Earth have caused many species to become extinct. Many others have evolved into new species, creating a great diversity of life on your planet.

A

B

C

About 120 000 years ago your species, Homo sapiens, evolved. At first you responded to your environment like other species, dying when conditions were bad for you. However, using your big brain, you developed tools that enabled you to live anywhere you wanted to. You have used the Earth's resources of space and materials for your own purposes. In the process you have crowded out other species, killed for fun and destroyed many others by the waste you produce. The rate of extinction of species on your planet is now hundreds, possibly thousands of times greater than the natural rate of extinction.

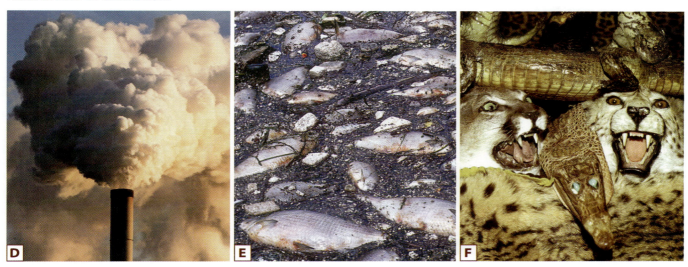

Now you plan to travel to other worlds and set up new colonies. You must prove to us that you can control your actions and not threaten other forms of life, otherwise we will not let you leave Earth.

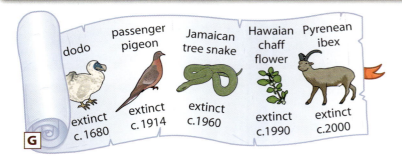

1 They say that life has evolved on Earth. Write a few sentences that explain what 'evolution of life' means to you.

2 People talk about the 'theory of evolution'. Theories need evidence. What evidence do you know for the theory of evolution?

3 The message tells us that millions of species have become extinct before our species evolved. This is what they mean by the 'natural rate of extinction'. Why is there a natural rate of extinction?

4 Make a list of five animals that once lived on Earth (including some that lived before humans evolved). If possible, give a reason why these animals are extinct now.

5 When humans first evolved, they were affected by the environment like other animals.
   a How are the numbers of individuals of a species affected by the environment?
   b Why are humans less affected by the environment than other species?

6 a In what ways do you think humans are increasing the rate of extinction?
   b What could we do to reduce this?

7 What do you need to find out more about to help you to give better answers to these questions?

Starting out

How did life on Earth start?

A These rocks in Greenland are over 3700 million years old. They contain no fossils.

Earth formed over 4500 million years (Ma) or 4.6 billion years (Ga) ago. At first it was just a large ball of rock but then water arrived, mostly from comets that crashed into the Earth. The oldest rocks on the surface of the Earth are around 4 billion years old. These contain no evidence of life.

The earliest signs of life are found in rocks that are over 3.5 billion years old. These rocks contain **fossils** of simple **cells** that look like **bacteria**. These cells may have arrived from other parts of our Solar System, or they might have developed‛ here on Earth. NASA scientists have shown that cell-like structures can form in the conditions found in deep space.

The **atmosphere** of the early Earth contained no free oxygen molecules. The most common gases were probably carbon dioxide, ammonia, methane and water vapour. These gases contain the elements carbon, hydrogen, oxygen and nitrogen which are the main elements in the compounds that make up living things.

B This meteorite landed on Earth after travelling from Mars. Some scientists think that the marks on it are fossils of bacteria (magnification ×30 000).

? **1 a** For how long has there been life on Earth?
　　 b What is the evidence for this?

The early Earth was hotter than today and there were constant lightning storms. Scientists can create conditions like these using apparatus similar to diagram C. After a few days the chemicals in the flask combine to form more complex molecules. These molecules included the building blocks for **DNA** and **proteins**.

DNA carries the instructions for building new cells in organisms. It is an important molecule because it can copy itself exactly. This allows cells to copy themselves so that an organism can grow or reproduce.

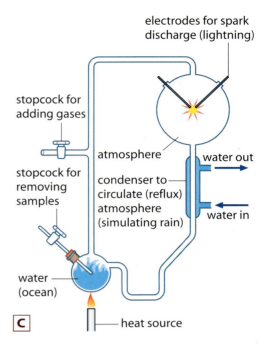

electrodes for spark discharge (lightning)

stopcock for adding gases

atmosphere

water out

stopcock for removing samples

condenser to circulate (reflux) atmosphere (simulating rain)

water in

water (ocean)

C

heat source

D These structures are called stromatolites. They contain photosynthetic bacteria. Fossils of structures like these have been found in rocks that are more than 2 Ga old.

Scientists estimate that there could be over 30 million **species** of living things on the Earth today. There are even more species that once existed but have become **extinct**. Most people believe that all these different species developed from the very simple cells that lived on Earth billions of years ago.

?

2 **a** Where is DNA found in cells and what is its role?
  b Why is it important that DNA can copy itself exactly?

3 Where are proteins found in animals, and what do they do?

4 Which is the odd one out: oxygen, water vapour, carbon dioxide? Explain your answers.

5 What evidence is there to suggest that life could have:
  a started on Earth
  b come from space?

6 For each answer you gave in question **5**, identify any assumptions that are made if we say:
  a life did evolve on Earth
  b life came from space.

Summary

Write a short paragraph to answer the question at the top of page 166. Include both possibilities, and the evidence for them.

Evolution of life on Earth

What is the evidence for evolution?

Fossils from rocks are evidence of the organisms that lived on Earth in the past. We can find the age of the rocks that fossils are found in, so we know how long ago they lived. The fossils show that the further we go back in time, the more different the organisms were from today's organisms.

Scientists can work out what the organisms looked like by studying the fossils, and work out which other fossils and living species they are related to. We can link related fossils and living species in an **evolutionary tree** to show how later organisms may have **evolved** from earlier ones.

A This drawing is a reconstruction from the fossil of *Eryops* which lived 230 Ma ago. It was a large predator (1.5 m long) that is most closely related to toads and frogs that are alive today.

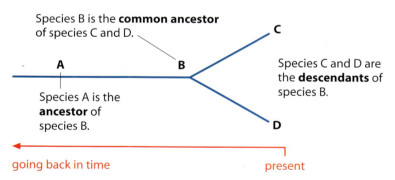

Species B is the **common ancestor** of species C and D.

A   B

Species A is the **ancestor** of species B.

Species C and D are the **descendants** of species B.

going back in time   present

C This evolutionary tree shows that fossil organism A evolved into fossil organism B which then evolved into C and D.

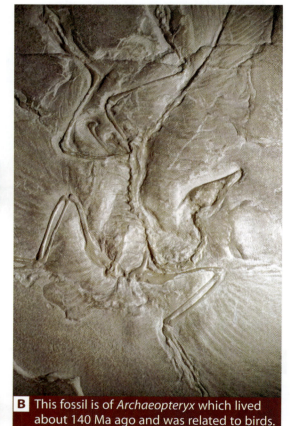

B This fossil is of *Archaeopteryx* which lived about 140 Ma ago and was related to birds.

?

1 **a** How do scientists study organisms that lived long ago?
   b How do they know when these organisms lived?

2 Look at photograph B.
   a Which features of the fossil are like birds?
   b Which features are different from birds?

3 How did scientists work out that *Eryops* (diagram A) was related to toads and frogs?

Scientists can analyse the DNA of living species. They have found that closely related species have DNA that is almost the same. We can draw a tree diagram to show how similar species are according to their DNA. These diagrams often look like the evolutionary trees made using evidence from fossils. By comparing how different the DNA is with how quickly DNA can change, we can estimate how long ago the living species had a common ancestor. Some DNA has been extracted from fossils, but this is very rare.

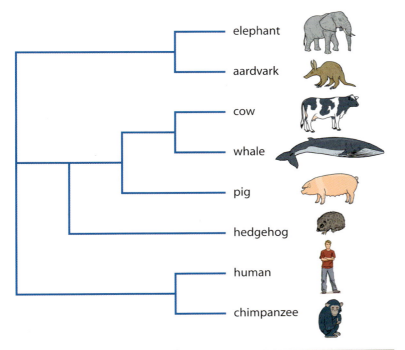

elephant

aardvark

cow

whale

pig

hedgehog

human

chimpanzee

E Scavengers will clear up the remains of this kill.

D This DNA tree diagram for apes and humans only shows living species. Species with similar DNA are shown closer together on the diagram.

Most organisms do not form fossils when they die, because they only form in special situations. The dead organism must be buried by sediment soon after death, and must remain buried for thousands or millions of years. This makes it very difficult to get enough information to draw an accurate evolutionary tree.

Summary

Fossils and DNA analysis provide information about evolution of species but still do not give a complete picture or one that is necessarily correct. Draw up a table to summarise the key points about using fossils or DNA to construct evolutionary trees, including the advantages and disadvantages of each.

?

4 Look at diagram D.
  a Which animal is most closely related to humans?
  b When did they last share a common ancestor?

5 Give one difference between an evolutionary tree diagram and a DNA tree diagram.

6 Many fossils are found in sediments that settled in water. Explain why aquatic organisms are more likely to form fossils than land organisms.

7 a What assumptions are made in the construction of each kind of evolutionary tree?
  b What evidence could help decide which tree is correct?

Evolution by natural selection

How does evolution happen?

The species today have different characteristics from species which lived in the past. In 1809 Jean-Baptiste Lamarck suggested these changes happen when a characteristic develops (is acquired) in an organism because it is used. This **acquired characteristic** would then be **inherited** by its offspring when it reproduces.

In 1858 Charles Darwin and Alfred Russel Wallace proposed a different idea based on these observations:
• There is **variation** between all the individuals in a species.
• Most offspring produced by an organism do not survive long enough to reproduce.

Darwin and Wallace concluded that only individuals that are best **adapted** to the environment survive and reproduce, and so pass their characteristics on to their offspring. Characteristics which increase the chance of survival are therefore more common in the next generation. This idea became known as evolution by **natural selection**.

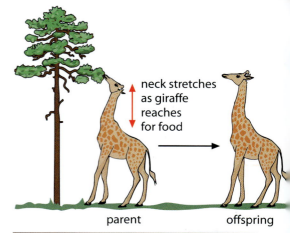

A Lamarck thought that giraffes now have long necks because their ancestors stretched to feed on tall trees.

?
1 According to Lamarck:
   a Which is the acquired characteristic in giraffes?
   b How did giraffes with very long necks evolve?

2 Suggest two things that might cause the death of an individual.

3 Why are there variations between individuals?

4 **a** What do we mean by 'adapted to the environment'?
   b Explain how characteristics that increase the chance of survival become more common in the next generation.

B How natural selection can lead to evolution.

Variation in the different forms or **alleles** of a **gene** happens when there is a **mutation** (change in the genetic code). Mutations happen naturally in any cell when there is a mistake in copying the DNA. Occasionally a mutation will produce a new characteristic.

Most mutations do not affect the organism. Some cause problems, such as sickle cell disease, and some may be advantageous. For example a mutation causes the peppered moth to be dark in colour rather than light. The moths rest on trees during the day and rely on camouflage to hide from predators.

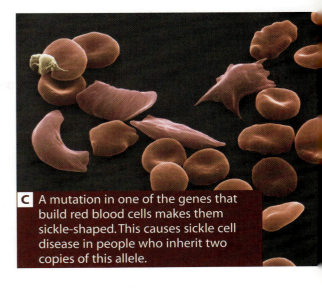

C A mutation in one of the genes that build red blood cells makes them sickle-shaped. This causes sickle cell disease in people who inherit two copies of this allele.

?

5 **a** Describe two factors that increase the natural rate of mutation.
 b When might one of these happen?

6 Mutations can happen in body cells and sex cells. Explain why only mutations in sex cells get passed on to offspring.

D In sooty areas the dark form of the peppered moth is better camouflaged.

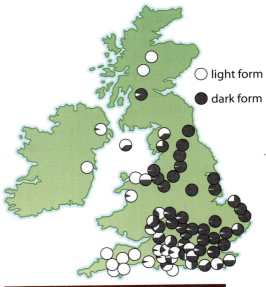

○ light form

● dark form

E Proportion of light and dark moths in the UK.

?

7 **a** Explain how the dark form of the peppered moth became more common when there was sooty pollution.
 b Predict what would happen to the proportions of dark and light moths in areas where the sooty pollution has been cleaned up.

8 How would you investigate the theory that the changing numbers of the different forms of peppered moths were due to natural selection through predation?

Summary

Write a short article for the school science magazine, describing how Lamarck and Darwin would have answered the question 'If I do weight-training and build up my muscles, will my children inherit my big muscles?'. Complete your article by explaining which answer is right and why.

171

Darwin's theory of evolution

When does a hypothesis become a theory?

A The wolf is the ancestor of all breeds of dog.

Wolfhound

Jack Russell Terrier

B Wolfhounds were bred for hunting large animals. Terriers were bred for hunting animals that live in burrows.

When Darwin suggested his **hypothesis** he had little **evidence** to support it. Darwin linked his idea with his knowledge that species can change over time through **selective breeding**. This is when breeders breed from individuals which show the characteristics they want. The offspring are more likely to have these characteristics. This made his hypothesis stronger because it showed a way that natural selection could happen.

Some scientists found it difficult to accept the hypothesis because nobody knew about genetics and how characteristics can be passed from generation to generation. Many religious people disliked the hypothesis because their explanation for all the different species on Earth, and all the fossils, was that God had created them. Many scientists soon accepted the hypothesis because it also explained other observations, such as fossils from recent rocks look more like living species than fossils from ancient rocks.

?

1 Which characteristics would have been selected in dogs:
   a for breeding wolfhounds
   b for breeding Jack Russell terriers?

2 Explain how selective breeding and natural selection are:
   a similar
   b different.

3 How does genetics explain how characteristics are passed on to the next generation?

4 Give two reasons why Darwin's hypothesis was not immediately accepted.

C Many people made fun of Darwin's ideas.

A hypothesis is an idea that can be tested scientifically. You can use it to explain a wide range of observations, or to make **predictions** and then test whether or not those predictions are correct. If the hypothesis can do these things then it becomes a **theory**.

Darwin used his hypothesis to explain how the finches he had seen on the Galapagos Islands had evolved. He suggested that a few individuals of one species got to the Galapagos Islands from South America over 500 km away. Over time, individual birds that were best adapted to feed on each kind of food survived and produced more offspring than those that were not so well adapted. Eventually 13 different species of finch evolved from the original single species.

D Two of the finches that Darwin observed.

The Galapagos finches are still studied. In 1977 Peter and Rosemary Grant used Darwin's theory to predict that after a period of drought, when only large seeds were left for one species to eat, the next generation would have slightly larger beaks. Measurements showed that the offspring had beaks that were 4% larger. This is the kind of **proof** that scientists need to test a theory.

Summary

Draw a flow chart that shows how a hypothesis becomes a theory. Include the bold words on these pages on your chart. Use examples from Darwin's hypothesis to explain the stages in your chart.

?

5 What is the difference between a hypothesis and a theory?

6 How does evolution by natural selection explain the evolution of the finch which can pick out insects from bark?

7 Explain how the Grants used Darwin's theory to make their prediction.

8 Some insects burrow deep into bark. How would this affect birds that feed on these insects? Explain how you would test your prediction.

Sensor and effector cells

How can organisms sense and respond to changes?

A Electric eels live in muddy water. They use pulses of electricity to navigate and to sense prey.

B Dolphins use pulses of high-pitched ultrasound to track and catch prey.

In order to survive, an organism needs to be able to sense changes in itself and in the environment around it. It then needs to respond to the change, or **stimulus**, in a way that improves its chances of survival. For example, if an animal feels hungry, it needs to find food, or if the temperature gets colder, it may need to find some way to keep warm.

The cells that sense changes are **sensor** (or **receptor**) cells, such as the cells in our eyes or skin. The cells that respond are called the **effector** cells. These include muscle cells. In single-celled organisms, like amoeba, the one cell is both the sensor and effector. In **multicellular** organisms, the cells are specialised to sense more complex stimuli, and respond to them in different ways.

A How can you find out if maggots respond to light?

?
1 Draw up a table for five of the human senses. Include a column to show where the sensor cells are found, and another for the stimulus that those cells respond to.

2 Name two senses that some animals have but humans do not.

In multicellular organisms the sensor and effector cells are usually in different parts of the body. Diagram C shows how information about a stimulus produces a reaction by the effector. Sometimes the information will pass directly to the effector, but in humans and other **vertebrates** the information will often go to the **brain** and then to the effector.

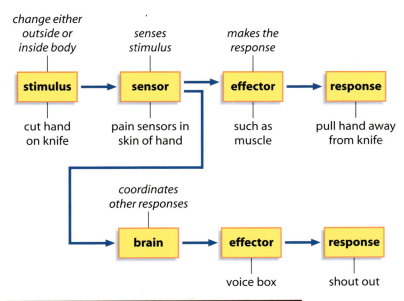

change either outside or inside body	*senses stimulus*	*makes the response*	
stimulus →	**sensor** →	**effector** →	**response**
cut hand on knife	pain sensors in skin of hand	such as muscle	pull hand away from knife

coordinates other responses

	brain →	**effector** →	**response**
		voice box	shout out

C Information about a stimulus passes to effectors.

In many reactions the information may be passed to several areas of the brain, so that you can compare the stimulus with memories of things like this, or with information that is coming from other stimuli. This means you can make choices about what to do next, so your response to the same stimulus may be different at different times. You may also respond in more than one way, so the brain **coordinates** the different responses.

D

? 3 Why do you think many messages in the body go to the brain?

4 You notice an insect biting your arm. Describe the path of the response you would have to this stimulus. Include which sensors and effectors will be used.

Summary

You see a friend across the street. Describe the path of response to this stimulus, starting with the sensor cells and ending with the effector cells. Identify any decisions you make before you respond to the stimulus.

? 5 Look at the boy in diagram D.
   a Which sensor cells have been stimulated?
   b Which effector cells might be used to respond?
   c Which part of his body is coordinating the responses?
   d Describe what choices he might make to coordinate responses and solve the problem.
6 You feel cold.
   a Describe all the different ways that you could respond to this stimulus.
   b How would these responses ensure your survival?
7 A blackbird sees a worm (its prey). Consider all the ways that it might respond to this.

What communications systems do organisms have?

Multicellular organisms have two communication systems for passing information around the body. The **nervous system** links sensors to effectors with nerves throughout the body. This system responds to changes in our surroundings.

In the nervous system, messages pass very quickly through nerves as tiny electrical signals. For example, if you tread on a pin, your brain will receive the message and send it on down to the muscles in your leg in much less than 1 second. The nervous system is the communication system that your body uses to respond very quickly to a stimulus.

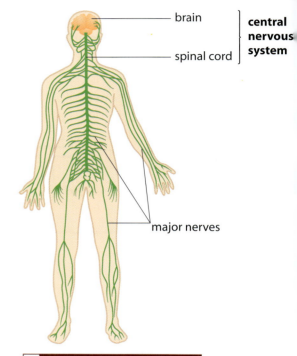

brain

spinal cord

central nervous system

major nerves

A The human nervous system.

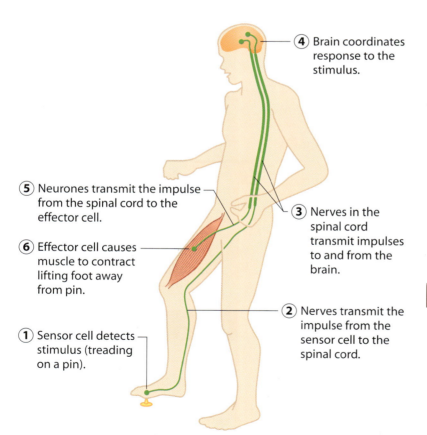

④ Brain coordinates response to the stimulus.

⑤ Neurones transmit the impulse from the spinal cord to the effector cell.

③ Nerves in the spinal cord transmit impulses to and from the brain.

⑥ Effector cell causes muscle to contract lifting foot away from pin.

② Nerves transmit the impulse from the sensor cell to the spinal cord.

① Sensor cell detects stimulus (treading on a pin).

B How the message passes through the nervous system after treading on a pin.

?

1 Name the main parts of the human nervous system.

2 Look at diagram B. Describe how the muscles in your leg would respond to the message from your brain in this situation.

3 Think of two situations where you would need to respond quickly to a situation. For each situation, explain how your nervous system helps you to respond.

Multicellular animals also have another communication system called the **hormonal system**. This system responds to some changes in the environment, but also to changes inside the body. It uses chemicals called **hormones** to act as messengers. These are **secreted** from the sensors, which are known as **endocrine glands**, straight into the blood. The hormones travel around the body until they reach **target cells** which then respond. Your body makes many different hormones from many glands.

Hormones may stay in the blood for several hours but they are eventually removed as they are excreted in urine and are broken down by enzymes.

Insulin is a hormone that is made in the pancreas when levels of glucose in the blood are too high. This is dangerous because it affects all body cells and can result in a **coma**. Insulin affects all cells in the body, by making them respire faster. It also causes muscle and liver cells to take glucose out of the blood until the level is back to normal.

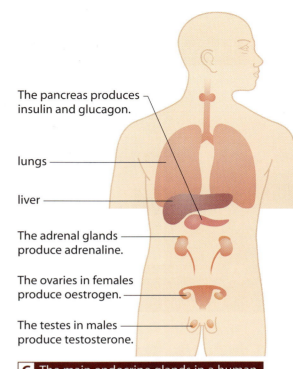

The pancreas produces insulin and glucagon.

lungs

liver

The adrenal glands produce adrenaline.

The ovaries in females produce oestrogen.

The testes in males produce testosterone.

C The main endocrine glands in a human body.

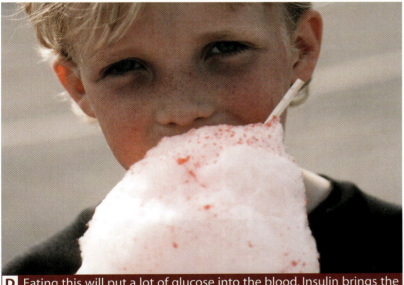

D Eating this will put a lot of glucose into the blood. Insulin brings the level of glucose back to normal.

Controlling the levels of chemicals in the body, such as blood glucose, at generally constant levels is known as **homeostasis**. This is important to keep the cells in the body working well. Both the nervous and hormonal systems play a role in homeostasis.

Summary

Draw up a table to list similarities and differences in the way the nervous system and hormonal system work.

?

4 List five human endocrine glands and the hormones that they make.

5 Describe the role of insulin in terms of the homeostasis of blood glucose levels after a meal.

6 Carbon dioxide levels in the blood are measured by receptors in blood vessels near the brain. If levels are too high, these send messages to the diaphragm and rib muscles to make you breathe faster. Explain why carbon dioxide levels vary, and how this response controls them.

Human evolution

How have humans evolved?

A These macaques learned to sit in hot spring water in winter by copying other macaques.

B The lions work together.

C This chimpanzee likes to eat biting ants.

All vertebrates have a brain and mammals have relatively large brains for the size of their bodies. This allows them to develop **complex behaviour**, such as:

• learning from experience by copying others
• working and communicating in groups
• using **tools**.

These kinds of behaviour improve the chances of survival.

The first **hominid** (human-like) species evolved from an ape-like ancestor around 7 million years ago. The hominids evolved differently from those ancestors who evolved into chimpanzees because they developed larger brains. They also began to walk more on two legs than on four. Around 2 million years ago they began to use tools.

?
1 Some macaques in Japan live near hot springs. How have they learnt to keep warm when the weather is cold?

2 How is being part of a group helpful to the animals in photo B?

3 How does using tools improve the chances of survival for the animal in photo C?

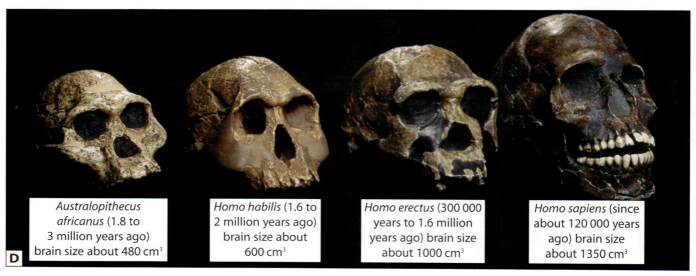

Australopithecus africanus (1.8 to 3 million years ago) brain size about 480 cm³

Homo habilis (1.6 to 2 million years ago) brain size about 600 cm³

Homo erectus (300 000 years to 1.6 million years ago) brain size about 1000 cm³

Homo sapiens (since about 120 000 years ago) brain size about 1350 cm³

D

? 4 Describe the differences in the skulls in photo D.

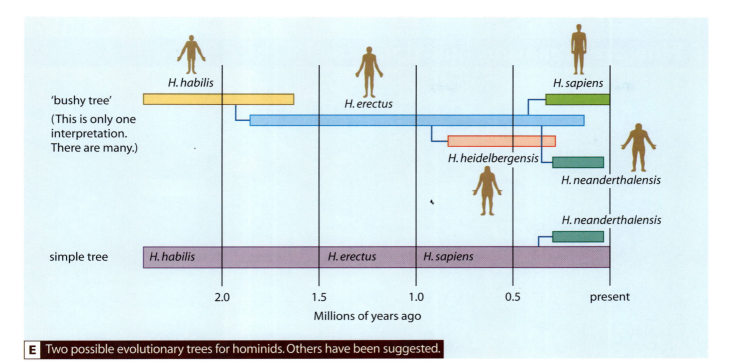

Many different species of hominid have evolved over the last 7 million years. More recent species have larger brains than older ones. They also show more complex behaviour, such as making more specialised tools, developing language and creating art.

Diagram E shows two ways of arranging the timelines for hominid species. Some scientists arrange these time lines simply to make as few branches on the evolutionary tree as possible because they think one species evolved into another. Others arrange them to make a very bushy tree because they think that didn't happen.

?

5 All species of humans (*Homo*) have used tools, including hand axes and choppers. How could these have improved their chances of survival?

6 Only one hominid species survives today.
 a Which is it?
 b What has happened to all the others?

7 A scientist who makes a simple evolutionary tree for hominids has a different explanation for what happened to *Homo erectus* than a scientist who draws a bushy tree. What are these two explanations and what do they say about human evolution?

8 a What further information would we need to decide which explanation in question 7 is the correct one?
 b Why might getting this information be difficult?

Summary

Write short notes to answer the question 'How have humans evolved?' at the top of the last page.

Food webs

How are organisms linked in a food web?

A

Diagram A shows a **community** of plants and animals from the edge of a woodland. The plants in this **habitat** grow here because they are adapted to the **environmental conditions**, especially light, water and temperature. The animals are here because they feed on these plants, or on other animals that feed on the plants.

All the animals and plants in a habitat are linked in **food chains** that show how energy from food is passed from one organism to another. Food chains can be joined together into a **food web** for the habitat.

?

1 **a** Name three factors in the environment that affect the growth of plants.
   b Explain how a change in each of these factors could affect the plants.

2 Name two plants that would not grow well in the habitat shown in diagram A, and give reasons for your answers.

3 How would changes to the plants affect the animals in the habitat? Explain your answer.

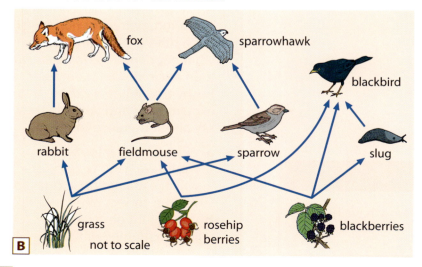

B   not to scale

In the food web in diagram B you can see that both blackbirds and fieldmice feed on rosehips. In a good year, when there are lots of berries, both species will have plenty to eat during the autumn and winter months. However, when there are very few berries there will be **competition** between the species. The most successful species will eat most of the berries.

The animals in a habitat compete with each other for resources, such as food, mates or nesting sites. The plants compete with each other for light, water and space to grow.

A How do environmental factors affect where a plant or animal species is found?
- Which habitats can you investigate?
- How will you sample the plants and animals?

Most animals in a food web feed on several kinds of food or prey and are called **generalist feeders**. However some, like the koala, only feed on one food. These are called **specialist feeders**.

C A fieldmouse also eats seeds.

D The trees in this woodland absorb most of the light, so that very few plants can grow on the ground beneath them.

E The koala only eats eucalyptus leaves.

? 4 Look at Diagram B.
  a If the blackbirds eat most of the berries, what can the fieldmice do?
  b If it has been a bad year for all kinds of fruit and seed, what else might happen to the fieldmice?

5 Think of a plus, a minus and an interesting point about this statement: The koala is the only animal that eats eucalyptus leaves.

6 Do you think specialist or generalist feeders are most likely to be successful? Explain your answer.

Summary

The food web shown in diagram B is part of an information leaflet for a nature trail. Write some words to go with the drawing to explain what a food web can tell us about a habitat and the organisms that live there.

Extinction

Why do species become extinct?

The fossil record contains many organisms that were once alive but are now extinct. There are many possible causes of extinction. Sometimes it happens because there is a big change in environmental conditions. Large changes in the environment can cause **mass extinctions**, when many species die out at the same time. For example, 250 million years ago about 95% of life on Earth died when global warming caused surface temperatures to rise between 5 and 10 °C.

If there is not much food or space available, there is more competition between different species. Occasionally this may happen on a large scale. Diagram B shows an example of this.

A Volcanic eruptions are natural ways of adding large amounts of carbon dioxide to the atmosphere.

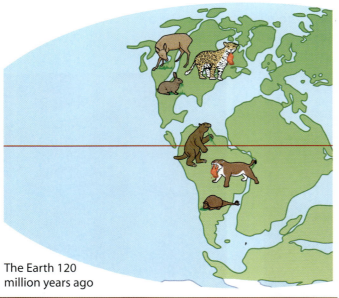

The Earth 120 million years ago

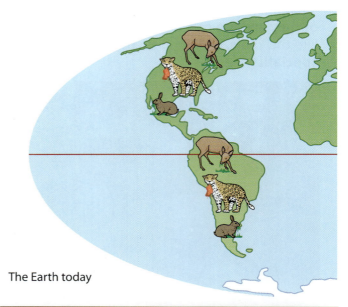

The Earth today

B Until about 5 million years ago, North America and South America were separate land masses with very different animal populations.

After North and South America joined together, the animals from both continents could compete with each other. Most of the marsupials of South America became extinct.

?

1 a What is global warming, and how is it caused?
  b List as many ways as you can that global warming might affect plants and animals.

2 Suggest why many animals in South America became extinct when it joined to North America.

3 At the same time, Antarctica was moving from about where South Africa is today towards the South Pole. How this would have affected the animals and plants living there?

Plants and animals may also die if they become infected with a disease or a parasite (organisms that live inside other organisms). This does not usually cause the extinction of a whole species. However, extinction might happen when a parasite or disease is introduced to an area where it did not exist before, where the plants and animals have not developed resistance, or where there are very small numbers of a species.

Changes in conditions select for different characteristics in the new species that evolve. If conditions had changed in a different way then different new species would have evolved.

4 Spring arrives 2 weeks earlier in the UK now compared with 40 years ago. Some organisms have changed to match this and others have not.
   a Look at the photo in C and use the information below it to describe what may happen to the numbers of great tits.
   b Explain your answer.

C

- Great tits lay their eggs at the same time every year.
- 40 years ago great tit eggs hatched when most caterpillars were around.
- Today most caterpillars are around nearly two weeks earlier in the year because they feed on young oak leaves that open as soon as it starts to get warm.

5 How could the introduction of a new parasite affect other organisms if it does not make them become extinct?

Summary

Use these table headings to make a table of all the factors that could cause a species become extinct.

Factors linked to non-living things	Factors linked to other species

Humans and extinctions

How do humans cause the extinction of other organisms?

A The numbers of giant panda are decreasing as we destroy the forests in which they live.

B The thylacine (marsupial wolf) of Tasmania was hunted to extinction in the early 1900s.

C Many ground-nesting birds in New Zealand are at risk of extinction from introduced predators like the rat.

D Galapagos penguins are at risk of extinction because of pollution in their habitat.

Homo sapiens is a very successful species. We can eat a wide range of plant and animal foods from many food webs and change our environment to make conditions suitable for us to live in. However, as we use the world to suit our needs we also affect the plants and animals around us. What we are doing is threatening other species with extinction. We say they are **endangered**.

Over the past 200 years the human population has risen from less than 1 billion to over 6 billion, and it is still rising rapidly.

Group	Number of known species	Percentage of known species threatened with extinction in 2003
mammals	4 842	23
birds	9 932	12
fishes	28 100	3
insects	950 000	0.06
flowering plants	199 350	3

E Species threatened with extinction.

?

1 Write down four ways that humans may cause the extinction of other species.

2 Which of the causes of extinction by humans is likely to be most important in the future? Explain your answer.

3 Look at table E.
   a Why do you think that a greater proportion of mammals are threatened than other groups? (*Hint*: look back at your answer to question **1**.)
   b Calculate the actual numbers of threatened species of each group.
   c Which group is probably most underestimated?
   Give a reason for your answer.

People are trying to protect and **conserve** endangered species in many different ways.

F The number of great crested newts is increasing because they are protected in the UK. You are not allowed to disturb ponds where they live.

G Elephants are killed for the ivory in their tusks. There is now a worldwide ban on trading in ivory to try to protect the African elephant.

H Crocodiles were once hunted for their skins. They are now being farmed so that wild animals are not killed.

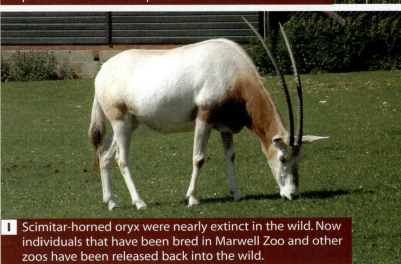

I Scimitar-horned oryx were nearly extinct in the wild. Now individuals that have been bred in Marwell Zoo and other zoos have been released back into the wild.

?

4 Describe four ways in which endangered species are now being conserved and protected.

5 Write down two problems that animals bred in captivity might have on being released into the wild, and suggest how they might be overcome.

6 In 2004 the scientist David Bellamy suggested that a monorail be built across the Galapagos Islands to encourage more people to visit this important site. However, another scientist, David Attenborough, argued that increasing the number of visitors would risk damaging this unique environment. Do you think the monorail should be built? Give reasons for your answer.

Summary

Write a short magazine article titled 'Humans and the last mass extinction'. Include examples of the way humans cause extinctions and how organisms can be protected from extinction.

Biodiversity

Why is biodiversity important?

A There are many more plant and animal species in the natural grassland than in the habitat that is being used for farming.

Biodiversity usually means the variety of living things within habitats. Some habitats, such as tropical forests and coral reefs, naturally have a higher biodiversity than others, such as moorland. When we change habitats to suit our needs, we usually reduce their biodiversity.

Habitats with high biodiversity have complex food webs. Many of the animals in them eat more than one kind of food.

We can reduce the damage we do to biodiversity by leaving natural, undisturbed areas where plants and animals can live. These areas must be large enough to allow the plants and animals space to grow well and reproduce. When we use the environment in a way that does not damage the long-term survival of the organisms that live there, we are using it in a **sustainable** way.

?

1 **a** How do we affect the biodiversity of a habitat when we clear land to grow crops?
  b Explain why the biodiversity changes.

2 What would happen to these animals if one kind of their food died out?

B This coral reef has a high biodiversity.

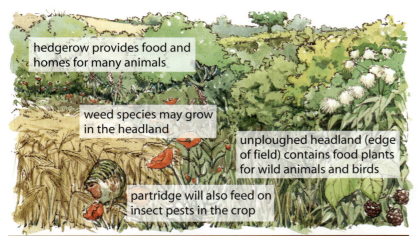

hedgerow provides food and homes for many animals

weed species may grow in the headland

unploughed headland (edge of field) contains food plants for wild animals and birds

partridge will also feed on insect pests in the crop

C Farmers are planting more hedgerows and leaving areas at the edges of fields uncultivated to encourage wild plants and animals to return to the area.

Biodiversity also refers to the amount of genetic variation in a species. In the crop field, the wheat plants all belong to the same species. What's more, they all belong to just one **variety** of that species of wheat, formed through selective breeding, so the genes in the wheat plants are all very similar. In the grassland, there are not only more different species of plants, there are different varieties of each species. If a disease kills one variety of grass plant in the grassland, the rest of the grass plants may not be affected.

D Wild potatoes contain many different genes that we might need in the future.

All the plants and animals that we use for food have varieties in the wild that contain different genes. In the future these genes could help us to improve our crops and farm animals, as they may carry characteristics for disease or pest resistance, for increased **yield**, or greater tolerance of drought.

?

3 Give one reason why planting hedgerows and leaving unploughed headlands can help wildlife.

4 **a** How could the farmer benefit from leaving headlands around crops?
   b What disadvantage might there be to leaving headlands?

5 About 80% of the wheat grown in the UK has been developed from one variety.
   a What is the importance of this fact in relation to disease?
   b Give at least two suggestions for how we could solve this problem.

6 The atmosphere may be getting warmer and drier in the summer in the UK. What would be the value of genes that give tolerance of drought?

7 Write a letter to a farmer explaining the benefits and possible drawbacks of sustainable farming.

Summary

Write an encyclopaedia entry explaining the two key meanings of the term biodiversity. Include in your entry an explanation of why maintaining biodiversity is important.

Earth, life and humans

What do you know about life on Earth and humans?

This is the trial of the species called 'human' on the planet they call 'Earth'. I am here to help the humans to defend themselves.

A

You should start by explaining how you think life started and evolved on your planet.

B

1 a What were conditions like on the early Earth?
  b How do scientists think that life started on the Earth?
  c What is the evidence for the earliest forms of life on Earth?

2 Living organisms have changed over time.
  a How do fossils show that species have changed over time?
  b How can scientists use fossils to work out how different species were related to each other?
  c Describe one difficulty in working out an accurate evolutionary tree using fossils.

  d What modern technique can be used to investigate the relationships between living organisms?

3 a How did Charles Darwin explain the evolution of different species? Describe his theory in as much detail as you can.
  b What evidence did Darwin have to support his theory?
  c Describe one other theory that has been used to explain how evolution happens.
  d Give two reasons why some people did not accept Darwin's theory when he first suggested it.

4 Darwin did not know about DNA and genes. How does our current understanding of genes help us to explain evolution? Explain in as much detail as you can.

5 a What is a food web?
  b What does 'competition' mean in terms of a food web?
  c Explain how a disease that kills one type of plant can affect all the other plants and animals in a food web.
  d How can a change in the climate cause some species to become extinct?

6 a How do humans detect changes in their surroundings?
  b Describe how the nervous system coordinates responses to stimuli. Use the following words in your answer: effector, receptor, brain, central nervous system.
  c What role does the hormone insulin play in the homeostasis of blood glucose, and why is this important?

7 Humans and some other animals can learn from their experiences, and they can also live as part of a group.
  a Describe two ways in which living as a group can help a species to survive.
  b Describe two skills that humans need to learn to live in a group.
  c Describe four ways in which tools can help humans survive.
  d Describe briefly how hominid species have evolved since 7 million years ago.

8 a Describe four different ways in which humans have caused the extinction of other species.
  b Suggest how we can try to stop extinctions being caused by human activities.

9 The time when many large Australian mammals became extinct correlates with the time that early humans were moving into this continent.
  a What does the word 'correlate' mean in the sentence above?
  b What evidence do scientists need to show that early humans caused the extinction of the large mammals?

10 a What are the two different meanings of the word 'biodiversity'?
   b How can biodiversity be maintained in farmland?
   c Why is it important to keep wild varieties of crop plants and rare breeds of farm animals?

Food matters

Why do we eat food?

FOOD BY PRESCRIPTION – IS THIS THE END OF FARMING?

Research scientists have told us that they can now make all the food that we need. They start with the main elements that make up food: carbon, hydrogen, oxygen, nitrogen and sulfur. They then use these elements to make all the things needed for a healthy diet: carbohydrates, fats, proteins, fibre and vitamins. When mixed with water and small amounts of minerals, they can produce a diet that will meet anybody's requirements.

Dr Margaret Jones says 'This will have a great impact on the way that we eat. What we need to eat can be measured electronically every month, and a special mix made up specially for each person. The requirements can be recorded digitally on people's identity cards, which can then be e-mailed to the chemist who will make up the correct mixture. This should avoid the health problems connected with diet, such as obesity, diabetes and high blood pressure.

It will, however, have a major impact on farming in Britain, as there will be much less demand for home-grown food. The long-term effects on such an important industry are yet to be fully studied'.

This is not a new idea. Over 120 years ago, a chemist suggested that in the year 2000: 'everyone will carry their food around with them as a little nitrogen pill, a little pat of fat, a little piece of starch and sugar, and a little jar of flavourings to suit their own taste'.

We eat food to obtain all of the chemicals that we need to stay alive. Our bodies need a variety of foods, and to be healthy we need these in the right amounts. Unfortunately many people eat too much of some foods, leading to the increasing problem of **obesity** in the UK and other developed countries. Meanwhile people in other countries, especially the developing world, eat too little, leading to **malnutrition**.

?
1   What would be the advantages and the disadvantages of eating your food as described above?

2   How would this change affect farmers?

3   Describe two examples of people who need special diets.

A A healthy meal.

B An unhealthy meal.

C These swollen bellies and stick-like arms are signs of a poor diet.

Many people are concerned about their diet, the fact that some people in the world do not have enough to eat, and also the way that food is produced. You need to know something about food and how it is grown and processed if you are going to make informed choices on these matters.

D Intensive farming.

E Free-range farming.

?

4 Describe two examples of times when a person may need to change the type or amount of food that he/she eats.

5 Think of a typical weekly food shopping trip for your family. List the main foods that you buy each week.

6 What do you think affects the choice of food that you or your parents buy? For example, price, packaging, speed of preparation, or something else?

7 Do you think about animal welfare issues when buying food?

8 **a** Does your family buy organic food?
   b If so, why?

Producing food

Why do we need fertilisers?

The world's population has increased rapidly in the past 200 years. This means that we must now farm much more intensively to get much more food from the same area of land.

Plants, like animals, need a balanced diet. They need water, carbon dioxide and light for the process of **photosynthesis**. Plant cells, like animal cells, contain protein molecules. They need **nitrogen**, in the form of **nitrates**, to make the protein molecules. A lack of nitrogen produces stunted plants and yellow leaves. Although air contains 80% nitrogen, most plants cannot use this directly. Some **nitrogen-fixing bacteria** can absorb nitrogen and convert it to nitrates. These bacteria live in the soil and also inside the roots of plants of the pea and bean family. Nitrates and other nitrogen compounds are continually recycled in the **nitrogen cycle**.

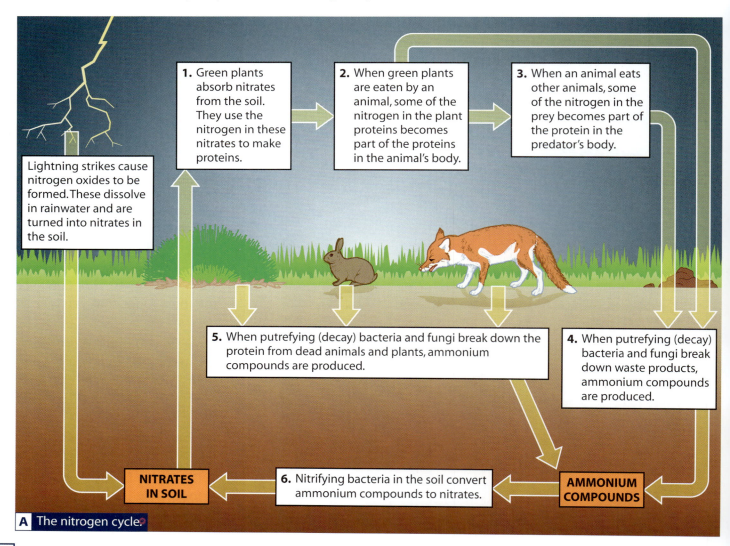

Lightning strikes cause nitrogen oxides to be formed. These dissolve in rainwater and are turned into nitrates in the soil.

1. Green plants absorb nitrates from the soil. They use the nitrogen in these nitrates to make proteins.

2. When green plants are eaten by an animal, some of the nitrogen in the plant proteins becomes part of the proteins in the animal's body.

3. When an animal eats other animals, some of the nitrogen in the prey becomes part of the protein in the predator's body.

5. When putrefying (decay) bacteria and fungi break down the protein from dead animals and plants, ammonium compounds are produced.

4. When putrefying (decay) bacteria and fungi break down waste products, ammonium compounds are produced.

NITRATES IN SOIL

6. Nitrifying bacteria in the soil convert ammonium compounds to nitrates.

AMMONIUM COMPOUNDS

A The nitrogen cycle.

Plants also need 12 other elements as nutrients, which they absorb from the soil water through their roots. The most important are:

- **potassium** – a lack of potassium leads to yellow leaves and dead patches
- **phosphates** – a lack of phosphates leads to poor root systems and small leaves.

A How can you show that plants grow better with added nitrates, potassium and phosphates?

B A plant lacking an essential nutrient.

When plants die they decay and return nutrients to the soil. However, when plants are harvested the nutrients cannot be returned to the soil. These nutrients need to be replaced or the land will gradually produce less and less food. **Synthetic fertilisers** contain specially balanced amounts of these nutrients.

Heavy use of fertilisers can cause problems. Nutrients in the soil dissolve in rainwater and soak deep into the ground or are washed away into streams, lakes and rivers. Here, they encourage the rapid growth of water plants, including algae. These block out light to plants below, which die. **Decomposers** feed on the dead plants and grow rapidly, using up all of the oxygen in the water. If this happens rapidly, other plants and animals cannot get the oxygen that they need and also die. This is called **eutrophication**. Overuse of nitrates can also lead to water pollution.

These problems can be avoided by using the right amount of fertilisers when the plants are growing rapidly and can absorb the chemicals quickly.

?
1. Describe two ways in which bacteria are important in the nitrogen cycle.
2. Why does the nitrogen cycle work best in well-aerated soil (i.e. soil with many pockets of air)?
3. Why do plants need nitrogen, potassium and phosphates?
4. What mineral is the plant shown in Photo B lacking?
5. Why do nitrates, potassium compounds and phosphates have to be added to the soil where crops are growing?
6. Think of a plus, a minus and an interesting point about this statement: Nitrates should not be added to soil.
7. a Why do you think that the levels of nitrates in drinking water have risen in recent years?
   b How could this be avoided?

C This river has been polluted with fertiliser.

Summary

Draw a flow diagram showing the nitrogen cycle. Include the following terms: ammonium compounds, consumer, decomposer, nitrates, producer.

Intensive farming

How do intensive farmers look after their crops?

A In Britain we try to produce as much wheat as possible, so that we do not have to import foreign wheat.

Fertilisers

Many farmers in Britain use synthetic fertilisers. These allow the farmer to grow the same crop in large fields every year. Farmers grow the crop that is most suited to the climate and soil type, or the one that will make most money.

Synthetic fertilisers increase the **yield** (the amount) of crops grown, but there are serious drawbacks. Growing the same crop every year can have severe effects on the soil structure. Soil usually has a crumbly structure which allows water and air to penetrate easily. This structure is destroyed by fertilisers and very fine, dusty soil is formed instead. Removing hedges to make the fields bigger and easier to manage also means that there are no windbreaks, so the soil is blown further. The use of fertilisers also discourages soil organisms such as worms. These organisms help to break down plant matter in the soil and release nutrients naturally.

B Winds blow the soil away and cause erosion.

?
1 What are the main components of fertilisers?

2 What problems can fertilisers cause? (*Hint*: you may also need to look back at the last topic.)

Pesticides

Growing similar crops close together causes problems if there is an infection of the crop. The pest or parasite will spread very quickly through the crops, especially in large fields where no natural methods are used to separate acres of land. Growing the same crop every year on the same land allows pests to attack earlier, especially if they have survived the winter in the soil or nearby wild plants.

Weeds will compete with crops, taking nutrients out of the ground and reducing the yield of the crop. Infections by fungi and insects such as aphids can cause severe damage to all sorts of plants.

An intensive farmer tries to control pests and diseases using **pesticides**. Chemicals used against weeds are called **herbicides**, those used against insects are **insecticides** and those used against fungi are **fungicides**.

Herbicides may also kill the crop that is being grown, and they also kill wild flowers. Some farmers use selective herbicides to kill the weeds but not the crop.

The use of pesticides can cause problems by killing insects that might be natural predators of the insects that do damage.

C Aphids damage plants by sucking their juices.

D Most of this field was sprayed with selective herbicide to kill the poppies without damaging the crop.

?

3 What do pesticides do?

4 What is the difference between insecticides, herbicides and fungicides?

5 What type of herbicide would you use on your lawn?

6 Wheat for milling is used directly from the farm. Why might this result in pesticide residues being found in the resulting flour?

7 Worms are sometimes used in compost heaps. Find out how a compost heap works.

Summary

Write down all the arguments for and against the use of pesticides and fertilisers.

Organic farming

What is organic farming?

Organic farming is farming without the use of any synthetic fertilisers or pesticides. Instead, **natural fertilisers** are added to the soil and wildlife is used to control pests.

An organic farmer sees the farm as a whole, with the individual parts depending on one other. If animals are reared, the manure from these is spread on the ground as a natural fertiliser. This avoids the problem of loss of soil structure found with synthetic fertilisers, but can lead to a lack of some nutrients in the soil which may decrease yield and result in poorer quality of produce. Manure may also be more expensive to buy and difficult to apply, and there is still a risk of pollution.

Pests can also be controlled naturally. If different crops are grown each year in a field, the number of pests cannot get very large as they die off in the years when the crop they feed on is not being grown. Pests can be controlled biologically by encouraging predators that feed on them.

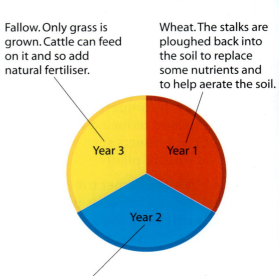

Fallow. Only grass is grown. Cattle can feed on it and so add natural fertiliser.

Wheat. The stalks are ploughed back into the soil to replace some nutrients and to help aerate the soil.

Beans. These make their own fertiliser from the air and so make the soil more fertile.

A Crop rotation helps to keep the soil fertile.

B These pheasants feed on insect pests in the crop. Organic farmers keep more hedges to provide shelter for pheasants.

An organic farm also looks different to an intensive farm:
• The fields tend to be smaller, with boundaries such as hedges and ditches to provide homes for natural predators.
• A variety of different crops is grown.

?
1 What are the advantages and disadvantages of using manure?

2 Describe each year of a crop rotation and explain why it is used.

3 Describe two organic methods of controlling pests.

4 How can you tell that a farm is organic by its appearance?

By 2005 there were 4010 organic farms in the UK, working about 4% of available farmland. More people want to buy organic food as they worry about production methods and the health risks of pesticide residues. However, organic food is more expensive as less is produced and yields vary. This means that it is more difficult for organic farmers to make a good living, especially when cheap imports from other countries are available. Government support and encouragement from supermarkets help.

All organic farms have to conform to standards set down by the UK Register of Organic Food Standards. They have to undergo a 2-year conversion process, and are then inspected regularly afterwards.

A Design a survey to find out whether people want to buy organic food, and their reasons for or against.

Organic Leeks
per kg
25% OFF
SAVE £1.20 ~~£4.79~~ £3.59
£3.59 kg

C The choice of organic food is steadily increasing, although its quality and appearance tend to vary.

?
5 Why do some people want to buy organic food?

6 Why do organic farmers make less money than intensive farmers?

7 Draw a table to show the advantages and disadvantages of organic farming and intensive farming.

8 Use the internet to find out if there are any organic farms near you.

Summary

Your uncle wants to start an organic farm. Your aunt isn't so sure. Try to put forward both sides of the argument.

Food additives

Why are food additives used?

Food additives are chemicals which are added to our food during its production. Although many people think that food additives are a 'modern invention', they have in fact been used for centuries. Saltpetre was used in the Middle Ages to preserve meat, especially important when there were no fridges or freezers. Nowadays nitrite, the active ingredient of saltpetre, is used. It prevents bacteria growing on meat that cause a rare but often deadly form of food poisoning called botulism.

If you look at the label on any type of processed food, you are likely to find a whole list of additives. These are grouped according to what they do.

- **Antioxidants** are added to most foods containing fats or oils, such as potato crisps. They prevent the oxidation by air of fats and oils, which would cause the fat to change colour and taste unpleasant.
- **Colours** make food look more attractive. Many are artificial, but some are natural, such as anthocyanin (red) and chlorophyll (green).

A Saltpetre was dug out of the ground and used to preserve meat.

B Strawberries and strawberry jam.

pickled chillies   pickled onions   pickled beetroot

C Vinegar has been used to preserve food for many years.

?
1 Why did people in the Middle Ages use saltpetre?

2 Look at photo B.
  a Which product has been artificially coloured?
  b Why do you think this was done?

- **Emulsifiers** and **stabilisers** keep ingredients mixed together when they would normally separate, for example oil and water in salad dressings, or fats and water in ice cream.
- **Flavour enhancers** have little flavour of their own, but bring out the flavour in a wide range of foods, for example monosodium glutamate is used a lot in Chinese cookery.
- **Preservatives** such as sorbic acid keep food safe for longer. Traditional methods of food preservation, such as drying, salting, pickling in vinegar and smoking are not always appropriate for all foods, although salt is often added as a flavouring.
- **Sweeteners**, such as saccharin, help to reduce the amount of sugar in processed foods and drinks.

D These foods all contain additives.

All additives are given **E-numbers** which means that they have passed a safety test and been approved for use in the UK and the rest of Europe. These must be clearly shown in the list of ingredients, either by name or E-number.

E-numbers are allocated in blocks, depending on what they are used for:
- E 100 series are colours, e.g. E160a carotene , an orange colour.
- E 200 series are preservatives, e.g. E220 sulfur dioxide.
- E 300 series are antioxidants, e.g. E300 ascorbic acid.
- E 400 + are other types, including emulsifiers, sweeteners, etc.

?

3 Look at photo D. What type of additives are in each of these foods?

4 Which of the additives from question **3** are needed on health grounds?

5 Think of a plus, a minus and an interesting point about this statement: No additives should be used in foods.

6 Bacteria need warmth, water and air to multiply. Why do drying, salting, pickling and smoking prevent the growth of bacteria on food?

Summary

Design an information leaflet about food additives for your local library.

Additives and safety

Are additives safe?

The companies that make our food often use additives to make them taste or look better, or to stop the food spoiling. However, although we know *how* to use additives to do these things, this does not mean that we *should*. Different people have different ideas about their use.

'My doctor told me that I should only buy food that has reduced salt. He says that if we eat too much salt we increase the risk of high blood pressure and heart attacks.'

'We use preservatives in all of our products to make the food keep longer. If we didn't there would be more wasted food, and we would have to charge higher prices.'

Mr Bowler – Fast Foods Ltd

Mrs Evans

'I've read that the average person in Britain eats about 35 kilos of added sugar in their diet each year. They say that being overweight is unhealthy, but I feel fine'.

'Some winemakers added antifreeze to their wine to make it sweeter. This was only discovered when one of them claimed a tax deduction on the antifreeze! That would never be allowed now.'

Ben

Mr Green

Maria

'We do not have any freezers and it is a long walk to get any food. We try to buy food that has preservatives in it, so that it does not rot in the heat.'

 A Debate the use of additives, and decide which ones should be allowed and which ones banned. Give reasons for all your decisions.

Pippa

Mrs Taylor

'My Nathan will only drink a certain kind of orange squash, and nothing else. I've been told that the colour in it may make him uncontrollable, but what else can I do? He can't go without drink.'

'I think that sweeteners are great. I can drink as much of this as I like without putting on any weight. I drink about eight cans a day.'

'I've read that too many colours are added to this Chicken Tikka Masala, but it doesn't seem to taste the same if the colours are left out'.

Dr Appleton

'I'm a chemist working for the **Food Standards Agency**. We check that food additives are safe, and make certain that laws on additives are kept up-to-date.'

John

?

1 List as many reasons as you can for putting additives in food.

2 Describe some reasons why additives should not be used.

3 Why do you think Ben is obese?

4 Do you think that Pippa is sensible to drink so much diet drink? Explain your answer.

5 Think of a plus, a minus and an interesting point about this statement: Some foods that are sold as 'health foods' contain lots of additives.

6 Does the need for additives vary from country to country? Explain your answer.

7 Why do we need regulations to make our food safe?

8 Suppose that the government banned the use of preservatives.
   a How would this affect the manufacturers?
   b How would this affect the consumers?
   c Who would benefit from the ban?
   d Who would end up paying for the ban?

Summary

Write a short article for the school newsletter arguing whether or not additives should be used in school dinners.

Chemical contaminants 1

Is unprocessed food safe to eat?

A Both these mushrooms are poisonous.

Not all plants are safe to eat. Many years ago, people often picked mushrooms in fields, but nowadays people are afraid of eating **toxic** (poisonous) mushrooms. The most deadly mushroom in this country is the Deathcap, which causes 90% of all deaths from fungus poisoning.

Some types of food are only safe to eat if they are properly cooked. For example, kidney beans must be boiled for at least 10 minutes to destroy the toxic haemagglutinins that they contain. This is not normally a problem as most people buy canned, cooked beans.

?
1 Why would more people die from eating Deathcap mushrooms than Fly Agaric mushrooms?

2 Why must kidney beans be boiled before being added to a dish?

3 Why is only sweet cassava on sale in this country?

B There are two varieties of cassava. The bitter one is poisonous unless properly cooked.

About 1–2% of the population are **allergic** to foods like peanuts or shellfish. If they eat even the tiniest amount of the food, the body reacts by producing histamines, which are special chemicals that cause a condition called **anaphylaxis**. In this, parts of the body including the mouth and tongue may quickly swell, causing difficulties in breathing and even death. Many people with these allergies carry a special injection containing adrenaline around with them, so that they can give themselves the antidote if it is needed. All foods that may cause allergic reactions must be labelled.

Some people are unable to eat certain foods because their bodies cannot deal with them. For example, some people cannot eat foods containing gluten (in wheat flour) or cow's milk.

Foods can be contaminated while they are being stored before use. For example, **aflatoxin** is a poisonous substance which may lead to liver cancer. It is produced by a mould that grows on crops like peanuts and cereals. It is a problem, particularly in undeveloped and developing countries. Any foods found to have this mould must be destroyed. About 25% of the world's food crops are affected by such moulds each year, and have to be destroyed.

C Epipens are always carried by people with severe food allergies.

D Supermarkets sell special foods for people with food allergies.

E Farmers must prevent mould growing on these peanuts.

People also worry about pesticides and herbicides that may remain in food produced by intensive farming.

?

4 What is anaphylaxis?

5 Why do people with mild allergies treat them with anti-histamine pills?

6 Why would farmers lose money if their crops were infected by disease?

7 Find out what people who cannot drink cow's milk use as an alternative?

8 Find out what other foods could be affected by aflatoxin.

Summary

Write an article explaining why raw food is not always safe.

Chemical contaminants 2
How can harmful chemicals get into food?

Most of the food that is bought in supermarkets has some sort of packaging.

Chemicals from the packaging can sometimes be absorbed by the food that it contains. For example, cling film contains chemicals that may be harmful to humans. However, these chemicals are only likely to get into foods if the cling film gets hot or if very fatty foods such as cheese or pastry are wrapped in the film.

A Do these cakes really need three layers of packaging?

B Not all food is packaged before it is sold.

Packaging is meant to be used only once, and with one type of food. This means that it may not be safe for other foods as the chemicals from the packaging could move into these new types of food. For example, bottles in which water is sold should not be used for fruit juice. This is because the juice is acidic and chemicals in the plastic bottle may react with these acids.

?
1 How could you stop harmful chemicals in cling film from getting into food?

2 What are the advantages and disadvantages of plastic packaging?

3 Could you keep vinegar in a water bottle? Explain your answer.

C These bottles should only be used for water.

Food cans are made of steel, coated with tin. The tin can slowly transfer into food, making people feel unwell. There is a legal limit to the amount of tin that can be present in food. To avoid this, a chemical called **bisphenol** is sometimes used to coat the inside of the can. When these cans are heated to kill bacteria, the bisphenol coating stops the tin from contaminating the food. However, bisphenols may interfere with our sex hormones. There are now strict rules which state that these bisphenols must only be used when they do not change the quality of the food.

Some harmful chemicals may form as the food is being cooked. Recently, scientists discovered high levels of **acrylamide** in starchy foods that had been cooked at high temperatures. These included potato crisps, bread and crispbread. Acrylamide is known to cause cancer in animals and its presence in foods may harm people's health. Although this worried people when it was discovered, the British Food Standards Agency has so far advised people not to change what they eat.

D The bisphenols inside this can may be harmful.

E The way in which these foods were made may have produced a harmful chemical.

Many people can reduce the amount of harmful chemicals that they are exposed to by eating a healthy diet. This means eating more freshly prepared food rather than lots of processed food, together with plenty of fresh fruit and vegetables.

?

4 Why are cans of food heated?

5 Steel is mainly iron. Why can't it be used by itself for cans?

6 Name two other foods that contain starch, but which are not cooked at such high temperatures.

7 Should processed food be sold at all? Explain your answer.

Summary

Write a pamphlet for your Health Centre explaining why fresh food is likely to be better than processed food for your health.

Digestion

What happens to food after we have eaten it?

Most of the food that we eat is in the form of **polymers**. These are large molecules that cannot be absorbed by the body in their natural state because the molecules are too big. **Starch** is a polymer made up of many **glucose** ($C_6H_{12}O_6$) units joined together. **Proteins** are also polymers, with many **amino acid** units joined together. Proteins contain carbon, hydrogen, oxygen, nitrogen and some sulphur. Both starch and proteins have to be digested and broken down into smaller molecules.

Cellulose is also a polymer of glucose units, but it is not digested. It is often called **fibre**, and helps waste products move easily through our intestines. Low-fibre diets are linked to many bowel disorders, including cancer.

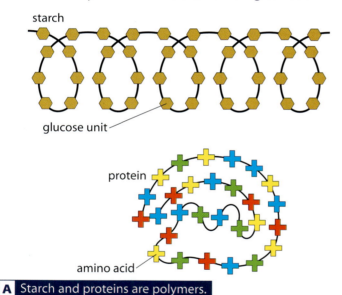

A Starch and proteins are polymers.

Digestion is helped by **enzymes**, which are produced and then added to food at various places in the gut. They help to break down these large insoluble food molecules into smaller soluble ones that can be absorbed.

There are three main types of enzyme found in the digestive system. Each of these helps to break down only one type of food, so we say that they are **specific**.

- **Amylases** help to break down carbohydrates such as starch to glucose.
- **Proteases** help to break down proteins to amino acids which are the building blocks of proteins.
- **Lipases** help to break down fats to smaller molecules of glycerol and fatty acids.

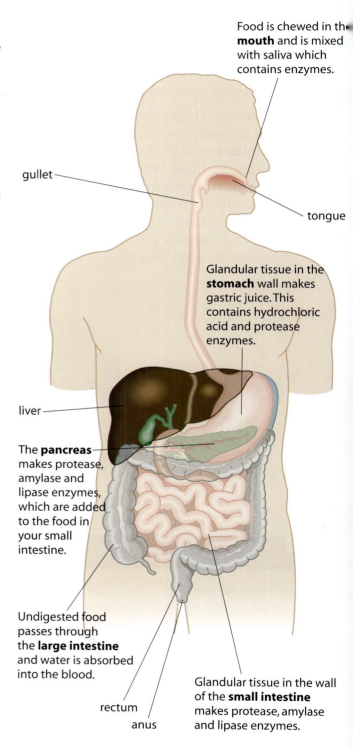

Food is chewed in the **mouth** and is mixed with saliva which contains enzymes.

gullet

tongue

Glandular tissue in the **stomach** wall makes gastric juice. This contains hydrochloric acid and protease enzymes.

liver

The **pancreas** makes protease, amylase and lipase enzymes, which are added to the food in your small intestine.

Undigested food passes through the **large intestine** and water is absorbed into the blood.

rectum

anus

Glandular tissue in the wall of the **small intestine** makes protease, amylase and lipase enzymes.

B The human digestive system and the chemicals added to food.

A The pH is different in each part of your digestive system.
- How could you find out whether the pH affects the way enzymes work?

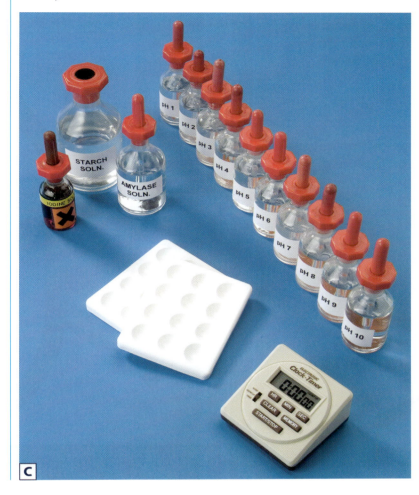

C

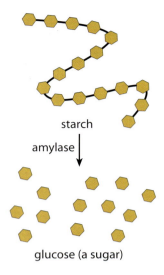

starch

amylase ↓

glucose (a sugar)

D Amylase breaks down starch.

The glucose, amino acids, fatty acids and glycerol formed are all small enough to be absorbed.

Different parts of the digestive system have different pHs. Saliva has a pH of about 8, while stomach contents have a pH of 2. When semi-digested food enters the small intestine this acid is neutralised by bile, causing conditions in this area to return to about pH 8 again. Enzymes work best in the pH conditions of the part of the digestive system where they are found.

Summary

Describe in detail what happens to a cheese sandwich made with wholemeal bread as it passes through the digestive system.

?

1 Why does food have to be broken down?

2 **a** What elements does starch contain?
 b What extra elements are found in proteins?

3 **a** How are starch and cellulose similar?
 b How are they different?

4 Draw a table to show where in the body each type of digestive enzyme is made.

5 In which pH conditions do amylases, proteases and lipases work best?

6 Which is the odd one out: glucose, protein, starch? Explain your answers.

7 Why would a piece of food dissolve more rapidly in digestive juices if it was chewed first?

Using food

How do our bodies use food?

Once food has been broken down into small, water-soluble molecules, it passes through the wall of the small intestine into the bloodstream. Larger molecules cannot pass through, and are egested in the faeces.

The molecules are then taken in the blood to all the cells of the body which need them.

All our cells need energy. They get this energy from glucose in a process called **respiration**. This energy is used to
• keep us warm
• help our muscles contract
• help us grow.

In fact, energy is used in almost every change that happens in our bodies.

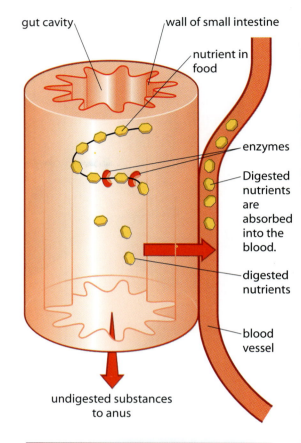

A Only glucose molecules are small enough to pass through the gut wall.

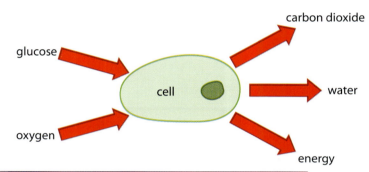

B The process of respiration happens inside every cell.

Some cells also use this energy to build up amino acid molecules into new, large protein molecules. Muscle, tendons, skin, hair, haemoglobin (which carries oxygen in the blood) and enzymes are all mainly proteins.

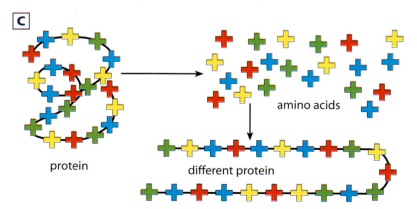

Amino acids from one type of protein in our food can be converted into totally different new proteins.

? 1 What happens to food when it has been broken down into smaller molecules?

2 Write a word equation for respiration.

Fatty acids and glycerol absorbed from our foods are converted back into fats. This fat is needed for energy and any that we do not need is stored under our skin. It can also clog up our arteries, leading to heart disease.

Any excess glucose that is not needed immediately for respiration is also converted to fatty acids and stored as fat.

Any amino acids that have not been turned into proteins can cause harm if they build up in cells. The body is able to **excrete** these. The amino acids are taken in the blood to the **liver**, where they are converted to **urea**, which is harmless. This urea is then taken to the **kidneys** and excreted as urine.

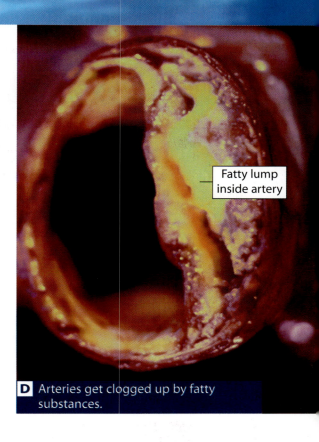

Fatty lump inside artery

D Arteries get clogged up by fatty substances.

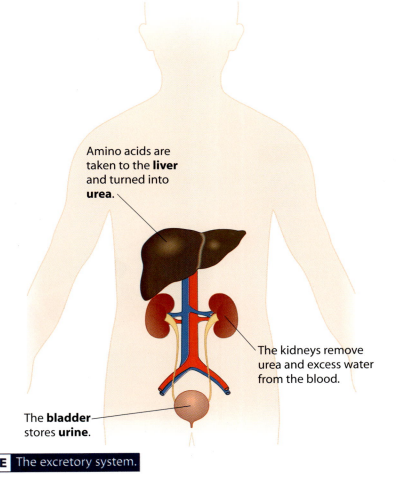

Amino acids are taken to the **liver** and turned into **urea**.

The kidneys remove urea and excess water from the blood.

The **bladder** stores **urine**.

E The excretory system.

Summary

Draw a flow diagram to show what happens to digested foods. Include information on what happens if there is an excess of digested products.

?

3 Describe how an amino acid in a piece of beef becomes part of a muscle cell.

4 What happens when we eat more fat than we need?

5 a Why do we need to excrete amino acids?
   b How does this happen?

6 Why might we become obese if we eat too much starch or sugar?

7 Many toxic substances are excreted in a similar way to excess amino acids, but some are not. Find out the names of two substances that are not excreted in this way.

Diagnose Diabetes

What is diabetes?

Many foods contain sugar, especially some processed foods. When we eat sugar it is broken down to glucose which is quickly absorbed into the bloodstream. This causes the amount of glucose in the blood to increase rapidly.

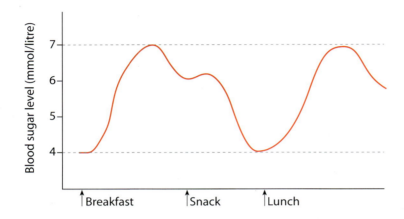

A The effect of a sugary meal on the amount of glucose in the blood.

Glucose levels are controlled by a **hormone** called **insulin**, which is made in the **pancreas** and released into the blood. Insulin helps cells to take glucose from the blood, which the cells then use for respiration. After a meal, more insulin is made to deal with the increased amount of glucose in the blood. The glucose levels in the blood fall back to normal as the cells take it in.

People with **diabetes** (called **diabetics**) do not have enough insulin to control the amount of glucose in their blood. This means that levels of glucose in the blood can get dangerously high and this can lead to serious health problems. Some of the first symptoms of diabetes are extreme tiredness, thirst and the presence of glucose in the urine. A common test for diabetes is to test urine for glucose using Clinistix.

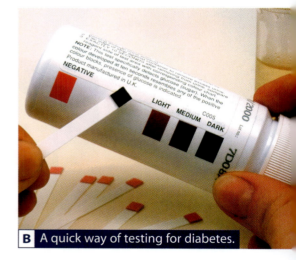

B A quick way of testing for diabetes.

?

1 How would blood glucose levels change when we eat ice cream?

2 What effect would a high-protein diet have on blood glucose levels?

3 Why do diabetics get so tired?

4 Why do you think that glucose is excreted in the urine of a diabetic?

There are two main types of diabetes. **Type 1 diabetes** develops in young people when the pancreas stops making enough insulin. About five in every 1000 people are affected. The illness develops very quickly, and is treated by insulin injections and eating a carefully controlled diet.

Type 2 diabetes affects at least 2% of the population. This illness develops more slowly. It happens when the body no longer responds to its own insulin or does not make enough insulin. Obesity is one of the risk factors for type 2 diabetes. It used to develop in some people after the age of 40, and is sometimes called **late-onset diabetes**. There is a lot of concern that children are now developing it because of their poor diets.

Many people with Type 2 diabetes control it by changing their diets. This means losing weight if they are overweight, because being overweight makes their blood glucose levels harder to control. They should also eat healthy low-fat, high-fibre meals at regular intervals and take lots of exercise. Type 2 diabetes can also be treated by tablets which help the body to control glucose levels, or if necessary, by insulin injections. The insulin used is made by genetically modified bacteria, which can produce very large amounts of this chemical.

C Insulin injections are essential for the health of a diabetic.

D Healthy puddings!

?
5 Can diabetics eat foods that contain sweeteners? Explain your answer.

6 Insulin is a protein. Why can't it be taken by mouth?

7 Why are some children now developing Type 2 diabetes?

Summary

Write an information leaflet for a doctor's surgery explaining the causes and symptoms of the two types of diabetes, and how they can be treated.

Diet and health

Does our diet affect our health?

We are given lots of information about what we should or shouldn't be eating. 'Don't eat too much fat', 'Don't eat too much salt', 'Eat five portions of fruit and vegetables each day'. All of these are very good advice, but many people do not really understand why they are so important.

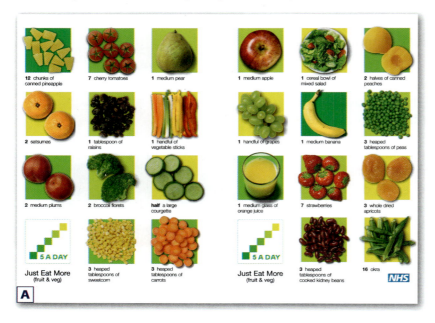

A

Many people today eat too much and don't exercise enough. This leads to obesity, which increases the risk of developing heart disease, high blood pressure, osteoarthritis and Type 2 diabetes. Many adults and over 1 million children in this country are obese. Obesity is linked to around 30 000 deaths a year in England alone.

Heart disease is caused when fatty substances build up in the arteries which supply blood to the heart muscle. The arteries narrow and the heart muscle does not get enough oxygen. If an artery gets blocked by a blood clot, a heart attack results. Heart disease is mainly caused by eating too much saturated fat.

? **1** What causes obesity?

B This extra weight puts strain on the heart and joints.

C Foods full of saturated fats.

High blood pressure can be caused by being obese and by eating too much salt. With this condition the heart has to work overtime pumping blood round the body. If it is not controlled, it can lead to heart disease and stroke. At the moment, 75% of the salt that we eat comes from processed food, such as biscuits, pizza and ready meals.

D You can compare foods by checking food labels and try to reduce salt intake.

Osteoarthritis occurs when the joints in our bodies wear away. This happens much more quickly if somebody is overweight, as the joints have to support more weight. Hip and knee joints can be replaced if the joints get very worn, although this is a serious operation.

There are other diseases linked with diet. A diet low in fibre may be linked with bowel cancer. This is one reason why we are advised to eat lots of fruit and vegetables each day. **Anaemia** is caused by a lack of iron and leads to tiredness. Red meat is the best source of iron, but vegetarians get enough from foods like beans, dried fruit, green vegetables and fortified breakfast cereals.

Some people feel that we should not be told what to eat. However, bad diets can lead to health problems, which cost a lot of money in terms of hospital treatment and lost working days.

E Foods containing iron help prevent anaemia.

?

2 a What causes heart disease?
   b How can we try to prevent it?

3 a Why do we add salt to our food?
   b Is it necessary to do so?

4 Why should we eat lots of fruit and vegetables?

5 Do you listen to warnings about diet? Explain your answer.

6 a Write down five healthy foods and five unhealthy foods. Explain your choices.
   b Do your five healthy foods form a balanced healthy diet? Explain your answer.

Summary

Write a letter to your school kitchen explaining why they should provide healthy food.

Food and its uses

How healthy is our food?

Gareth and Jack are organising the food for their Bronze Duke of Edinburgh's Award expedition. They have to plan menus for two lunches, one hot supper and a hot breakfast. This is their shopping list

brown bread for sandwiches and breakfast

cheese – 250g.

dried 'Super Noodles' – 6 packs for supper

baked beans – 2 large cans

bacon – 250 g

sausages – 8

crisps – 8 packs – mixed flavours

chocolate bars – 10

B

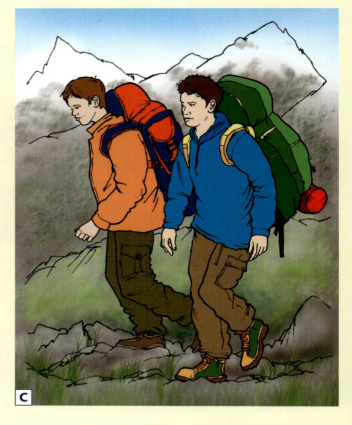
C

1 It said on the packet of sausages said that they contained preservatives. Why do you think these were added to the sausages?

2 a How is the protein in the bacon digested?
   b What happens to any excess amino acids that the body does not require?

3 Describe why eating brown bread helps the food pass through the gut.

4 a Why is it a good idea to include so many chocolate bars?
   b Should people normally eat so much chocolate? Explain your answer.

5 Should the boys pick any mushrooms to have with their sausages? Explain your answer.

6 a Would this diet be suitable for a diabetic?
   b If a Year 10 boy had Type 1 diabetes, what would he have to carry with him on the expedition?
   c What causes this type of diabetes?

One of the packets of crisps had the following food label.

NUTRITION INFORMATION PER PACK	
ENERGY	92 KCAL
PROTEIN	1.0 G
CARBOHYDRATE	13.7 G
FAT	3.7 G
FIBRE	1.1 G
SALT	0.8 G
ADDITIVES	

D

7 What health problems are linked with eating too much salt?

8 Part of the label has been torn off.
  a What additives would you expect to find in a packet of crisps?
  b What do these additives do?
  c Describe the other four main types of additives.

9 What is the name of the chemical that might have formed in the crisps when they were cooked?

10 Gareth's father says that they shouldn't be eating food that contains additives. Give two arguments in favour of additives, and two against.

11 Another boy in their group is allergic to peanuts.
  a What would happen if he ate peanuts?
  b What should the group do to avoid this?
  c What chemical may be produced by a mould that grows on peanuts?

Jack was telling Gareth that his mother wanted to open a stall at the local market, and was trying to decide whether or not to concentrate on selling organic produce.

E

12 How is organic farming different to conventional farming?

13 **a** What nutrients must be added to the soil to help healthy plants grow?
  b What is the difference between synthetic and natural fertilisers?

14 How would the prices for organic food differ from those for food grown on an intensive farm? Explain your answer.

15 The school's PE staff organised this expedition. What are the health benefits of walking?

Radioactive materials

What are the uses and risks of radioactive materials?

I am an engineer in a nuclear power station. I am amazed that people still think that nuclear power stations are dangerous. When I designed the power plant, I made sure that the power station could not become a nuclear bomb! Using nuclear fuel to produce electricity means that there are times when dangerous radiation is produced, but each step is closely monitored so that people inside and outside the power station are not at risk. We also produce nuclear waste, which has to be stored safely.

My name is Kamran and I work in the medical physics department of a hospital. I use nuclear medicine to try and kill cancer cells. It is very important that the patient receives the right amount of this medicine as too much or too little could cause the patient to get very ill. I need to consider the activity, half-life and toxicity of any medicine that I use.

My name is Michael. Here at Isotron we use radiation to sterilise food. We can sterilise fruit, vegetables, spices and fish. Sterilised food lasts longer, but sometimes the radiation kills some of the useful nutrients that are in the food. However, the food itself does not become radioactive or dangerous, so there is no need to worry about that!

My name is Jean and I work for a company called Oxford Safety. We train teachers and lab technicians so that they know how to use radioactive sources properly. I visit schools and run courses to show people how to handle, store and use radioactive materials safely. If radioactive sources are not used properly, people could become very ill as the radiation can kill or damage the cells in their body.

I'm called Yao-Tsan and I work for a company that makes smoke alarms. Inside the smoke alarm there is a radioactive source that sends out a stream of charged 'alpha' particles. When these charged alpha particles are detected the alarm does not make a sound. However, when smoke gets into the alarm, the smoke stops the charged particles from reaching the detector and the alarm sounds.

?

1 What are some of the uses of nuclear radiation? Do you think that they are all entirely safe? Explain your answer.

2 **a** Put the uses of nuclear radiation from these two pages into a league table with the best one at the top and the worst one at the bottom.
   b Explain your reasons for placing them in this order.

3 What is your opinion about nuclear power? Do you think we should use nuclear fuels to generate electricity?

4 Do you think that we should eat food that has been irradiated with nuclear radiation? Explain the reasoning behind your answer.

5 Who is the odd one out: Kamran, Jean or Yao-Tsan? Explain your answers.

I'm not sure about these nuclear power stations. One simple mistake and we could all be killed! Just look what happened to all of those people in Russia in 1986 when the Chernobyl nuclear reactor exploded. I'm much happier getting my electricity from a coal-fired power station. I know that nuclear power stations pollute the atmosphere less, but a single accident could release enough radiation to kill a whole city!

Radioactivity

What is radioactivity?

A Some foods are naturally radioactive, including certain nuts, milk, salad oil, peanut butter and alcoholic drinks. Different foods and drinks give out different amounts of radiation.

Radiation is all around us. It is in the air, in our food, in buildings – it is even inside our own bodies! This is called **background radiation**. It does not harm us, in fact scientists believe that a low level of radiation may actually be good for us.

Certain foods such as Brazil nuts, salad oil and peanuts are naturally radioactive because they have taken in **radioactive** material from the soil when they grow. Our homes are constantly receiving radiation from a gas called **radon** that is found in rocks underneath our houses. We are constantly breathing in this radioactive gas. Some rocks, such as granite, are naturally radioactive and give out radiation.

?

1 Name three things that give out radiation.

2 What is background radiation?

3 **a** What is radon?
   b Name one place where it comes from.

4 Why is granite radioactive?

B These houses are made from granite. Granite contains uranium which is radioactive.

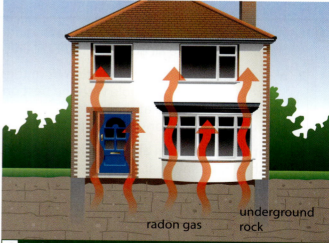

radon gas

underground rock

C Radon is a radioactive gas and a major contributor to background radiation. It seeps into houses from underground rocks.

Where does this radiation come from?

Everything around us is made from atoms. We cannot see atoms because they are so small. Atoms are made up of smaller particles with positive and negative **charges**. **Protons** are positively charged particles found in the **nucleus** of an atom. **Electrons** are tiny, negatively charged particles which move around the nucleus. The number of positive charges found in an atom is always the same as the number of negative charges, so they balance each other out and the atom is **neutral**. The nuclei of most atoms also contain **neutrons** which have no charge.

Each element has its own type of atom, and all the atoms of that element have the same number of protons. However atoms of an element may have different numbers of neutrons. Atoms of the same element with different numbers of neutrons are called **isotopes**.

The atoms of many elements are very **stable**, and they never change. For example, iron is a stable metal so its atoms do not change. However, the atoms of some elements are **unstable** and they emit radiation from the nucleus. When this radiation is emitted the atom becomes more stable and may turn into a different element. This emission of radiation will continue until the atom becomes completely stable.

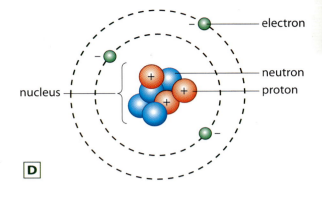

D

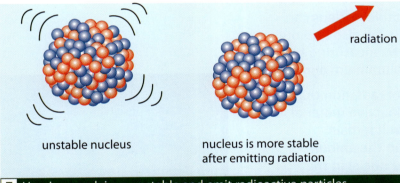

unstable nucleus

nucleus is more stable after emitting radiation

radiation

E Uranium nuclei are unstable and emit radioactive particles. Eventually, uranium turns into a stable metal called lead.

F Uranium ore.

?

5 Which particles are present in:
   a the atom
   b the nucleus?

6 A nucleus has a charge but an atom does not. Explain this statement.

7 Which part of the atom does radiation come from?

8 Why do unstable atoms give out radiation?

9 **a** Find the names of five types of stable atom and five types of unstable atom.
   b State one use of each of the five unstable atoms.

Summary

A member of your family asks you where radiation comes from. Explain this to them, using no more than seven bullet points.

Three types of radiation

What are the three types of radiation?

Unstable atoms give out radiation from their nuclei. When radiation is emitted, the element undergoes **radioactive decay**.

An unstable nucleus can emit three types of radiation, called **alpha**, **beta** and **gamma** radiation. The properties of the three types of radiation are shown in table A.

Type of radiation	alpha particles (α)	beta particles (β)	gamma radiation (γ)
charge	+2	−1	0
mass	4	0	0
penetrating effect	not very penetrating; stopped by a thick sheet of paper, by skin, or by a few cm of air	penetrating, but stopped by a few mm of aluminium or other metal	very penetrating; never completely stopped, though lead and thick concrete will reduce intensity

A The main properties of alpha, beta and gamma radiation

The radiation that is given out by an unstable nucleus can be measured using a **Geiger counter**. You can also find out which type of radiation is being emitted by measuring how much of the radiation penetrates paper, aluminium and lead.

It is not possible to change the amount of radiation that an unstable element emits. If a piece of radioactive material is crushed, heated or dissolved in water, it will remain radioactive and there will be no change in the amount of radiation that it emits. This is because the nuclei in the atoms have not changed.

Even if the element is chemically reacted with another element to form a new compound, the new compound will have no change in its radioactivity.

?
1 Name the three types of radiation.

2 Which one of the three types of radiation is:
   a heaviest
   b most penetrating?

3 Why do you think that heating, crushing or dissolving a radioactive material has no effect on the amount of radiation that it emits?

B Coal contains a few radioactive carbon atoms. When it is burned in air, carbon dioxide is produced. The carbon dioxide gas emits the same amount of radiation as the coal did before it was burned.

Radioactive decay

When an unstable atom undergoes radioactive decay, it becomes more stable. Heavier radioactive elements emit different particles from lighter ones. All nuclei that are unstable after the emission of a particle can become more stable by also emitting a gamma ray. The gamma ray takes energy away from the nucleus without it losing any mass.

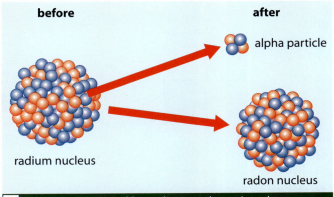

D Heavier elements, like radium and uranium, become more stable by losing an alpha particle.

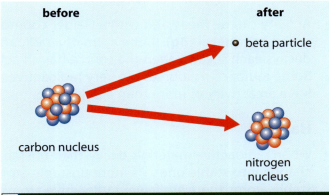

E Lighter elements, like radioactive carbon, become more stable by emitting a beta particle.

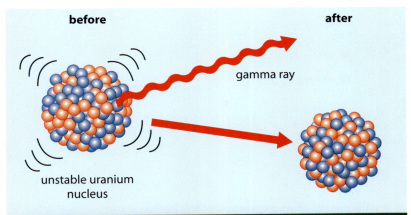

F An unstable nucleus can become more stable by emitting a gamma ray.

?

4 Plutonium is a heavy, unstable element. Which of type of radiation do you think it is most likely to emit?

5 A sample of radioactive material is thought to give off all three types of radiation. What equipment would you need to test if this was actually true?

6 A beta particle is the same as an electron in many ways, but how are they different?

7 Which is the odd one out: alpha, beta or gamma? Explain your answers.

8 Why do you think that alpha particles are more dangerous than gamma rays if swallowed, but less dangerous than gamma rays if the source is outside the body?

Summary

You have been asked to design a poster to make people aware of alpha, beta and gamma radiation. Design your poster using diagrams and the bold words on these two pages.

Activity and half-life

What happens to a radioactive material over time?

Radioactive elements constantly give out radiation. The **activity** of a **source** is the number of atoms that decay each second. The more radiation given out each second, the greater the element's activity will be.

Activity can be measured with a Geiger counter in units called **becquerel** (**Bq**). If one atom of a radioactive source decays each second, then the source has an activity of 1 Bq. Some radioactive sources are very radioactive and may have an activity of more than a million Bq.

Half-life

When radioactive materials decay, their unstable atoms change into stable ones. As more unstable atoms turn into stable atoms there are fewer radioactive atoms left to decay so the activity of the source decreases. The time taken for the activity to decrease to half its original value is called the **half-life** of the material.

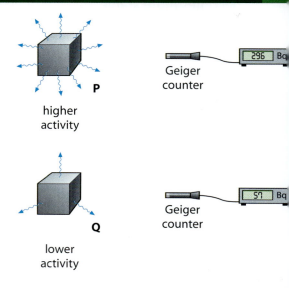

higher activity

lower activity

A Source P has a greater activity than source Q.

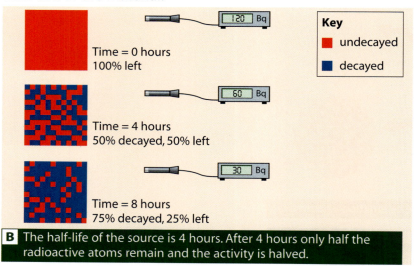

Key

- undecayed
- decayed

Time = 0 hours
100% left

Time = 4 hours
50% decayed, 50% left

Time = 8 hours
75% decayed, 25% left

B The half-life of the source is 4 hours. After 4 hours only half the radioactive atoms remain and the activity is halved.

?

1 Material X gives out 350 radioactive particles each second. Material Y gives out 280 radioactive particles each second. Which one has the greater activity?

2 A piece of rock has a half-life of 8 hours. What proportion of atoms in the rock will remain radioactive after:
   a 8 hours
   b 16 hours
   c 1 day?

3 A radioactive isotope has a half-life of 4 hours. If its initial activity is 240 Bq, what will its activity be in 12 hours' time?

The half-life of a particular radioactive source is always the same. For example, if the half-life of a material is 2 hours, then its activity will halve every 2 hours. Graph C shows what happens.

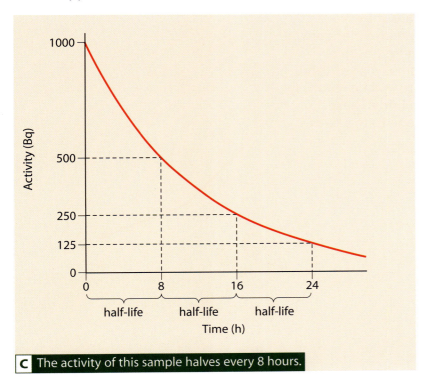

C The activity of this sample halves every 8 hours.

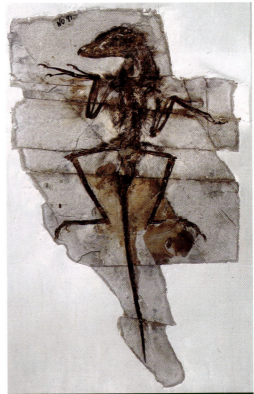

D Radioactive decay can tell us that this young *Dromaeosaurus* died about 70 million years ago.

Not all radioactive materials have the same half-life. Some materials have fairly short half-lives and these are used in hospitals to treat people with illnesses. One example of this is technetium-99 m, which has a half-life of 6 hours. Other materials, such as carbon-14, have very long half-lives and these can be used to tell how old rocks, fossils and old relics are. Nuclear waste, such as plutonium, also has a long half-life, which means that it can remain dangerous for thousands of years. It needs to be stored in a safe place in a container underground, well away from people.

Summary

Some radioactive materials are used in medicine. Design a leaflet for a hospital explaining that it is safe to use these materials. You should include an explanation of activity and half-life in your leaflet.

?

4 Why is it important to bury nuclear waste and keep it well away from people?

5 How can the activity of a sample of rock help us work out how old it is?

6 A sample of technetium-99 m has an activity of 48 Bq. What would the activity be after:
  a 6 hours
  b 12 hours
  c two days?

7 Why would technetium-99 m not be useful when trying to find out how old a rock is?

8 The activity of a sample at time 0 is 72 Bq. Twenty-four hours later its activity is 9 Bq. What is the half-life of the sample?

What is ionisation?

Atoms have no overall charge which means they are neutral. When radiation hits an atom it can lose electrons from its outer shell. The atom then has more positive charges than negative charges and becomes a positively charged **ion**. This ion is now more likely to react chemically with molecules in the cells of the human body. These chemical reactions can cause great damage to the body.

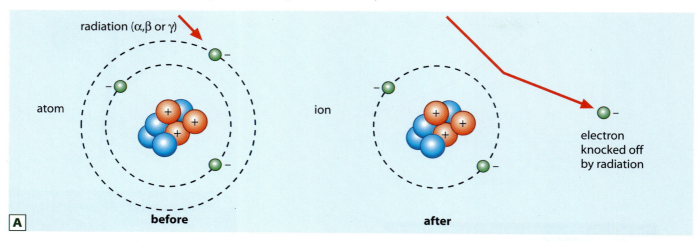

A

Alpha, beta and gamma radiation can all collide with atoms and turn them into ions. These three types of radiation have different ionising capabilities. Alpha particles are slow and heavy, so they can knock electrons off atoms very easily. This makes them the most ionising of the three types. Beta particles are faster than alpha particles, but they are less ionising because they don't have as much mass. Gamma radiation is the least ionising of the three because it has no mass. However, gamma radiation does have some energy and can knock electrons off atoms.

Uses of ionising radiation

Ionising radiation has many uses:
- Gamma rays can be used to sterilise surgical equipment by killing the dangerous bacteria that can live on the surface of surgical instruments. If this is not done, patients could become very ill.
- Beta radiation can be used to preserve fruit. This makes it last longer by killing any harmful bacteria that are on the fruit.
- Alpha radiation can be used to kill cancer cells in the human body. Alpha particles cannot travel very far, so they are relatively harmless outside the body.

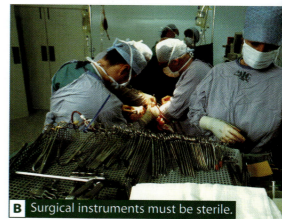

B Surgical instruments must be sterile.

?
1 What is an ion?

2 How is a positive ion formed?

3 a Which type of radiation is most ionising?
  b Explain why.

4 a Which type of radiation is most likely to damage living cells?
  b Which type is least likely to damage cells?

C Irradiated fruit lasts longer.

Dangers of ionising radiation

Cancer is caused when the damage to cells causes them to divide abnormally. Radiation **dose** is a measure of how much damage radiation does to the body, and depends on both the amount of radiation and the type. It is measured in units called **sieverts** (**Sv**). The greater the dose that a person is exposed to, the higher the chance of suffering from radiation-linked diseases such as cancer.

Dose (Sv)	Effect on body
0.0025	average dose received each year by people in the UK; seen as 'safe'
3	radiation burns to skin; sterility to men and women; blood cells damaged
20	radiation sickness; damage to nervous system; almost certain death in days

D Damage caused by different doses of radiation.

?

5 **a** Name three uses of ionising radiation.
   b Explain why each use requires a suitable type of radiation.

6 Why do alpha particles cause more damage than gamma rays inside the body?

7 Think of a plus, a minus and an interesting point about this statement: All radiation should be ionising.

8 Why might a number of low-energy rays be more suitable for killing cancer cells than one single high-energy beam?

Summary

Draw a table to show how ionising radiation can be useful and harmful to humans.

Exposure to radiation

How are we exposed to radiation?

All around us there is natural radiation that comes from rocks, the air, food and cosmic rays from outer space. This is called background radiation. This radiation is not harmful, but it is always present. It comes from unstable atoms when they undergo radioactive decay. The level of background radiation depends on where you are.

You can absorb radiation in different ways. **Direct irradiation** is when a body is exposed to radiation from an external source. During **exposure** this radiation can be absorbed by the body or it can pass straight through. The body does not become radioactive following direct irradiation.

Contamination means that radioactive materials in the form of gases, liquids or solids are released into the environment where they can then affect people through physical contact. Contamination can affect the body internally if radioactive material gets into the body through the lungs, stomach or a wound.

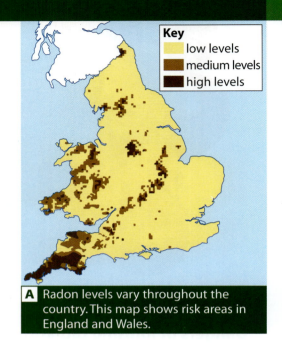

Key	
	low levels
	medium levels
	high levels

A Radon levels vary throughout the country. This map shows risk areas in England and Wales.

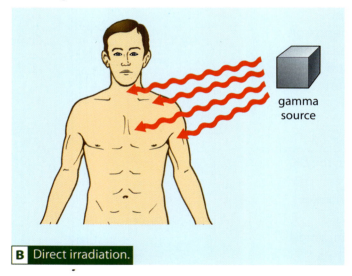

gamma source

B Direct irradiation.

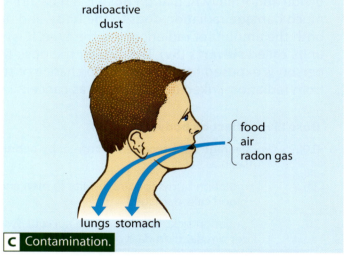

radioactive dust

food
air
radon gas

lungs stomach

C Contamination.

Exposure to radiation

All of us are exposed to direct irradiation and we are all contaminated by the gases that we breathe in and the liquids and solids that we drink and eat. However, some people are at a higher risk of exposure and they need to take special precautions. For example underground workers, medical physicists and workers in power stations are all at risk of **occupational radiation**.

?

1 a Where does background radiation come from?
  b Are you at risk from breathing in radon? Explain your answer.

2 a What is direct irradiation?
  b Give an example.

3 a What is contamination?
  b Give an example.

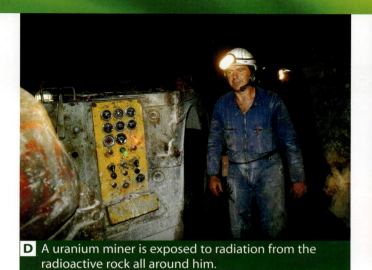

D A uranium miner is exposed to radiation from the radioactive rock all around him.

E This person works in a nuclear power station.

People who work with nuclear radiation monitor their exposure with devices called **film badges** which show how much beta and gamma radiation a person has been exposed to. Health and safety laws require that people most at risk need to have their radiation levels checked frequently. The film badges are checked regularly and any workers who have received too much radiation will be told.

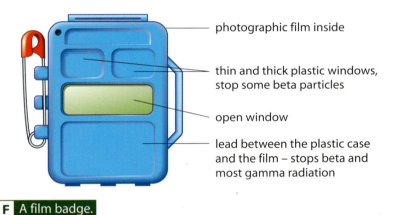

photographic film inside

thin and thick plastic windows, stop some beta particles

open window

lead between the plastic case and the film – stops beta and most gamma radiation

F A film badge.

?

4 Which people are most at risk from radiation?

5 Which types of radiation cause the least damage to the body?

6 a Which type of radiation causes most damage to the body?
  b Why is this?

7 a How can workers check that they have not received too much radiation?
  b Why do workers need to check their film badges on a regular basis?

8 Look at diagram E and explain, in detail, how a film badge works.

Summary

Make a mind map concerning radiation using the words below. You can use more words if you need to.

radiation   background
contamination   direct irradiation
exposure   granite   monitoring
film badge   Geiger counter
radioactive   health

P3.7 Are we safe?
Can anything be 'completely safe'?

A Which is the biggest risk, playing on the beach near a nuclear power station or travelling on a wet motorway?

Most of the radiation around us is harmless, but it is not possible to state that it is 'completely safe'. Much of it is natural radiation and some of it comes from human activities. The **actual risk** associated with background radiation is very low because it has a low energy so the dose that a body receives is very small. However, if you were to mention to people that nuclear power stations contribute to the background radiation, they might become quite frightened, even though they are very safe. This fear is due to the person's **perceived risk** – a risk that somebody believes to be true.

The **precautionary principle** can be explained by the phrase 'better safe than sorry'.

Precautionary principle

- People have a duty to try and stop something bad, if they think it is going to happen.
- The dangers of a new technology are the responsibility of the inventor.
- Before using a new technology, people have the right to use alternatives or nothing at all.
- Decisions involving the precautionary principle need to be open and they must involve all people.
- The risks and benefits of anything new must always be considered.

The precautionary principle should be followed when new technologies, products, chemicals or processes are being developed for use by many people.

?
1. a What is the difference between actual risk and perceived risk?
   b Give one example of each.

2. Why is the precautionary principle important?

3. How might the precautionary principle be applied to:
   a nuclear power stations
   b treating skin cancer?

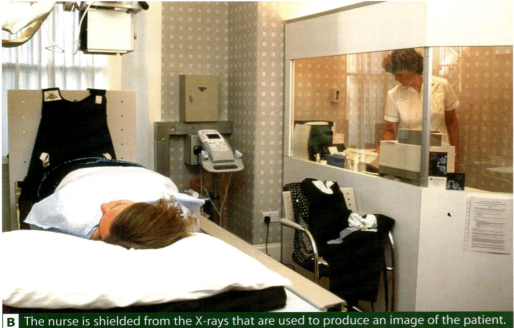

B The nurse is shielded from the X-rays that are used to produce an image of the patient.

Exposure to radiation should be kept to a minimum. The **ALARA** principle states that this should be **A**s **L**ow **A**s **R**easonably **A**chievable. The principle is based on the assumption that a radiation dose, no matter how small, may have a harmful effect. So every reasonable means of lowering exposure should be used. To minimise exposure to radiation we need to look at:

• time – shorter exposure time means a lower dose
• distance – as distance from the source doubles, exposure decreases by a factor of four
• shielding – protective shielding greatly reduces the dose.

Most activities have some risk. We need to think about whether the risk is worth taking.

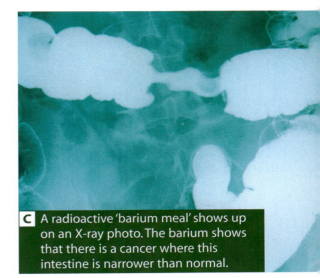

C A radioactive 'barium meal' shows up on an X-ray photo. The barium shows that there is a cancer where this intestine is narrower than normal.

?

4 Look at photo C. For someone having a barium meal:
  a what are the risks
  b what are the benefits?

5 Would doctors give a barium meal to someone who is not ill? Explain your answer.

6 **a** What is the ALARA principle?
  b How might the ALARA principle be employed in a nuclear power station?

7 Give another example of where the ALARA principle might be used.

8 How might modern life be different if the precautionary principle was not employed?

Summary

A scientist has developed a new form of radiation that she believes might be a cure for certain diseases. Write her some notes explaining what the precautionary and ALARA principles are and how they apply to her new discovery.

Fossil fuels and electricity

How is electricity produced from fossil fuels?

A fuel is a substance that releases heat energy when it is burned. It is a store of chemical energy. The three **fossil fuels** are coal, oil and natural gas. These fuels can be used in power stations to produce electricity. Since electricity is produced from another energy form, it is called a **secondary energy source**.

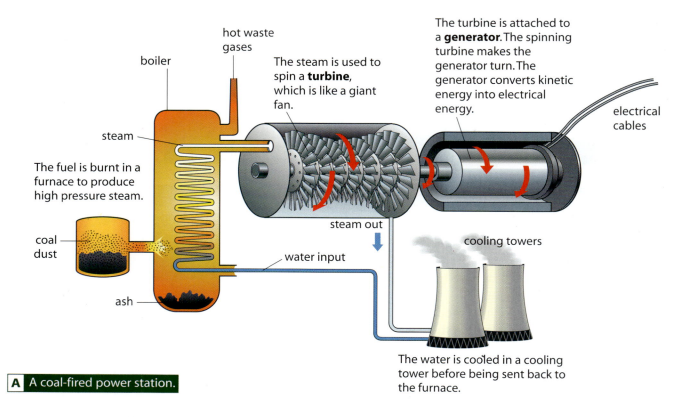

boiler

hot waste gases

The steam is used to spin a **turbine**, which is like a giant fan.

The turbine is attached to a **generator**. The spinning turbine makes the generator turn. The generator converts kinetic energy into electrical energy.

electrical cables

steam

The fuel is burnt in a furnace to produce high pressure steam.

coal dust

ash

steam out

water input

cooling towers

The water is cooled in a cooling tower before being sent back to the furnace.

A A coal-fired power station.

B Electricity is sent around the country through the National Grid. About 2% of the energy carried by the National Grid is wasted as heat.

?

1 **a** What is a fuel?
  b Name three fossil fuels.

2 Why is electricity called a secondary energy source?

3 Describe the stages involved in the production of electricity in a power station.

4 How is electricity transported across the country?

5 List the ways in which energy is wasted when electricity is generated and sent around the country.

Electricity is a very convenient form of energy because:
- it can be used in many ways, by many different devices.
- it is easy to transmit long distances across the country.
- it does not produce any polluting gases when it is being used.

The main problem with electrical energy is that it is very difficult to store, so it needs to be generated all of the time.

Fossil fuels are a very convenient way of producing electricity. The fuels contain a large amount of energy and they are readily available. If more electricity is needed, more fuel is burned in the furnace. However, there are also problems associated with burning fossil fuels:
- they produce large amounts of carbon dioxide gas when they burn, which causes **global warming**.
- sulphur in the fuels produces sulphur dioxide gas, which dissolves in water to make **acid rain**.
- they are **non-renewable** which means that once they have been used up they cannot be replaced.

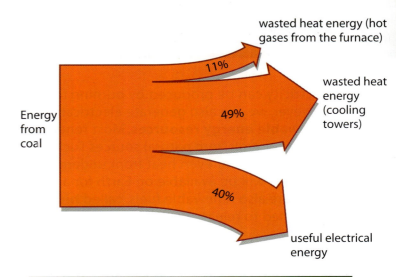

C A power station is not very efficient. Over half of the energy originally in the coal is wasted.

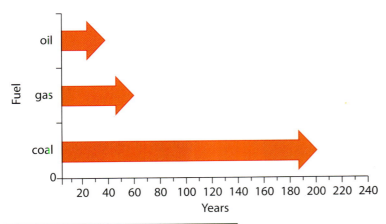

D How long different fossil fuels will last.

Summary

Write an article for a scientific magazine entitled: 'The good side and the bad side to fossil fuels'.

?

6 Name two ways in which fossil fuels are useful for producing electricity.

7 **a** Name two polluting gases that are released when coal and oil are burned.
   b What effects do these polluting gases have, and why is this a problem?

8 What is the main problem with using non-renewable energy resources?

9 Complete this statement in as many different ways as you can think of: Electricity is a secondary energy source…

10 Imagine that you could develop your own 'perfect' fuel for use in a power station.
   a Describe what this fuel would be like.
   b Explain how it would be 'perfect'.

Renewable energy resources
What are renewable energy resources?

Electricity can be produced by burning fossil fuels. However, we can also generate electrical energy using **renewable energy resources**. Most renewable resources convert energy from natural sources such as the Sun, the wind, the tides or even heat from underground. Renewable resources will be available on Earth for a very long time. There are also renewable fuels, called **biofuels**, which can be burned to release energy.

Wind power

In a wind turbine, the kinetic energy of the wind turns the turbine blades, which drive a generator to produce electricity. Large generators can send electricity to the National Grid so that it can then be used in places such as homes and offices. Small generators can be used to generate electricity in isolated places.

Geothermal energy

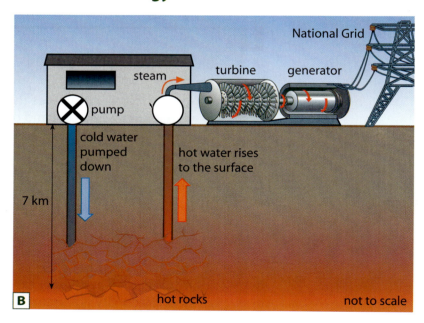

B   hot rocks   not to scale

A

In some places such as Iceland, Mexico and New Zealand the rocks beneath the ground are very hot as a result of natural radioactivity. This heat energy can be used to generate electricity.

> **?**
> 1 Name three things that are sources of renewable energy.
>
> 2 Do renewable energy resources require a fuel? Explain your answer.
>
> 3 How does a wind turbine produce electricity?
>
> 4 How is this electricity used?
>
> 5 What are the advantages and disadvantages of a small wind turbine?
>
> 6 Look at diagram B. Describe how a geothermal power station produces electricity.

Hydroelectric power

Hydroelectric power uses water that is stored high up behind a dam. When the valves are opened, water rushes down from the dam at high speed to turn turbines, which drive a generator. Hydroelectric power stations are usually found in hilly areas.

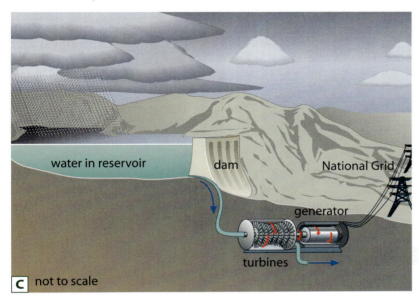

water in reservoir   dam   National Grid

generator

turbines

C not to scale

Biofuels

Biofuels include wood, methane, animal dung, cereals such as maize and sorghum and other crops such as cassava and cane sugar. Wood is obtained from forests that are managed for this purpose and methane is obtained from farm waste. Animal dung and cane sugar can be **fermented** (broken down by microorganisms) to produce bio-alcohol. In Brazil, this **biomass** provides a cheap alternative to petrol.

Other renewable energy resources include **solar power**, **tidal power** and **wave power**.

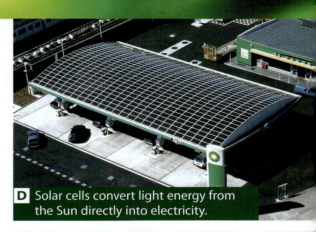

D Solar cells convert light energy from the Sun directly into electricity.

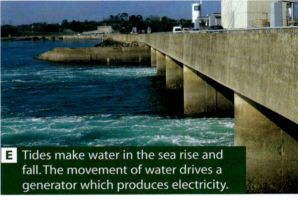

E Tides make water in the sea rise and fall. The movement of water drives a generator which produces electricity.

F Generators are driven by the up and down movement of waves.

?

7 Why do hydroelectric power stations need to be in hilly areas?

8 When and where might solar power:
   a be very useful
   b be no use at all?

9 Which renewable energy resource do you think is the best? Write a paragraph explaining your choice.

Summary

Your local council has informed you that the electrical energy for your home will now be provided by renewable resources instead of a power station. Write down seven questions that you would want to ask the leader of the local council before you telephone him to discuss this proposal.

Nuclear power

What are the benefits and drawbacks of nuclear power?

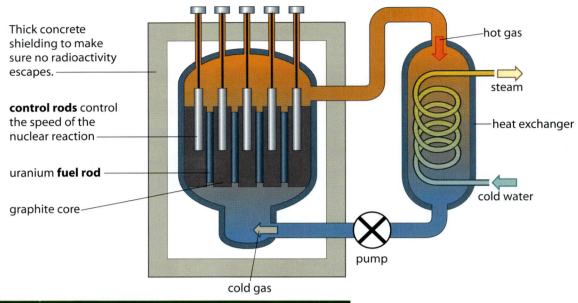

Thick concrete shielding to make sure no radioactivity escapes.

control rods control the speed of the nuclear reaction

uranium **fuel rod**

graphite core

hot gas

steam

heat exchanger

cold water

pump

cold gas

A A nuclear power station has a nuclear reactor instead of a furnace.

Certain radioactive materials can be used in a nuclear power station to produce electricity. However, unlike fossil fuels, the **nuclear fuel** is not burned. Instead, it is used in a nuclear reactor where a process called **nuclear fission** takes place, releasing a huge amount of heat energy. The energy released when a kilogram of **uranium** undergoes nuclear fission is nearly 100 million times greater than the energy released when 1 kg of coal, oil or natural gas burns.

In nuclear fission a large nucleus is split up into two smaller nuclei by a slow-moving neutron. When a uranium-235 nucleus is bombarded with slow-moving neutrons, it splits into two smaller nuclei and some neutrons. Gamma radiation is also emitted. It is important that this does not get out of the nuclear reactor as it can cause damage to human cells.

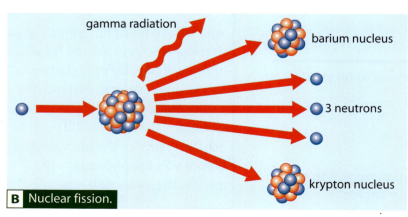

gamma radiation

barium nucleus

3 neutrons

krypton nucleus

B Nuclear fission.

?

1 How is the design of a nuclear power station different from a coal-fired power station?

2 What does 'nuclear fission' mean?

3 a Why must gamma rays not be allowed to escape from the reactor?
   b Why is the shielding in a nuclear reactor built from lead or concrete?

Each one of the neutrons produced goes on to produce another fission reaction. This is called a **chain reaction**. If this was allowed to continue, then the fission process would grow out of control and the nuclear reactor would become a **nuclear bomb**. On average, one of these neutrons goes on to sustain a chain reaction and the surplus neutrons are absorbed by **control rods**. The nuclear reactor also needs to be kept cool by pumping a coolant around it. If this did not happen, then the reactor would melt and a serious nuclear accident could occur.

B The Chernobyl accident in 1986 killed 32 people immediately, and many more in the months that followed the clear-up.

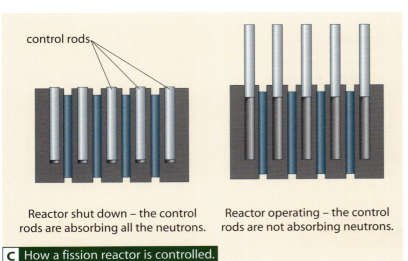

Reactor shut down – the control rods are absorbing all the neutrons.

Reactor operating – the control rods are not absorbing neutrons.

C How a fission reactor is controlled.

Nuclear waste

Used nuclear fuel is often taken to a **reprocessing plant** where the unused fuel is removed so that it can be used again. What is left is called **nuclear waste**. It has a long half-life so it will remain radioactive for many thousands of years. Some materials and parts of the reactor also become radioactive. Nuclear waste is not considered safe until its radioactivity is similar to the level of background radiation. Table D shows the different kinds of nuclear waste. There are strict rules about how the different kinds of radioactive waste must be disposed of.

Waste Category	Examples
Low level waste	• used protective clothing
Intermediate level waste	• reactor components
High level waste	• the parts of used nuclear fuel that cannot be reprocessed

?

4　Why are the following items needed in a nuclear reactor:
　a control rods
　b coolant?

5　**a** Why does nuclear waste need to be buried deep underground and not just stored in a warehouse?
　b Why does it need to be stored for a long time?

6　Think of a plus, a minus and an interesting point about this statement: All of our electrical energy should come from nuclear power stations.

7　Find out what 'decommissioning' means and why it is necessary.

Summary

Design a poster that shows the process, uses and dangers of nuclear fission.

Renewable or non-renewable?

Which resources should we use?

The electrical energy that we use in our homes can come from fossil fuels, from nuclear fuels or from renewable energy resources. Homes, hospitals and factories receive most of their electrical energy from power stations that use fossil fuels or nuclear fuels. The advantages and disadvantages of nuclear and fossil fuels are shown in table A.

Fuel	Advantages	Disadvantages
fossil fuels (coal, oil and natural gas)	• reliable and easy to obtain • do not produce harmful radiation	• produce greenhouse gases • non-renewable
nuclear fuel	• reliable and easy to obtain • does not produce greenhouse gases	• non-renewable • produces radioactive waste • dangerous if accident occurs • nuclear power stations expensive to build and decommission

A The advantages and disadvantages of nuclear and fossil fuels.

?

1 a What are the advantages shared by fossil fuels and nuclear fuels?
  b What are the shared disadvantages?

2 Which do you think is best – nuclear fuel or coal? Explain your answer.

3 Why might some people be 'frightened' of nuclear fuel?

B This is the nuclear power station at Three Mile Island in the USA. Many people think it is an eyesore.

Fossil fuels and nuclear fuels have many advantages, especially the fact that they are very convenient. However, these fuels will eventually run out and our energy needs will ultimately have to be provided by renewable resources. The advantages and disadvantages of renewable resources are listed in table C.

Advantages	Disadvantages
• renewable – will not run out • do not produce greenhouse gases • no fuel costs (except biofuels) • low maintenance	• unreliable – e.g. solar power does not work at night, wind power does not work when it is not windy • inefficient – low energy output • can be expensive to set up (geothermal) • can be unsightly and noisy (wind farms) • can take up large areas of land, though you can still farm beneath them (wind farms) • can damage the environment (hydroelectric/tidal)

C Advantages and disadvantages of renewable energy resources.

D Some people are concerned that birds may be killed by wind turbines.

?
4 a How are renewable resources better than fuels?
   b How are fossil fuels considered to be better than renewable resources?

5 Why might some people not be in favour of building wind farms, hydroelectric dams and tidal barrages?

6 Why do you think geothermal energy is so expensive to set up?

7 Which do you prefer – non-renewable or renewable resources? Explain your answer.

8 Complete this sentence in as many different ways as you can: Electrical energy can be produced …

9 Which characteristics would a 'perfect' energy resource have? Explain why it would be better than any of the current renewable and non-renewable resources.

Summary

Write a letter to your MP explaining why the government should invest in renewable energy resources for the school.

Sustainable development

What is sustainable development?

In developed countries, it is taken for granted that we have access to electricity. However, over two billion people in the world (which is one person in three) do not have access to electricity. They must rely on fuel sources such as firewood or kerosene for cooking.

When talking about energy resources, **sustainable development** means developing new technologies which will enable us to obtain enough energy for our needs, without more pollution of the Earth's atmosphere and water supplies. There are two issues to consider here:

- **technical feasibility** – what *can* be done, based on the technology that is available
- **values** – what *should* be done based on what is morally right for everyone.

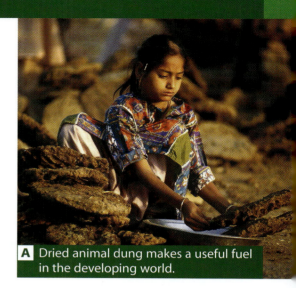

A Dried animal dung makes a useful fuel in the developing world.

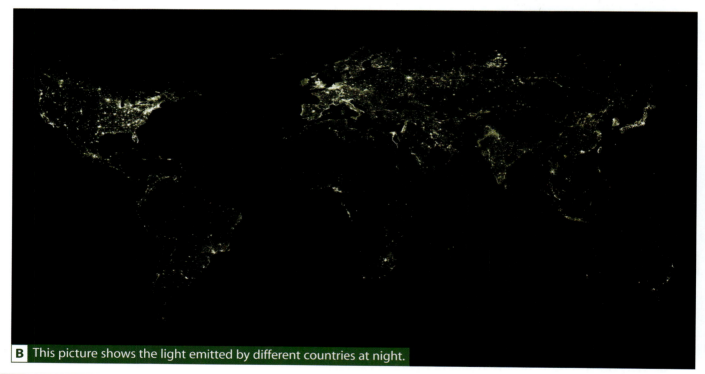

B This picture shows the light emitted by different countries at night.

?

1 **a** How many people in the world do not have access to electricity?
   b What proportion of the world's population is this?

2 Which types of resources are the fuels that people in developing countries use to cook?

3 Look at picture B. What does this tell you about the availability of electricity?

4 What is meant by the term 'sustainable development'.

People representing the governments of the world have met to discuss the most important issues surrounding sustainable development. They have agreed that there are a number of urgent areas that need to be addressed. These include:

- increasing the number of renewable energy resources throughout the world
- developing new technologies that will produce electrical energy without releasing greenhouse gases
- stopping government subsidies for companies that produce electricity from non-renewable energy resources
- producing cleaner fossil fuels, and vehicles, that are less polluting
- making modern biomass and wood technologies available to more people
- helping poorer countries develop and use new energy technology.

The World Summit on Sustainable Development in 2002 looked at ways to improve people's lives while protecting the environment. Over 100 world leaders addressed the summit. In total, 193 countries were involved in discussions, and over $1000 million was made available to try to solve the world's energy problems.

C

?

5 a What do governments believe are the most important issues for sustainable development?
 b Which of these do you think is most important? Explain your answer.

6 Why do you think so many countries are involved in discussions such as the World Summit for Sustainable Development?

7 a What are the technically feasible ways in which rich countries could help poorer countries to become more developed?
 b Which values should be taken into account when deciding what help to provide?

8 What are the reasons for and the desired outcomes of a programme of sustainable development?

9 Sustainable development also includes the development of water and sanitation, health and agriculture. What problems might occur here and how should they be addressed and improved?

Summary

Write a 250 word television script that explains what 'sustainable development' is.

Power for the people

Which energy resources should be used to generate electricity?

The population of Copperwheat City has increased by nearly 250 000 over the last 20 years. As a result, the government has decided that a new power station is needed to meet the extra demand for electrical energy. The nuclear power company 'Powerfuel' will build a nuclear power station on the outskirts of Copperwheat City.

1 **a** What is radioactive decay?
   b Name the three types of radiation that can be produced by radioactive decay.
   c Describe the properties of each type of radiation.
   d Give one use for each type of radiation.

2 **a** Describe how the process of nuclear fission is used to generate electricity.
   b How is a fossil-fuelled power station different from a nuclear power station?

3 Why does Copperwheat City need another power station?

4 What are the advantages of nuclear power?

There are different opinions about whether the new power station should be built.

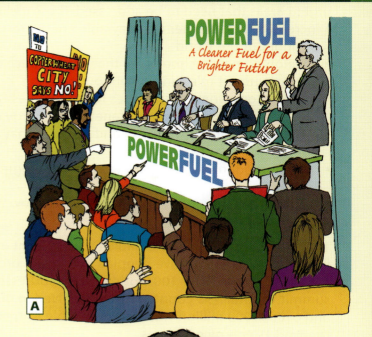

A

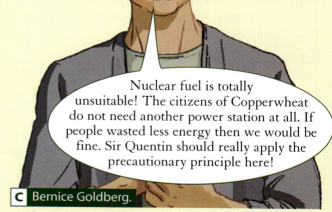

B Sir Quentin Jones.

The new nuclear power station will provide many jobs and will meet the extra demand for electricity. The power station will be completely safe and nuclear fuel will be transported to the power station from Russia.

Nuclear fuel is totally unsuitable! The citizens of Copperwheat do not need another power station at all. If people wasted less energy then we would be fine. Sir Quentin should really apply the precautionary principle here!

C Bernice Goldberg.

5 Is Sir Quentin correct when he says that the new power station will be completely safe? Explain your answer.

6 Why might Bernice think that nuclear fuel is 'unsuitable'?

7 What does Bernice mean when she says that Sir Quentin should apply the precautionary principle?

Nuclear power is not suitable for this location. The coastal area is much better suited to a wind farm. The local background radiation levels will not be affected if wind turbines are used.

D Professor Robert Storey.

Powerfuel has been in trouble in the past for not following the correct safety procedures when storing and transporting radioactive waste. They also do not support schemes of sustainable development in other parts of the world.

E Dave Brookes

8 a Why is wind energy referred to as a renewable resource?
b Name three other renewable resources.
c Give one advantage and one disadvantage of each of the resources that you named in part b.

9 a List two advantages of wind farms compared to nuclear power.
b Describe one disadvantage of wind farms compared to nuclear power.

10 a What is background radiation?
b Name three sources of background radiation.

11 Could other renewable resources be used in this location? Explain your answer.

12 a What is the half-life of a radioactive material?
b Why is the long half-life of radioactive waste a problem?
c How is high-level nuclear waste dealt with?

13 a How can radiation harm the body?
b Name two jobs where workers may be exposed to occupational radiation.
c Explain the ALARA principle.
d How are people who may be exposed to occupational radiation monitored?

14 What might the inhabitants of Copperwheat feel when they learn about the problems that 'Powerfuel' have had?

15 a Explain what is meant by sustainable development.
b How can sustainable development be encouraged throughout the world?

Glossary

abortion Stopping a pregnancy by removing the fetus.

absolute magnitude The true brightness of a star.

absorb Take in, such as when infrared radiation is absorbed by your body and you feel warmer.

acceptable theory An explanation for an outcome that agrees with the evidence and is accepted by the majority of scientists.

acid rain Rainwater which is more acidic than normal (with a pH often as low as 3 or 4). It is produced when sulfur dioxide from burning fuels dissolves in rainwater.

acquired characteristic Characteristic that is developed by use and passed on to offspring, as defined by Lamarck.

acrylamide A chemical produced when starchy foods are cooked at high temperatures.

active immunity When the body produces its own antibodies and memory cells.

activity The number of unstable nuclei that decay each second.

actual risk The risk that is actually present, as opposed to the risk that someone thinks is present.

adaptation Characteristic which is successful in an environment; which allows the organism to survive and breed.

aflatoxin A poisonous substance produced by certain moulds.

AIDS Acquired immune deficiency syndrome – a disease caused by the HIV virus which attacks and weakens the body's immune system.

air A mixture of gases that covers the surface of the Earth.

ALARA principle The idea that any unavoidable risks should be As Low As Reasonably Achievable.

alleles Different forms of a gene for the same characteristic, e.g. alleles for red flowers and white flowers.

allergic When a food produces an unpleasant reaction in the body.

alpha radiation Radiation consisting of positively charged particles given out by an unstable nucleus.

amino acids The units which make up proteins, and which proteins turn into during digestion.

amylase The enzyme that converts starch into smaller sugar molecules.

anaphylaxis A severe reaction to foods that cause an allergy.

ancestor An organism that evolved into a more recent organism.

angina Chest pains caused when the coronary artery gets partly blocked.

antibiotic resistant Bacteria that are no longer killed by antibiotics.

antibiotics Chemicals used to kill or stop the growth of microorganisms inside the body.

antibodies Chemicals made by white blood cells, which destroy particular microorganisms.

antigens Chemical markers on the outside of cells that identify where the cells come from.

antioxidants Chemicals added to food to prevent oxidation of fats.

apparent magnitude How bright a star appears to be when seen from Earth.

arteries Blood vessels with thick muscular walls that carry blood away from the heart.

asexual reproduction Reproduction involving only one parent, producing offspring that are genetically identical to each other and to the parent.

asteroid A small rocky body that orbits the Sun.

asthma A disease in which something triggers the airways to become narrow, making breathing difficult.

atmosphere A layer of gases that surrounds the Earth.

atom A particle which is the smallest part of an element that can exist.

background radiation Naturally occurring radiation that is present all around us. It comes from buildings, rocks, food and cosmic rays from outer space.

bacterium (plural bacteria) A single celled microorganism much smaller than an animal cell. Bacteria were the earliest life forms.

becquerel (Bq) The unit of activity. 1 Bq is equal to one atom decaying every second.

best estimate The mean of a set of data which is likely to be closest to the true value of the quantity.

beta particle Radiation consisting of negatively charged particles given out from an unstable nucleus.

bias Having a particular point of view that affects how results are interpreted.

Big Bang The idea that the Universe was created in a huge explosion and has been expanding ever since.

Big Crunch A possible end for the Universe when everything is pulled back together.

biodiversity Either the number of different plant and animal species within a habitat, or the genetic variety within a species.

biofuel Any fuel that is produced from plants or animal waste.

biomass Plant or animal material that can be burned to release heat.

bisphenol A chemical used to coat the inside of food cans.

blind trial Where patients in a trial don't know which dose of a medicine they are receiving.

booster A top-up dose of a vaccine.

brain Part of the central nervous system which coordinates responses to stimuli.

brittle A material that tends to break rather than change shape when a force acts on it.

carbon cycle How carbon is cycled between living organisms and the air.

carrier A person that has one allele for a disease, but does not have the disease itself. Carriers can pass the faulty gene on to their offspring.

catalytic converter Using a catalyst to speed up chemical reactions which reduce the amount of pollutants in vehicle exhausts.

cause A factor that produces a change in another factor.

cell cultures A collection of cells grown in the laboratory that new medicines can be tested on.

cell The basic unit which living things are made of.

cellulose (plants) A carbohydrate that makes up plant cell walls that together can form a fibre.

cellulose (food) A polymer containing many glucose units which cannot be digested.

central nervous system The spinal cord and brain which coordinate messages in the nervous system.

chain reaction A series of nuclear changes started by a single nuclear fission, resulting in the release of heat, neutrons and new nuclei.

characteristics Features that an organism has, e.g. curly hair.

charge A property of a particle that allows it to exert a force on another charged particle. Charges can be positive (+) or negative (−).

chemical reaction A chemical change in which new substances are formed but there is no change in the number of atoms of each element.

chlorophyll The green chemical in plants that absorbs light energy for photosynthesis.

chromosomes Thread-like strands found in the nucleus of a cell. Chromosomes are made of DNA and contain the 'instructions' for a living thing.

clinical trials Trials in which a new drug is tested on humans to find out whether it is safe and whether it works.

clone An organism produced by asexual reproduction. A clone has exactly the same genes as the organism it was made from.

colours Chemicals added to food to enhance their colour.

coma Being completely unconscious.

combustion The scientific word for burning.

comet A body made of frozen gases and bits of rock that has a long, elliptical orbit.

common ancestor An ancestor shared by two or more descendants.

community A group of different species living in the same habitat.

competition Fighting for the same resource, such as food, space or a mate.

complex behaviour Behaviour which requires learning or thinking, rather than just responding to the environment.

compound A substance containing two or more elements chemically joined together.

compression A force that tries to squash a material.

conservative plate boundary A plate boundary where two plates are sliding past each other.

conserve Protect species from dying out.

contamination The process whereby radioactive materials in the form of gases, solids or liquids get into the human body.

continent A large area of dry land.

continental crust The type of crust that forms the continents.

continental drift The idea that the continents can move around, as explained by Wegener.

control rods Rods that can be moved up or down in the core of a nuclear reactor to control the rate of the chain reaction.

convection current A flow caused by part of a material being heated or cooled more than the rest.

convergent plate boundary A place where two tectonic plates are moving towards each other.

coordinate Link together or organise, as the brain organises how we respond to stimuli.

coronary arteries Arteries that supply the heart muscles with blood, providing oxygen and nutrients for the muscle cells.

correlation When two factors show a similar pattern of change. For example, when one factor increases the other does as well.

corroborate Agree with, or back up.

crater The hole in the ground made by an asteroid or meteorite hitting the Earth or other body. (Craters also form in volcanoes.)

critical mass The mass of the Universe that will just stop it expanding.

cross-links The bond between two polymer molecules.

crude oil A mixture of hydrocarbons formed from dead organisms by heat and pressure over millions of years.

crust The top, solid layer of the Earth.

crystal A solid material in which the particles are arranged in a regular pattern.

crystalline A material that has some regular arrangement of particles.

cuttings Parts cut from a plant that can be grown into new plants.

cystic fibrosis An inherited disease that causes cells to produce sticky mucus. It is caused by a recessive allele.

decompose To break down or split up a compound into two or more substances.

decomposers Organisms that break down dead organisms (e.g. bacteria and fungi).

deform To change shape.

density The mass of a specific volume of a substance, e.g. the mass in kg of 1 m³ of the substance. Density = mass/volume.

descendant An organism that evolved from an ancestor.

designer babies Babies whose genes have been modified to give them particular characteristics, such as being good looking, or good at sport.

detector Something which can detect radiation of a particular wavelength, such as an eye or photographic film.

diabetes A condition where the amount of glucose in the blood is higher than normal.

diabetic A person with diabetes.

digestion Breaking down large food molecules into smaller ones that the body can use.

direct irradiation The process whereby the human body is exposed to an external radioactive source.

divergent plate boundary A place where two tectonic plates are moving apart and new oceanic crust is being formed.

DNA The molecule that carries all the instructions for living organisms; can copy itself.

dominant A dominant allele always shows itself in the offspring.

dormant (volcano) A volcano that has not erupted for many years.

dose A measure of the amount of damage radiation does to the body. It depends on the type of radiation and how much of it there is. Dose is measured in sieverts.

double blind trial A clinical trial in which neither the doctor nor the patient knows whether the patient is taking the new drug.

ductile Property of a material that allows it to be drawn into a wire or fibre.

durable A durable material will not wear out quickly in use.

duration The length of time that something lasts.

effector Cells which carry out the response to a stimulus, such as muscle cells.

efficient Does not waste much energy as heat.

elastic Property of a material that allows it to return to its original shape and size when a force acting on it is removed.

electromagnetic radiation Electromagnetic waves given out by an object, such as light or radio waves.

electromagnetic spectrum The whole range of electromagnetic waves, from gamma rays to radio waves.

electron A particle with a negative charge found outside the nucleus of an atom.

element A substance that cannot be broken down into anything simpler by chemical reactions. An element consists of one type of atom.

embryo The ball of cells that grows from a fertilised egg.

embryonic stem cells Unspecialised cells in an embryo that can develop into any other kind of cell.

emission Something given off by an engine, a factory, etc.

emit To give out (radiation).

emulsifiers Chemicals that bring about emulsification in food.

endangered At risk of becoming extinct, because there are only a few individuals left.

endocrine gland Sensors in the hormonal system which secrete hormones into the blood system.

engulf Scientific word for swallowing. It is what white blood cells do to harmful microorganisms.

E-numbers Numbers given to food additives to show that they have been approved.

environmental conditions Physical conditions of a habitat, such as amount of light, water and wind, as well as all the biological conditions, such as food, competition for space with other organisms, etc.

environmental factors Things such as the amount of food or diseases, that can affect the growth and development of an organism.

enzymes Substances made of protein that speed up chemical reactions in living organisms.

epicentre The place on the surface of the Earth directly above the location of an earthquake.

epidemic A disease that affects many people in a community.

epidemiological studies Study of a large number of people to look for links between a disease and the factors that may cause it.

erosion Wearing away of the land surface or the movement of broken bits of rock.

error The difference between a measurement and the true value.

ethical decisions Decisions about what is right or wrong.

ethical issues Ideas about whether certain things are right or wrong, and whether they should or should not be done.

eutrophication Bacteria multiply by feeding on dead material and use up all the oxygen in the water.

evidence Data or information that can be used to support an idea.

evolutionary tree A diagram which shows how organisms are related to each other through evolution.

evolve Change characteristics over time.

excretion Ridding the body of toxic waste substances.

exposure How much radiation we receive.

extinct A species that no longer exists.

factor A quantity that can be measured, changed or controlled.

fermented When sugar is converted to alcohol by the process of fermentation.

fertilisers Substances added to soil to replace lost nutrients and help plant growth.

fibre (materials) A material which has been drawn into a thread or filament.

fibre (plants) A more common word for cellulose.

film badge A badge, containing photographic film, worn by people who work with radioactive materials. The photographic film is used to check whether people have been exposed to harmful levels of radiation.

flavour enhancers Food additives that are used to improve flavour.

flexibility How bendy a material is.

focus (earthquake) The place where the earthquake starts.

food additives Chemicals added to food during its production.

food chain A diagram which shows how energy is transferred from a producer to the animal that eats it, to the animal that eats that animal and so on.

Food Standards Agency A government organisation that oversees all food standards and safety.

food web A diagram showing how all the food chains within in an environment link together.

formula A short way of showing the atoms in a compound.

fossil fuels Non-renewable fuels such as coal, oil and gas that have formed over millions of years from dead animals and plants.

fossil Preserved remains of organisms, such as bones, found in rocks.

fractional distillation The separation of the components of a mixture which have different boiling points.

fractionating column/tower The tube in which separation of the substances in crude oil takes place. It has a high temperature at the bottom and a lower temperature at the top and collecting trays at various heights.

fractions Parts of crude oil which have boiling points within a certain range.

fuel rods Rods made of uranium used in a nuclear reactor.

fuel A material that is used to release energy.

fungicides Chemicals used to kill fungi and moulds.

fungus A type of microorganism; some of which grow on skin.

fuse When an egg cell and a sperm cell join in fertilisation.

fusion When the nuclei of atoms join together and release energy.

galaxy Millions of stars grouped together.

gametes Sex cells, e.g. sperm cells or egg cells.

gamma radiation Radiation that is given out by an unstable nucleus in the form of photons that travel at the speed of light.

gamma rays A form of electromagnetic radiation with very high energy photons.

Geiger counter A device used to detect radiation.

gender Whether an organism is male or female.

gene therapy Curing an inherited disease by putting correctly working alleles into a person.

gene Part of a chromosome. One gene contains the 'instructions' for a particular feature such as flower colour.

generalist feeder An animal which feeds on many foods.

geohazard A hazard or danger caused by the Earth, such as a volcano or earthquake.

geothermal energy Energy from hot rocks under the Earth's crust.

global warming The gradual warming of the Earth's atmosphere due to the extra carbon dioxide that humans are putting into the atmosphere.

glucose The small unit which makes up cellulose and starch, and which starch turns into during digestion.

greenhouse effect When gases in the atmosphere trap heat energy/ infrared radiation and keep the Earth warm.

greenhouse gas Gases such as carbon dioxide and methane that trap heat in the atmosphere.

habitat A place where a community of plants and animals lives that has a particular group of environmental conditions.

haemophilia An inherited disease that stops blood clotting properly.

half-life The time taken for the activity of a material to halve from an original value.

hardness How difficult it is to scratch or cut a material.

hazard A property of something that could cause harm to health or the environment.

hazcards A set of cards that lists the hazards of substances and ways of dealing with them.

heart attack When the coronary arteries become blocked and the supply of blood to the heart muscle is interrupted, damaging the heart muscle.

heart disease May be caused by a build up of fatty substances in the arteries leading to the heart.

herbicides Chemicals used to kill weeds and other unwanted plants.

heterozygous When two alleles for a characteristic in a cell are different.

high blood pressure Where the heart is having to work harder than it should.

HIV Human immunodeficiency virus – the virus that causes AIDS.

homeostasis Maintaining conditions inside the body at constant levels, such as blood glucose level.

hominid Human-like organism.

homozygous When two alleles for a characteristic in a cell are the same.

hormonal system The part of the body which carries messages from sensor cells and to effector cells using hormones.

hormone A chemical secreted into the blood by an endocrine gland. Hormones control processes in the body.

human trials Trials where new medicines are tested on humans.

Huntington's disease An inherited disease that attacks the nervous system. It is caused by a dominant allele.

hydrocarbon A compound containing only carbon and hydrogen atoms.

hydroelectric power Electrical energy produced when water in a high reservoir is allowed to move quickly downhill and drive a generator.

hypothesis An idea or explanation that can be tested scientifically.

identical twins Making copies of an organism with identical genes to the parent organism.

immune system A system in your body that includes white blood cells, that protects your body from infections.

immune When you can make antibodies to fight a disease quickly so you don't become ill.

impact A collision, such as when a meteorite hits the Earth.

incineration Burning a material completely.

infectious disease A disease that is caused by microorganisms and can pass from one person to another.

influenza An infectious disease caused by a virus that affects the respiratory system.

infrared Electromagnetic radiation with lower photon energies than visible light. We can feel this as heat.

inherit Receive from your parents.

inherited disease A disease that is passed on from parents to offspring by a particular allele.

inherited Characteristics that have come from a parent.

inner core The central, solid part of the Earth.

insecticides Chemicals used to kill insect pests.

insulin A hormone that controls the level of glucose in the blood.

intensity The amount of energy carried by radiation – more intense radiation carries more energy.

ion An atom that has become charged.

ionising radiation Radiation that causes atoms to becomes ions.

ions Charged particles.

isotope Isotopes are atoms of the same element with different numbers of neutrons.

IVF In Vitro Fertilisation. The technique where an egg cell is fertilised in the laboratory, instead of inside the woman's (or animal's) body.

kidneys Organs that clean the blood and remove urea and other molecules for excretion.

lahar A mudflow caused by a volcanic eruption.

landfill Burying rubbish in holes in the ground.

late onset diabetes Another name for Type 2 diabetes.

lattice A regular pattern or arrangement of objects in rows and columns.

lava Molten rock on the surface of the Earth.

Life Cycle Assessment An examination of every stage in the manufacture and use of a material for a particular purpose, comparing its economic and environmental costs with other potential materials.

life cycle (materials) The sequence of events that happen to a material from obtaining the raw materials for its manufacture to its disposal as waste.

life cycle (stars) The changes a star goes through from when it is formed to the end of its life.

lifestyle factors Factors that are affected by the way a person lives their life.

light pollution Light from streetlights or other sources that interferes with observations made using telescopes.

light year The distance that light travels during one year.

lipases Enzymes that help to digest fats.

lithosphere The rigid part of the Earth's surface, consisting of the crust and the upper part of the mantle.

liver The organ that makes and destroys chemicals in our body.

magma Molten rock beneath the surface of the Earth.

magnetic field The space around the Earth where its magnetic effect can be detected.

malleable Property of a material that allows it to change shape when hammered or squeezed.

malnutrition Lacking in essential nutrients.

mantle The layer of the Earth just beneath the crust.

mass extinction When many species become extinct over a short time from a geological point of view (e.g. less than a million years).

mass vaccination When many people in a population are vaccinated against a disease.

Medical ethics committee A group of doctors who decide whether it is right that something should be done just because it can be done.

melting point the temperature at which a solid changes to a liquid.

memory cells White blood cells left in the blood after infection. They make antibodies quickly if you are infected again by that microorganism.

metal A material that is malleable and ductile, conducts electricity and heat and can be shiny.

meteor A small piece of rock that burns up as it passes through the atmosphere.

meteorite A piece of rock that is not burnt up in the atmosphere and hits the Earth.

microorganism Any organism that you can only see clearly with a microscope.

microwaves Electromagnetic radiation with photon energies between infrared and radio waves. Can be used for mobile phone communication and cooking food.

Milky Way The name of the galaxy that our Sun is part of.

mixture A substance composed of two or more elements or compounds not joined together.

molecule A particle made up of two or more atoms joined together.

monomer A small molecule which can combine with itself or other monomers to make a polymer.

multicellular organisms Organisms made of many cells, i.e. almost all the plants and animals you see.

mutation Error in copying a gene which creates a new allele; this may or may not affect the organism, depending on how great the error is.

naphtha The fraction of crude oil with a boiling range of 100–150 °C, used in chemical manufacture.

natural fertiliser A fertiliser made from animal and plant waste.

natural selection When variations in characteristics are selected by the environment, and only individuals with successful characteristics survive to breed.

natural Occurs in nature.

nervous system The part of the body which carries messages from sensor cells and to effector cells along nerves.

neutral Something that has no charge.

neutron A particle with no charge found in the nucleus of an atom.

nitrates Compounds containing nitrogen that plants absorb and use.

nitrogen cycle The way that nitrogen is cycled in nature.

nitrogen The element most necessary for plant growth.

nitrogen-fixing bacteria Bacteria which can remove nitrogen directly from the air.

non-biodegradable Cannot be broken down by organisms in the environment.

non-renewable A non-renewable fuel cannot be replaced and will eventually run out.

NO$_X$ General term for the oxides of nitrogen, i.e. nitrogen oxide and nitrogen dioxide.

nuclear bomb A nuclear weapon in which a chain reaction is not controlled so a huge amount of energy is released at once.

nuclear fission The process of splitting nuclei in a nuclear power station to release large amounts of heat energy.

nuclear fuel The fuel used in nuclear power stations, especially uranium.

nuclear waste The waste materials from a nuclear power station.

nucleus (physics) The central part of an atom.

nucleus (biology) The 'control centre' of a cell. It contains the chromosomes.

obesity Being very overweight.

occupational radiation Radiation that people are exposed to in their place of work.

oceanic crust The type of crust that forms the ocean floors.

oceanic ridge A ridge in the middle of an ocean where new oceanic crust is being created.

oceanic trench A deep part of the ocean caused when one plate moves down beneath another.

osteoarthritis When the joints wear away.

outcome The result of an action or change in a factor.

outer core A liquid layer in the Earth, which lies above the solid inner core.

outlier A measurement that is very different from the other readings in a set of data.

ovaries Female sex organs which produce eggs.

ozone layer Part of the atmosphere where ozone is concentrated.

ozone Three oxygen atoms in one molecule.

pancreas The organ that makes insulin.

parallax A way of finding the distance to stars by measuring the angle of a star at different times of year.

particles The smallest bits of matter that exist in a solid, liquid or gas.

particulate carbon Tiny pieces of solid carbon.

particulates Tiny pieces of solid material.

passive immunity Immunity given by an injection of ready-made antibodies into the body.

perceived risk The risk that someone thinks is present.

pesticides Chemicals used to kill pests that destroy crops.

pH A measure of the acidity of a solution; the lower the pH number the stronger the acid.

phosphates Chemical compounds containing phosphorus needed for healthy plant growth.

photon A 'packet' of energy carried by electromagnetic radiation.

photosynthesis The chemical reaction that happens in plants. It uses light energy to convert carbon dioxide and water into sugar and oxygen.

placebo Looks like the drug being tested in clinical trials but contains no actual medicine.

planet Something that orbits a star. The Earth is a planet.

planetary nebula A shell of dust and gas thrown off at the end of the red giant part of a star's life.

plaque Fatty lump that can develop on the inside wall of a blood vessel and block it. In a coronary artery, this leads to a heart attack.

plastic Property of a material that allows it to keep its new shape and size when a force acting on it is removed.

plasticiser Small molecules mixed with a polymer to keep the polymer molecules apart.

plastics A commonly used word for polymer materials.

plate tectonics The theory that parts of the surface of the Earth move around.

pollutant A substance present in the environment as a result of human activity that can harm the environment or health.

pollution index A number based on the mean amounts of each pollutant present.

polymer A material made up of very long molecules formed when lots of small molecules join together.

polymerisation The process in which monomer molecules join together to form a polymer.

positive In terms of a medical or genetic test, a positive result means that the person has the disease or the allele that could cause a disease.

potassium A chemical element needed for healthy plant growth.

precautionary principle An idea that new technology should be thoroughly tested before people are allowed to use it. Often explained by the phrase 'better safe than sorry'.

predict Say what will happen in the future, based on a theory.

prediction Something that a hypothesis or theory says will happen under certain conditions and can be tested.

pre-implantation genetic testing When an embryo from IVF is tested for genetic diseases before being implanted into a woman.

preservatives Chemicals added to food to prevent the growth of bacteria and fungi.

product The substances formed during a chemical reaction.

proof Evidence which shows that a prediction is correct.

proteases Enzymes that break down proteins into amino acids.

protein A polymer made up of amino acids, containing carbon, hydrogen, oxygen and nitrogen. Our genes carry the instructions for making proteins.

proton A positively charged particle found in the nucleus of an atom.

prove Show that something is definitely right.

public authorities Governments or local councils who are responsible for people's safety.

pyroclastic flow A fast-moving cloud of hot gases, ash, dust and rock caused by a volcanic eruption.

radiation Particles and rays that are given out by radioactive materials.

radio waves Electromagnetic radiation with low photon energies. Used to transmit TV and radio programmes.

radioactive Any material that gives out alpha, beta or gamma radiation.

radioactive dating A way of dating a rock or other material by measuring the amount of different radioactive materials in it.

radioactive decay The process whereby an unstable nucleus turns into a more stable nucleus by giving out alpha, beta or gamma radiation.

radon A radioactive gas.

range The difference between the largest and smallest value in a set of data.

reactant The substances present at the start of a reaction.

receptor Another word for sensor.

recessive A recessive allele only works when both chromosomes in a pair have the same allele.

recycling Reusing a material over and over again.

red giant A star that has used up its hydrogen fuel and expanded.

refining The separation and purification of materials obtained from a natural resource.

reflect Bounce something back from a surface.

reliable Results that can be trusted because the study was carried out properly.

renewable energy resources Renewable resources will not run out.

reprocessing plant A building where useful nuclear fuel is recycled or extracted from nuclear waste for reuse in the nuclear reactor.

residence time The length of time a substance remains in an environment.

respiration The chemical reaction that happens in all living cells to release energy by converting sugar and oxygen into carbon dioxide and water.

risk An estimate of how dangerous a hazard is in a particular situation.

rubber A material that is elastic and deforms relatively easily.

seafloor spreading The formation of new crust at oceanic ridges, which causes oceans to become wider.

secondary energy source A source of energy that is produced from another primary source. For example, electricity is a secondary source because it is produced using other forms of energy (such as by burning fossil fuels).

secrete Release a substance made by a cell, such as a hormone.

sedimentation When sediments are deposited.

sediments Bits of rock formed by weathering.

seismic waves Waves that move through and around the Earth after an earthquake.

selective breeding When humans choose which characteristics they want and breed from organisms which show them.

sensor (measurement) An instrument that can detect a change in some property of the environment and give a reading, e.g. a thermometer, carbon monoxide sensor.

sensor (biology) Cells which respond to a stimulus, such as cells in the eye or ear, also called receptor.

sex chromosomes Either of the X or Y chromosomes that determine the sex of an organism. In humans, a female has XX sex chromosomes and a male has XY sex chromosomes.

sexual reproduction Reproduction that involves a male and a female. Sex cells from each parent fuse at fertilisation.

side-effects The unwanted effects on the body of a vaccine or medicine.

sievert (Sv) The unit of dose.

solar power Energy from the Sun. Light energy from the Sun is converted into electrical energy by solar cells. Some solar panels use the Sun's heat energy to heat buildings.

Solar System The Sun and all the planets, asteroids and comets that are orbiting it.

source Something that gives out electromagnetic waves or radiation.

specialised A cell that has features that help it to carry out its function.

specialist feeder An animal which feeds on only one type of food.

species (in evolution) a group of organisms with the same characteristics; (living) a group of organisms with the same characteristics that can breed with each other and produce fertile offspring.

specific Something that works on only one thing. For example, each enzyme will only work on one type of substance, and each antibiotic will only control one type of microorganism.

stabilisers Chemicals that keep foods emulsified.

stable A material that does not change.

star A large ball of gas that produces heat and light energy.

starch A polymer made up of glucose units, which can be digested. It contains carbon, hydrogen and oxygen.

stimulus A change in the environment that an organism responds to.

strain A new form of a microorganism.

strength Property of a material that determines the force required to break it.

structural protein Proteins that make up parts of the body such as muscles, skin or hair.

subduction zone A zone where an oceanic plate is moving down beneath another plate.

sustainability The ability of a resource to be used and replaced without damage to the wenvironment.

sustainable Can continue for many years without damaging the environment.

sustainable development A programme of developing new energy technology that does not harm the environment.

sweeteners Chemicals added to foods to make them sweeter.

symptoms Effects of disease on the body.

synthetic fertiliser A fertiliser made by a chemical process.

synthetic Manufactured from other substances.

target cell The effector in the hormonal system, where a hormone makes something happen.

tax A sum of money that people have to pay to the government for a service.

technical feasibility What can be done, based on what technology is available.

tectonic plates Sections of the surface of the Earth that can move around.

tension A force that tries to stretch a material.

terminate To stop – this usually refers to stopping a pregnancy (having an abortion).

testes Male sex organs which produce sperm.

theory An idea that is tested and explains a wide range of observations.

therapeutic cloning Cloning an adult human so that stem cells from the resulting embryo can be used as a treatment for illness.

thrombosis A 'clot' of blood causing a blockage.

tidal power Energy from the tides.

tool An object which is used to make something else happen.

toughness Property of a material that allows it to resist change of shape when a force acts on it.

toxic Poisonous.

toxins Poisonous chemicals released by harmful microorganisms.

trace A tiny amount of a substance in a mixture.

transmit Send or allow energy or waves to go through something.

Type 1 diabetes Diabetes that occurs when the pancreas does not make any insulin.

Type 2 diabetes Diabetes that occurs when the pancreas does not make enough insulin.

ultraviolet Electromagnetic radiation with higher photon energies than visible light. It can give us a suntan or skin cancer.

uncertainty The difference between a reading and the true value.

unstable A material that becomes more stable by giving out radiation.

uranium A radioactive material used in nuclear reactors.

urea The waste product of the breakdown of unwanted amino acids.

vaccinate Introduce a vaccine into the body to give you immunity to a disease.

vaccination Giving someone a vaccine.

vaccine Weakened or dead microorganisms which are put into the body to make you immune to a disease.

values What should be done based on ethical issues.

variation Differences in characteristics, such as colour of eye, length of neck.

variety A subgroup of a species which has a slightly different set of characteristics.

veins Large blood vessels that carry blood back to the heart.

vent (volcano) The part of a volcano where lava or gases and ash come out.

vertebrate Animals with backbones.

virus Very small type of microorganism that can only reproduce inside the cells of another organism.

viscous Does not flow easily.

visible spectrum The part of the electromagnetic spectrum that is detected by our eyes.

wave power Energy from waves on the sea.

wavelength The length of one complete wave.

weathering The process of breaking up rocks.

white blood cells Cells that help destroy harmful microorganisms which have invaded the body.

white dwarf A small star that forms when a red giant collapses.

wind power The use of wind turbines to generate electricity.

X-rays High energy electromagnetic radiation. Can be used to detect broken bones.

yield The amount of useful substance produced by a crop plant.

Index

abortion **23–5**
acid rain **48–9, 231**
acrylamide **205**
activity (radioactive materials) **222–3**
adaptation **170**
additives **198–201**
aflatoxin **203**
AIDS **87, 95**
air pollution **34–59**
ALARA principle **146, 229**
alleles **18–19, 171**
allergies **203**
alpha radiation **220, 224**
amino acids **206, 209**
amylases **206**
anaemia **213**
anaphylaxis **203**
angina **107**
antibiotics **100–1**
antibodies **92, 94**
antigens **92, 95**
antioxidants **198**
argon **39**
arteries **106, 212**
asexual reproduction **12–13**
asteroids **74, 76–7**
asthma **35, 40, 51, 59**
atmosphere **38–9, 76, 148, 166**
atoms **42, 219, 224**

background radiation **218**
bacteria **12, 88, 100**
becquerel (Bq) **222**
best estimates **37, 115**
beta radiation **220, 224**
bias **103**
Big Bang **82**
biodegradable materials **132**
biodiversity **186–7**
biofuels **232–3**
bisphenol **205**
breathing **34–5**
brittle materials **118**

cancer **145–7, 213, 224–5**
capillaries **106**
carbon cycle **152–3**
carbon dioxide
    atmosphere **39**
    carbon cycle **152–3**
    global warming **158–9**
    greenhouse effect **154–5**
    molecules **42–3**
    photosynthesis **150–1**
    pollution **45, 49**
carbon monoxide **41, 46**
carriers **21**

cars **35, 54–5**
catalytic converters **55, 58**
cell specialisation **16–17, 174**
cellulose **206**
central nervous system **176**
CFCs **149**
characteristics **10, 170**
charged particles **219**
chemical reactions **42–3**
chlorophyll **150**
chromosomes **10, 14–15, 17**
climate change **156**
clinical trials **102**
clones **12–13, 28–9**
coal **44, 47–8, 50**
colourings **198**
combustion **44–7, 152–3**
comets **75, 166**
communication systems **176–7**
competition **181–2**
complex behaviour **178**
compounds **42–3, 112**
compression **118**
conservation **185**
contamination **202–5, 226**
continental drift **64–5**
convection currents **67**
cooking **143**
cork **127**
coronary arteries **107**
correlations **50–2, 108–9, 158–9**
craters **75**
critical mass **83**
crops **157, 195**
cross-linking **130**
crude oil **122–5**
crust **62**
crystallinity **129–30**
cultures **102**
cystic fibrosis **21–2**

decomposers **152, 193**
defences **90–1**
density **117**
designer babies **27**
diabetes **210–11**
diet **211–13**
digestion **206–7**
dinosaurs **77**
diphtheria **89**
disease **20–3, 50, 88–9, 157, 183**
DNA **10–11, 95, 167, 169**
Dolly the sheep **28**
dominant alleles **18–20, 22**
ductile materials **118**
durable materials **118**
dust **39, 46**

E-numbers **199**
Earth **62–3, 74, 154–7, 166–7**
earthquakes **72–3**
effector cells **174–5**
egg cells **14–15**
elasticity **118**
electricity **52–3, 55, 230–1**
electromagnetic spectrum **140–1**
electrons **219, 224**
elements **42–3, 81, 112, 219**
embryonic stem cells **17, 29–31**
embryos **17, 27, 30–1**
emissions **55, 159**
emulsifiers **199**
endangered species **184**
endocrine glands **177**
energy **128, 142, 208**
environmental factors **10, 13**
enzymes **11, 206–7**
epidemics **95, 97**
epidemiological studies **108**
erosion **62–3**
errors of measurement **37**
ethene **126, 128**
ethical issues **9, 24–5, 30–1, 87, 103–5**
eutrophication **193**
evolution **168–73, 178–9**
excretion **209**
extinction **77, 157, 164–5, 167, 182–5**

farming **194–7**
fat **209, 212**
fermentation **233**
fertilisers **192–4**
fibre (nutrition) **206**
fibres (materials) **120–1**
film badges **227**
flavour enhancers **199**
flexibility **119**
food **190–215, 218**
food webs **180–1, 186**
formulae **42**
fossil fuels **44–7, 52–3, 153, 230–1**
fossils **64, 166, 168, 182, 223**
fractional distillation **124–5**
fuels **44–7, 52–5, 125, 152–3, 230–1**
fungi **88, 100, 195**
fusion **80**

Galapagos finches **173**
galaxies **60, 82–3**
gametes **10, 14**
gamma radiation **141, 146, 220–1, 224, 234**
gases **38–9, 44, 149, 154–5, 158–9, 166**
Geiger counters **220, 222**
gender **14–15**
gene therapy **26–7**
generalist feeders **181**
generators **230**
genes **8–13, 26–7, 171, 187**
genetic testing **23–5**
geohazards **70–3**
geothermal energy **232**

global warming **139, 155–61, 231**
glucose **177, 206–10**
gravity **74, 80, 83**
greenhouse effect **154–5**
greenhouse gases **154–5, 158–9**

habitats **180, 186**
half-life **222–3**
hardness **119**
hazards **40–1, 70–3**
health **50–1, 212–13**
heart attacks **107–9**
heart disease **106–7, 212**
heat **142–3**
herbicides **195**
heterozygous organisms **18–19**
high blood pressure **213**
HIV **95**
homeostasis **177**
hominid species **178–9**
homozygous organisms **18–19**
hormones **17, 177, 210**
Huntington's disease **20, 22**
hydrocarbons **44–5, 122–3**
hydroelectric power **233**
hydrogen sulfide **41**
hypothesis **172–3**

immunity **92–3, 95**
incineration **132**
infection **92–3**
influenza **95**
infrared radiation **141–3, 154–5, 159**
inheritance **12, 20–3, 170**
insects **157, 195**
insulin **177, 210–11**
intensive farming **194–5**
ionising radiation **146–7, 224–5**
ions **146, 224**
isotopes **219**
IVF **8–9, 15, 23**

lahars **71**
landfills **132**
lava **70**
laws **53, 56**
Life Cycle Assessment (LCA) **134–5**
life cycles
    polymers **132–3**
    stars **81**
lifestyle **107**
light **140**
light years **78**
lipases **206**
lithosphere **66**

magma **67, 70**
magnetism **66**
magnitude **79**
malleable materials **118**
malnutrition **190**
mantle **66–7**
manure **196**

mass **117**
materials **112–37**
mean **37**
medicines **102–3**
melting points **116, 126**
memory cells **93–4**
meteor(ite)s **75**
methane **154–5, 159**
microorganisms **87–93, 100**
microwaves **141, 143–5**
Milky Way **60, 82**
mobile phones **144–5**
molecules **42–3, 112, 122–3, 128, 167**
monomers **126**
mountains **64–5**
mutations **95, 171**

natural gas **44**
natural selection **170–1**
nervous system **20, 176**
neutrons **219**
nitrite **198**
nitrogen **38–9, 192–3**
nitrogen oxides **41, 47, 59**
non-renewable resources **231, 236–7**
nuclear power **234–5**
nuclear waste **223, 235**
nuclei **10, 80, 219**

obesity **190, 212**
oceans **49, 66–7**
organ transplants **29**
organic farming **196–7**
osteoarthritis **213**
outliers **37, 115**
oxygen **38–9, 45–6, 148**
ozone **39, 148**
ozone layer **148–9**

packaging **204**
Pangaea **65**
parallax **79**
parasites **183, 193**
particles **112, 219**
particulates **39, 46, 48**
penicillin **100**
pesticides **195, 197**
pests **195–6**
pH **207**
phosphates **193**
photons **140–2**
photosynthesis **39, 49, 150–1, 192**
placebos **103**
plankton **150**
plants **12–13, 18–19, 150–1, 192–3**
plasticisers **131**
plasticity **118**
plastics **120–1**
plate tectonics **66–7**
pollution **34–59**
polymers **126–35, 206**
polythene **126, 128**
potassium **193**

power stations **52–3**
precautionary principle **145, 228**
predictions **68–9, 173**
preservatives **199**
proof **69, 173**
properties **116–21**
proteases **206**
proteins **11, 192, 206, 208**
protons **219**
pyroclastic flows **71**

radiation **78, 138–63, 218–21, 224–9**
radio waves **141, 144**
radioactive dating **66**
radioactive decay **220–1**
radioactivity **216–29**
radon **218**
range **37, 115**
recessive alleles **18–19, 21–2**
recycling **133**
red giants **81**
refining **124**
reliability **109**
renewable resources **232–3, 236–7**
reproduction **8–9, 12–13**
resistance **100**
respiration **150, 177, 208**
ringworm **89**
risks **41, 147, 228**
rocks **62, 166, 218, 223**
rubbers **120–1**
rubella **89**

sea levels **156**
seafloor spreading **67**
sedimentation **63**
seismic waves **72**
selective breeding **172**
sensor cells **174–5**
sex organs **17**
sexual reproduction **12–13**
sickle cell disease **171**
side-effects **94, 97**
sieverts (Sv) **225**
skin cancer **147**
smog **50**
smoking **109**
soil **194**
Solar System **60, 74–5**
soot **39, 46, 48**
specialised cells **16–17, 174**
specialist feeders **181**
species **167, 182–5**
sperm cells **14–15**
stabilisers **198**
stable elements **219**
starch **206–7**
stars **60, 78–9**
steel **118**
stem cells **17, 29–31**
stiffness **119**
stimuli **174–5**
strength **118**

structural proteins **11**
sulfur dioxide **40–1, 47, 55, 59**
Sun **60, 74, 80–1, 142, 150**
sustainability **134, 186, 238–9**
sweeteners **199**
symptoms **89**

tectonic plates **66–7, 72**
temperature **128**
tension **118**
testing treatments **102–5**
theories **51, 68–9, 128, 130, 173**
therapeutic cloning **29**
tin **205**
tough materials **118**
toxicity **41, 202**
toxins **89–90**
trace gases **39**
transport **54–5**
treatments **102–3**
twins **28**

ultraviolet radiation **141, 146–9**
Universe **82–3**
unstable elements **219–21**
uranium **219, 234**
urea **209**

vaccination **86–7, 93–9**
variation **170–1**
veins **106**
viruses **88, 100**
visible radiation **141**
volcanoes **40, 70–1**
volume **117**

waste disposal **132–3**
water vapour **38, 154–5**
weathering **62–3**
weeds **195**
white blood cells **92**
white dwarfs **81**
whooping cough **96–7**
wind power **232**

X-rays **141, 146**

Pearson Education
Edinburgh Gate
Harlow
Essex
CM20 2JE
UK
www.longman.co.uk

First published 2006
Fifth impression 2009
ISBN 978-0-582-85335-5

Project management and development editor	Sue Kearsey
Editor	Liz Jones
Design and production	Roarr Design
Illustration	Oxford Designers & Illustrators Ltd
Picture research	Charlotte Lippmann
Indexer	Indexing Specialists (UK) Ltd

Printed in China   GCC/05

The publisher's policy is to use paper manufactured from sustainable forests.

Acknowledgments

The publisher would like to thank Basil Donnelly, Leonie Garratt, Christina Garry, Ben Green, Miles Hudson, Peter Kennett, Alison Knowles, Colin Lever, Alistair Sandiforth and Dorothy Warren, for their help in the production of this book.

We are grateful to the following for permission to reproduce photographs:

Advertising Archives: pg109; **Agripicture**: pg196 (Peter Dean); **Alamy**: pg10 (Photofusion/Liam Bailey), pg18(t) (Imagebroker/Martin Siepmann), pg31(t) (Imagestate/Pictor International), pg31(m) (Network Photographers), pg32(t) (Comstock Images), pg35(l) (Robert Harding), pg36 (Keith Dannemiller), pg44(m) (Carlos Davila), pg48(br) (Phototake Inc./ Mauritius, GmbH), pg86(l) (ImageBroker/Harald Theissen), pg86(m) (Phototake Inc./Yoav Levy), pg87(b) (David Young-Wolff), pg102(br) (Agstock USA, Inc./Ed Young), pg103 (Tetra Images), pg108 (John Powell), pg112(tr) (Robert Harding Picture Library/Glyn Genin), pg112(ml) (1Apix), pg113(ml) (Jeff Morgan), pg114(l) (Plainpicture GmbH & Co. KG/Sebastian), pg117(t) (Dominic Burke), pg118(bl) (Adrian Muttitt), pg118(br) (Janine Wiedel), pg120(r) (Network Photographers), pg122 (Holt Studios International Ltd), pg132(l), pg142(m) (Bilderlounge/BreBa), pg144 (Acestock Ltd.), pg147(b) (David Sanger), pg177 (Noel Yates), pg185(ml) (Terry Whittaker), pg194(t) (Alistair Balderstone), pg212(tr) (Dennis MacDonald), pg216(t) (Image 100), pg216(m) (John Foxx), pg216(b) (Image Source), pg217(tr) (Image 100), pg217(tl) (Dymanic Graphics Group/IT Stock Free), pg217(r) (Pictor International), pg220 (Powered By Light RF), pg228(t) (Clynt Garnham), pg228(r) (Medicolors), pg230 (LGPL/Jim Gibson), pg232 (Paul Glendell); **Anthony Blake Photo Library**: pg116(t); **Ardea**: pg14(t) (Pat Morris), pg171(mr) (John Mason); **BP**: pg124; **Collections**: pg48(tl) (Brian Shuel), pg54(mr), pg57(b), pg138, pg139, pg181(bl), pg218; **Corbis**: pg16(t) (LWA/Dann Tardiff), pg23 (LWA/Dann Tardiff), pg30(t) (George Shelley), pg30(bl) (George Shelley), pg31(b) (Michael Prince), pg32(b) (Rob Lewine), pg40 (Roger Ressmeyer), pg44(r) (Toby Melville/Reuters), pg48(tr) (WildCountry), pg48(bl) (Ted Spiegal), pg54(b) (SABA/Tom Wagner), pg69 (Ralph White), pg70 (Bettmann), pg71(l) (Roger Ressmeyer), pg71(r) (Alberto Garcia), pg73 (Underwood & Underwood), pg86(r) (Karen Kasmauski), pg93 (Jose Luis Pelaez, Inc.), pg96(l) (Steve Raymer), pg112(tl) (Reuters), pg118(m) (Marc Lecureuil), pg119 (Martyn Goddard), pg135(tr) (Bettmann), pg142(t) (Royalty-Free), pg159(tr) (Reuters/ Toby Melville), pg202(bl) (Adam Woolfitt), pg202(br) (Wolfgang Kaehler), pg215 (Paul Barton), pg227(l) (Sygma/Bernard Bisson), pg227(r) (Charles O'Rear), pg236 (Bettmann), pg235 (Igor Kostin); **Crown Copyright**: pg98, pg212(tl); **Custom Medical Stock Photo**: pg20(t), pg20(b) (Jan Leestma); **Ecoscene**: pg34(t) (Amanda Gazidis), pg34(m) (Jon Bower), pg193 (Nick Hawkes); **Eduardo Kac**: pg27 (GFP Bunny, 2000. Alba the fluorescent Bunny); **FLPA**: pg150(r) (David Wilson), pg159(b) (Peter Davey), pg172(tr) (Jean Michel Labat), pg173(l) (Minden Pictures/Tui de Roy), pg173(r) (Michael Gore); **Food Features**: pg117(m), pg213(m), pg218;

Galaxy: pg75(m) (Kipp Teague/David Wood/NASA), pg76(bl) (Andrew Stewart), pg82(l) (Howard Brown-Greaves); **Getty Images**: pg8 (Keystone), pg26(l) (TimeLife Pictures/Ted Thai), pg50 (Keystone), pg100(t) (TimeLife/ W. Eugene Smith), pg191(tm) (Digital Vision); **GLKS**: pg187 (Klaus Dehmer); **Holt Studios**: pg18(m) (Nigel Cattlin), pg193, pg195(t), pg195(b); **Manchester Metro**: pg55; **Marwell Preservation Trust**: pg185(mr) (Bill Hall); **Mickie Gelsinger**: pg26(r); **Mike Lippmann**: pg135; **Missouri State University**: pg76(t) (Kevin R. Evans); **Mountain Camera**: pg49 (John Cleare), pg62(bl) (John Cleare), pg62(br) (John Cleare), pg63(tl) (John Cleare), pg63(tr) (John Cleare), pg64(tl) (John Cleare), pg65 (John Cleare), pg84 (John Cleare), pg166(l) (John Cleare); **NASA**: pg74, pg78(b), pg80(tl), pg80(tr), pg81, pg166(b); **Natural History Museum**: pg68, pg223; **Nature Picture Library**: pg174(r) (Jeff Rotman), pg184(tm) (Dave Watts), pg185(tl) (Paul Hobson); **NHPA**: pg12(m) (George Bernard), pg13(l) (George Bernard), pg152 (Jordi Bas Casas), pg154 (Alberto Nardi), pg164(t) (Daniel Zupanc), pg164(r) (Martin Harvey), pg164(b) (B. Jones & M Shimlock), pg167 (A.N.T. Photo Library), pg168 (Daniel Heuclin), pg169 (Christophe Ratier), pg171(ml) (Stephen Dalton), pg172(tl) (David Middleton), pg172(mr) (Yves Lanceau), pg174(l) (Mark Bowler), pg178(tm) (Jonathan & Angela Scott), pg178(tr) (Steve Robinson), pg181(t) (Stephen Dalton), pg181(br) (Steve Toon), pg183 (Melvin Grey), pg184(m) (A.N.T. Photo Library), pg184(r) (David Middleton), pg185(tr) (Martin Harvey), pg186(tr) (Ernie James), pg186(b) (Trevor MacDonald), pg191(b) (Ernie James), pg202(tl) (Guy Edwardes), pg202(tr) (George Bernard); **Oxford Scientific**: pg13(r) (Kent Breck); **Panos**: pg238(r) (Mark Henley); **Photofusion**: pg56(b) (Paul Ridsdale); **Photographers Direct**: pg237 (Anders Carlsson); **Reuters**: pg159(tl) (Utpal Baruah); **Rex Features**: pg54(t) (Philippe Hays), pg57(t) (Shout), pg72 (Sipa Press), pg102(t) (Hayley Madden), pg114(r) (Matt Baron); **Ronald Grant Archive**: pg61(r); **Science Photo Library**: pg9(t) (Bsip, Laurent), pg9(m) (Hank Morgan), pg11 (Michael Donne), pg12(b) (David Scharf), pg14(b) (Biophoto Associates), pg16(bl), pg16(bm) (Bioogy Media), pg16(br) (Francois Paquet-Durand), pg17(t) (Andy Walker, Midland Fertility Services), pg17(m) (Steve Allen), pg21 (Hattie Young), pg28(t) (Helen Mcardle), pg28(b) (Gusto), pg35(m) (Ian Boddy), pg35(r) (James King-Holmes), pg39(m) (Robert Brook), pg42 (Shelia Terry), pg43 (Andrew Lambert), pg44(l) (Steve Allen), pg56(t) (Nasa), pg60(m) (M-Sat Ltd), pg60(b) (Planetary Visions Ltd), pg64(tr) (Jerry Lodriguss), pg75(b) (John Sanford), pg76(br) (Julian Baum), pg77 (D. Van Ravensway), pg78(t) (David Parker), pg79, pg80(b) (Frank Zullo), pg82(r) (Robert Gendler), pg83 (Emilio Segre Visual Archives/American Institute of Physics), pg87(t) (CDC), pg88(l) (Dr. Linda Stannard, UCT), pg88(m) (Andrew Syred), pg88(r) (Dr. M.A. Ansary), pg94(l) (Ian Hooton), pg94(r) (Samuel Ashfield), pg95 (Andy Crump/TDR,WHO), pg96(m), pg96(r) (Dr. M.A. Ansary), pg99(l) (CC Studio), pg100(m) (Scott Camazine), pg101 (Damien Lovegrove), pg102(bl) (BSIP, Laurent H. Americain), pg110 (Mark Clarke), pg113(t) (Agstock/Harris Barnes Jr.), pg116(b) (Heine Schneebeli), pg121(m) (Alexis Rosenfeld), pg128 (Alex Bartel), pg133 (David Nunuk), pg135(mr) (Philippe Psaila), pg140 (Duncan Shaw), pg141 (Ted Kinsman), pg146(t) (Sinclair Stammers), pg146(b) (Scott Camazine), pg147(t) (Erika Craddock), pg161 (D. A. Peel), pg165(l) (Jeremy Walker), pg171(r) (Eye of Science), pg172(r) (Pascal Goetcheluck), pg178(b) (Pat & Tom Lesson), pg184(l) (Pat & Tom Lesson), pg203(t) (Mark Thomas), pg209 (BSIP, VEM), pg210 (Cordelia Molloy), pg211(t) (Samuel Ashfield), pg212(b) (Shelia Terry), pg219 (Astrid & Hanns Frieder), pg224 (James King-Holmes), pg225 (Cordelia Molloy), pg229(t) (Antonia Reeve), pg229(r) (Dr. P. Marazzi), pg233(l) (Martin Bond), pg233(m) (Martin Bond), pg233(t) (Martin Bond), pg238(b) (M-Sat Ltd.); **Skyscan**: pg60(t); **Still Pictures**: pg39(l) (Jeff & Alexa Henry), pg46 (UNEP/Anil Risal Singh), pg52 (Jorgen Schytte), pg53 (Das Fotoarchiv/ Manfred Vollmer), pg54(ml) (Das Fotoarchiv/Friedrich Stark), pg61(l) (Shezad Noorani), pg61(m) (UNEP/Robert T. Wells), pg85 (Peter Arnold), pg99(r) (Lineair), pg132(r) (Paul Glendell), pg135(l) (Paul Glendell), pg150(l) (Martin Bond), pg165(m) (Jean-Luc Ziegler), pg165(r) (Martin Wendler), pg178(tl) (Steve Kaufman), pg182 (Otto Hahn), pg191(tr) (Lineair Fotoarchief), pg191(m) (UNEP), pg203(b) (Das Fotoarchiv); **TopFoto**: pg198(t) (Heritage Image Partners); **Warren Photographic**: pg12(l) (Jane Burton); **Woodfall Wild Images**: pg186(tl) (David Woodfall), pg194(b) (Peter Wilson); **www.glofish.com**: pg26(t).

The following photographs were taken on commission © **Pearson Education Ltd. By:**
Rick Chapman: pg34(r), pg47, pg112(m,r), pg120(t, r), pg121(t), pg127, pg136, pg142, pg143(t,m), pg144, pg153, pg191(t), pg197, pg198(l,mr), pg199, pg203(mr), pg204(all), pg205(all), pg211(t), pg213 (t), pg214; **Trevor Clifford**: pg87(t), pg100(b), pg115, pg119, pg125 (t), pg131, pg207.

Front cover photos:
Main image: ©David Trood / The Image Bank / Getty Images
Inset: (top)©Denis Scott / Taxi / Getty Images; (middle) ©Bryan Peterson / Taxi / Getty Images; (bottom) Punchstock / Digital Vision (royalty-free).

Licence Agreement: *21st Century Science GCSE Higher CD-ROM*

Warning:
This is a legally binding agreement between You (the school) and Pearson Education Limited of Edinburgh Gate, Harlow, Essex, CM20 2JE, United Kingdom ('PEL').

By retaining this Licence, any software media or accompanying written materials or carrying out any of the permitted activities You are agreeing to be bound by the terms and conditions of this Licence. If You do not agree to the terms and conditions of this Licence, do not continue to use the CD and promptly return the entire publication (this Licence and all software, written materials, packaging and any other component received with it) with Your sales receipt to Your supplier for a full refund.

21st Century Science GCSE Higher CD-ROM consists of copyright software and data. The copyright is owned by PEL. You only own the disk on which the software is supplied. If You do not continue to do only what You are allowed to do as contained in this Licence you will be in breach of the Licence and PEL shall have the right to terminate this Licence by written notice and take action to recover from you any damages suffered by PEL as a result of your breach.

Yes, You can:
1. use or install *21st Century Science GCSE Higher CD-ROM* on Your own personal computer as a single individual user:

No, You cannot:
1. copy *21st Century Science GCSE Higher CD-ROM* (other than making one copy for back-up purposes);

2. alter *21st Century Science GCSE Higher CD-ROM,* or in any way reverse engineer, decompile or create a derivative product from the contents of the database or any software included in it:

3. include any software data from *21st Century Science GCSE Higher CD-ROM* in any other product or software materials;

4. rent, hire, lend or sell *21st Century Science High   D-ROM*;

5. copy any part of the documentation except where specifically indicated otherwise;

6. use the software in any way not specified above without the prior written consent of PEL

Grant of Licence:
PEL grants You, provided You only do what is allowed under the Yes, You can table above, and do nothing under the No, You cannot table above, a non-exclusive, non-transferable Licence to use *21st Century Science GCSE Higher CD-ROM.*.

The above terms and conditions of this Licence become operative when using *21st Century Science GCSE Higher CD-ROM.*

Limited Warranty:
PEL warrants that the disk or CD-ROM on which the software is supplied is free from defects in material and workmanship in normal use for ninety (90) days from the date You receive it. This warranty is limited to You and is not transferable.

This limited warranty is void if any damage has resulted from accident, abuse, misapplication, service or modification by someone other than PEL. In no event shall PEL be liable for any damages whatsoever arising out of installation of the software, even if advised of the possibility of such damages. PEL will not be liable for any loss or damage of any nature suffered by any party as a result of reliance upon or reproduction of any errors in the content of the publication.

PEL does not warrant that the functions of the software meet Your requirements or that the media is compatible with any computer system on which it is used or that the operation of the software will be unlimited or error free. You assume responsibility for selecting the software to achieve Your intended results and for the installation of, the use of and the results obtained from the software.

PEL shall not be liable for any loss or damage of any kind (except for personal injury or death) arising from the use of *21st Century Science GCSE Higher CD-ROM* or from errors, deficiencies or faults therein, whether such loss or damage is caused by negligence or otherwise.

The entire liability of PEL and your only remedy shall be replacement free of charge of the components that do not meet this warranty.

No information or advice (oral, written or otherwise) given by PEL or PEL's agents shall create a warranty or in any way increase the scope of this warranty.

To the extent the law permits, PEL disclaims all other warranties, either express or implied, including by way of example and not limitation, warranties of merchantability and fitness for a particular purpose in respect of *21st Century Science GCSE Higher CD-ROM.*

Governing Law:
This Licence will be governed and construed in accordance with English law.